Third Workshop on Evaluation and Comparison of NLP Systems (Eval4NLP 2022)

Online
20 November 2022

ISBN: 978-1-7138-6315-1

Printed from e-media with permission by:

Curran Associates, Inc.
57 Morehouse Lane
Red Hook, NY 12571

Some format issues inherent in the e-media version may also appear in this print version.

Printed with permission by Curran Associates, Inc. (2023)

Association for Computational Linguistics
209 N. Eighth Street
Stroudsburg, Pennsylvania 18360

Phone: 1-570-476-8006
Fax: 1-570-476-0860

acl@aclweb.org

Additional copies of this publication are available from:

Curran Associates, Inc.
57 Morehouse Lane
Red Hook, NY 12571 USA
Phone: 845-758-0400
Fax: 845-758-2633
Email: curran@proceedings.com
Web: www.proceedings.com

Introduction

Welcome to the Third Workshop on Evaluation and Comparison of NLP Systems (Eval4NLP 2022).

Fair evaluations and comparisons are essential for tracking development and identifying issues of NLP systems. In particular, recent NLP research has become increasingly dependent on fine-tuning pre-trained language models to perform downstream tasks, which has resulted in a considerable increase in the number of published state-of-the-art results. Such findings would be meaningless or even detrimental to the community without appropriate evaluation of all research aspects, including, but not limited to methodologies, datasets, metrics, and setups. To address these challenges, the Eval4NLP workshop series takes a broad and unifying perspective on the subject matter. The third edition of Eval4NLP workshop collocated with AACL 2022 continues to offer a forum for showcasing and discussing the most recent developments in NLP evaluation methods and resources.

Our workshop has attracted a lot of attention from the community with 20 research papers being submitted. After thorough consideration by the program committee and the workshop organizers, 11 papers were selected for presentation. This year's program covers a variety of topics in NLP evaluation and comparison, including new evaluation metrics (e.g., resource-performance tradeoff, summarization); systematic analyses over existing NLP models and techniques (e.g., GPT-2, stance classification baselines, data augmentation); new benchmark datasets for tasks like word segmentation, part-of-speech tagging, chat translation error detection, and multilingual referring expression generation; and critical analyses over existing evaluation benchmarks (e.g., STS) and metrics (e.g., SMATCH); and a novel adversarial example generation method.

We would like to thank all of the authors for their contributions, the program committee for their thoughtful reviews, the keynote speakers for sharing their perspectives, and all the attendees for their participation. We believe that all of these will contribute to a lively and successful workshop. Looking forward to meeting you all (virtually) at Eval4NLP 2022!

Eval4NLP 2022 Organization Team,
Daniel Deutsch, Can Udomcharoenchaikit, Juri Opitz,Yang Gao, Marina Fomicheva, Steffen Eger

Organizing Committee

Daniel Deutsch, Google Research, United States
Can Udomcharoenchaikit, Vidyasirimedhi Institute of Science and Technology, Thailand
Juri Opitz, Heidelberg University, Germany
Yang Gao, Google Research, United Kingdom
Marina Fomicheva, University of Sheffield, United Kingdom
Steffen Eger, Bielefeld University, Germany

Program Committee

Timothy Baldwin, MBZUAI and The University of Melbourne
Gerard De Melo, Hasso Plattner Institute and University of Potsdam
Daniel Deutsch, Google Research
Li Dong, Microsoft Research
Zi-Yi Dou, University of California, Los Angeles
Rotem Dror, School of Engineering and Applied Science, University of Pennsylvania
Steffen Eger, Bielefeld University
Ori Ernst, Bar-Ilan University
George Foster, Google
Anette Frank, Ruprecht-Karls-Universität Heidelberg
Yang Gao, Google Research
Yunsu Kim, Pohang University of Science and Technology
Lucy H. Lin, Spotify
Nitika Mathur, Oracle
Juri Opitz, Heidelberg University
Ines Rehbein, Universität Mannheim
Ehud Reiter, University of Aberdeen
Leonardo F. R. Ribeiro, Amazon Alexa AI
Ori Shapira, Amazon
Julius Steen, Institute for Computational Linguistics, Heidelberg University
Can Udomcharoenchaikit, Vidyasirimedhi Institute of Science and Technology
Shiyue Zhang, The University of North Carolina at Chapel Hill

Keynote Talk: SMART: Sentences as Basic Units for Text Evaluation

Reinald Kim Amplayo
Google

Abstract: Widely used evaluation metrics for text generation do not work well with longer multi-sentence texts. In this talk, I will introduce a new metric called SMART to mitigate such limitations. SMART treats sentences as basic units of matching instead of tokens, and uses a sentence matching function to soft-match candidate and reference sentences. Candidate sentences are also compared to sentences in the source documents to allow grounding (e.g., factuality) evaluation. Results show that system-level correlations of our proposed metric with a model-based matching function outperforms all competing metrics on the SummEval summarization meta-evaluation dataset, while the same metric with a string-based matching function is competitive with current model-based metrics. The latter does not use any neural model, which is useful during model development phases where resources can be limited and fast evaluation is required. SMART also outperforms all factuality evaluation metrics on the TRUE benchmark. Finally, extensive analyses show that our proposed metrics work well with longer summaries and are less biased towards specific models.

Bio: Reinald is a research scientist at Google working on text generation. Prior to that, he was a PhD student at the University of Edinburgh working with Mirella Lapata on opinion summarization. He was also affiliated with Yonsei University and Ateneo de Davao University.

Keynote Talk: Questioning Implicit Assumptions in our Evaluation Methodologies

Maxime Peyrard
EPFL

Abstract: Research in NLP/ML is driven by evaluation results, with attention and resources being focused on methods identified as state-of-the-art. The proper design of evaluation methodologies is thus crucial to ensure progress in the field. In this talk, we will discuss and review several assumptions implicitly made by our standard evaluation methodology and show that these assumptions may not be justified and have a significant impact on which systems are promoted to SotA.

Bio: Maxime Peyrard is a Post-Doc at EPFL in the data science lab. He is working at the intersection between NLP, and data science with a particular focus on methodological aspects like "how to obtain valid causal answers from data?" and "how to properly evaluate machine learning models?"

Table of Contents

Program

Sunday, November 20, 2022

10:30 - 10:45 *Opening Presentation*

11:30 - 12:15 *Paper Presentation Session 1*

Why is sentence similarity benchmark not predictive of application-oriented task performance?
Kaori Abe, Sho Yokoi, Tomoyuki Kajiwara and Kentaro Inui

Better Smatch = Better Parser? AMR evaluation is not so simple anymore
Juri Opitz and Anette Frank

Chat Translation Error Detection for Assisting Cross-lingual Communications
Yunmeng Li, Jun Suzuki, Makoto Morishita, Kaori Abe, Ryoko Tokuhisa, Ana Brassard and Kentaro Inui

13:15 - 14:00 *SMART: Sentences as Basic Units for Text Evaluation (Keynote Talk by Reinald Kim Amplayo)*

14:00 - 15:00 *Paper Presentation Session 2*

A Japanese Corpus of Many Specialized Domains for Word Segmentation and Part-of-Speech Tagging
Shohei Higashiyama, Masao Ideuchi, Masao Utiyama, Yoshiaki Oida and Eiichiro Sumita

Evaluating the role of non-lexical markers in GPT-2's language modeling behavior
Roberta Rocca and Alejandro de la Vega

From COMET to COMES – Can Summary Evaluation Benefit from Translation Evaluation?
Mateusz Krubiński and Pavel Pecina

Random Text Perturbations Work, but not Always
Zhengxiang Wang

15:30 - 16:15 *Questioning Implicit Assumptions in our Evaluation Methodologies (Keynote Talk by Maxime Peyrard)*

16:15 - 17:15 *Paper Presentation Session 3*

Eval4NLP 2022

Evaluation and Comparison of NLP Systems

Proceedings of the Third Workshop

November 20, 2022

A Japanese Corpus of Many Specialized Domains for Word Segmentation and Part-of-Speech Tagging

Shohei Higashiyama[1], **Masao Ideuchi**[1,2], **Masao Utiyama**[1], **Yoshiaki Oida**[2], **Eiichiro Sumita**[1]

[1]National Institute of Information and Communications Technology, Kyoto, Japan
[2]FUJITSU LIMITED, Tokyo, Japan
{shohei.higashiyama,masao.ideuchi,mutiyama,eiichiro.sumita}@nict.go.jp,oida.yoshiaki@fujitsu.com

Abstract

We present a Japanese morphological corpus of sentences from 27 specialized domains for the two tasks of word segmentation and part-of-speech tagging. Experiments on the corpus demonstrated that recent neural models with domain adaptation techniques and pretrained language models achieved accurate performance for the two tasks for many specialized domains.

1 Introduction

Because the Japanese language has no explicit word delimiters, word segmentation (WS) and part-of-speech (POS) tagging are fundamental and important steps for downstream natural language processing (NLP) tasks, such as linguistic analysis and text mining. In previous studies, researchers devoted much effort to developing WS and POS tagging systems (Kudo et al., 2004; Neubig et al., 2011; Tolmachev et al., 2020), often as Japanese morphological analysis, which simultaneously performs WS, POS tagging, and lemmatization. However, the majority of existing systems were evaluated on general domains, such as news and the web.

Although researchers constructed morphologically annotated corpora of specialized domain text, the domains in publicly available corpora are limited, for example, Mori et al. (2014, 2016); Harashima and Hiramatsu (2020). Moreover, researchers proposed domain-specific or domain-independent adaptation methods (Tsuboi et al., 2008; Fujita et al., 2014; Sudoh et al., 2014; Kameko et al., 2015; Higashiyama et al., 2020); however, they evaluated their systems on one or a few specialized domains. Therefore, a benchmark corpus that includes text for many specialized domains is beneficial for conducting comprehensive system evaluation and developing robust adaptation methods for many domains.

In this paper, we present a Japanese Corpus of Many Specialized Domains (JCMS) for WS and POS tagging. The corpus consists of 32,310 sentences annotated with word boundary and POS tag information for 27 specialized domains. Using our corpus, we evaluated existing morphological analysis and WS systems, including popular non-neural systems and recent neural cross-domain systems. Our experiments demonstrated that (1) most systems trained with general source domain resources resulted in degraded performance for specialized target domains; however, (2) domain adaptation (DA) techniques and pretrained language models (PLMs) contributed to robust performance without annotated text for target domains.[1]

2 Construction of the JCMS

2.1 Data Sources and Domains

To construct a multi-domain corpus with public availability and domain diversity, we extracted raw sentences from several publicly available corpora with their sentence segmentation.

To include various science and engineering text (SCI) in our corpus, we used the ASPEC[2] (Nakazawa et al., 2016), NITCIR-9 PatentMT test collection[3] (Fujii et al., 2010), and NTCIR-11 MedNLP-2 test collection[4] (Aramaki et al., 2014). The ASPEC is a parallel corpus of paper abstracts in various scientific fields; we extracted 24K Japanese sentences for 20 domains (from AGR to TRA, as shown in Table 1). The PatentMT data form a parallel corpus of patent documents (PAT); we extracted 1K sentences. The MedNLP-2 data consist of pseudo electronic medical records (EMR); we used all 1.4K unique sentences.

To include other domain text, we used the BC-

[1]The JCMS will be available at https://github.com/shigashiyama/jcms.

[2]https://jipsti.jst.go.jp/aspec/

[3]http://research.nii.ac.jp/ntcir/permission/ntcir-9/perm-en-PatentMT.html

[4]https://research.nii.ac.jp/ntcir/permission/ntcir-11/perm-en-MedNLP.html

Proceedings of the 3rd Workshop on Evaluation and Comparison of NLP Systems, pages 1 - 10
November 20, 2022 ©2022 Association for Computational Linguistics

Group	Domain		Sent.	Word
SCI	AGR	agriculture, forestry, fisheries	900	19.3k
	BIO	biology	1,000	20.2k
	CHE-B	basic chemistry	1,700	38.3k
	CHE-E	chemical eng.	750	18.2k
	CHE-I	chemical industry	950	18.7k
	CON	construction eng.	1,700	39.0k
	ELC	electrical eng.	2,000	39.3k
	ENE	energy eng.	1,360	37.5k
	ENV	environmental eng.	870	19.0k
	ETH	earth and space science	800	19.2k
	INF	information eng.	900	18.9k
	MAN	eng. management	1,500	36.8k
	MEC	mechanical eng.	1,750	38.3k
	MED	medicine	1,300	20.0k
	MIN	mining eng.	640	19.1k
	NUC	nuclear eng.	800	18.6k
	PHY	physics	1,000	17.8k
	SYS	system control eng.	1,500	36.8k
	THM	thermal eng.	1,500	38.3k
	TRA	traffic and transportation eng.	1,430	37.7k
	PAT	patent	1,000	19.1k
	EMR	electronic medical record	1,362	28.7k
GOV	LAW	law	1,060	37.9k
	DIE	diet minute	650	36.3k
	PRM	PR magazine	1,238	19.1k
OTH	TBK	textbook	1,650	17.7k
	VRS	verse	1,000	15.9k
	Total		32,310	726k

Table 1: Statistics of the JCMS SUW data. Scientific (SCI), government document (GOV), and other (OTH) domains are grouped.

CWJ[5] (Maekawa et al., 2014) non-core data and extracted 3K sentences from three government documents (GOV): letter of the law (LAW), minutes of the national diet (DIE), and public relations magazines of local governments (PRM). Additionally, we extracted 2.7K sentences from two other domains (OTH): textbooks (TBK)[6] and Japanese verse (VRS).

As shown in Table 1, the JCMS included 27 domains and 16–40K words per domain. We regard PAT and TBK data as single domains, although they include text in multiple academic or industry fields.

2.2 Segmentation Criteria and POS Tag Sets

Regarding the word boundary and POS tag annotation, we adopted two WS criteria (and corresponding POS tag sets). One is the short unit word (SUW). The SUW was designed by the National Institute for Japanese Language and Linguistics (NINJAL) to achieve consistent WS and has been adopted in various NINJAL corpora (Oka et al., 2020). Additionally, we defined a new criterion, SUW-SC, by separating conjugate words (verb, adjective, verbal/adjectival suffix, and auxiliary verb) into stems and conjugation endings, similar to EDR (2001) and Mori et al. (2014).[7] This criterion has the advantage that different conjugation forms of (regular) conjugate words (e.g., 読-む *yo-mu* 'read', 読-ま *yo-ma*, and 読-み *yo-mi*) can be treated as the same stem token (e.g., 読 *yo*) without an additional lemmatization process. The SUW-SC POS tags that differ from the SUW POS tags are shown in Appendix A.

2.3 Annotation and Checking Process

Using auto-analyzed sentences with SUW-SC information, five experienced annotators at an annotation company annotated sentences with word boundaries and POS tags, following the SUW-SC criterion and the BCCWJ annotation guidelines (Ogura et al., 2011a,b).[8] After the annotation, the annotators performed (1) unknown word checks to detect erroneous out-of-dictionary words and (2) full-sentence checks to detect any erroneous words, and then fixed annotation errors. Finally, we automatically converted SUW-SC information to SUW information by merging adjacent conjugate word stems and conjugation endings.[9] As a result, we obtained 32,310 sentences with 726k SUW tokens (771k SUW-SC tokens), as shown in Table 1, of which 10,520 sentences included one or more words modified by the annotators.

Through the annotation process, we also found approximately 350 character errors in the original sentences, which may have been caused by, for example, OCR and typographic errors,[10] and replaced them with the correct strings, while retaining the original strings as meta information.

To assess the quality of SUW-SC annotation, the first author randomly sampled and checked 200 annotated sentences comprising 4,928 words. The author found 15 erroneous (multi-) word spans. The F1 scores of the annotators' annotation were 99.75 (WS), 99.64 (top-level POS), and 99.56 (full POS)[11] when the annotation refined by the author

[5] `https://clrd.ninjal.ac.jp/bccwj/en/index.html`

[6] The BCCWJ compiles textbooks on ten subjects for elementary, middle, and high schools. The JCMS used sentences from Japanese textbooks for elementary schools.

[7] We did not separate words with irregular conjugations, such as する *suru* 'do;' we treated them as single words.

[8] We ignored word attributes, such as the base forms of conjugate words because of the high annotation cost.

[9] If conjugation type and form information are available, SUW annotation can also be converted to SUW-SC annotation using several simple rules. We will publish the conversion script together with the JCMS data.

[10] For example, we found ヌクレチド and フログラム but correct forms were assumed to be ヌクレオチド 'nucleotide' and プログラム 'program.'

[11] This check was done on the manually annotated sentences. This means that the reported F1 scores were not inter-annotator agreement on the auto-analyzed sentences.

System		GEN		SCI Avg.		GOV Avg.	
		Seg	POS	Seg	POS	Seg	POS
MeCab	D_s	**99.6**	99.0	97.9	97.2	98.0	**97.6**
KyTea	D_s	99.1	98.4	98.5	96.8	97.5	96.6
	D_s, D_t	99.1	98.4	98.6	97.1	97.5	96.7
BiLSTM	–	98.7	98.1	98.0	97.2	97.6	96.9
BiLSTM-LF	D_s	99.4	98.8	98.1	97.3	97.9	97.3
	D_s, D_t	99.4	98.8	98.1	97.3	97.9	97.3
BiLSTM-LWP	D_s, D_t, U_t	98.9	98.3	98.9	98.1	97.7	97.1
BERT	–	99.4	**99.1**	**99.3**	**98.7**	**98.1**	**97.6**
BERT-WM	–	99.4	–	**99.3**	–	98.0	–
	U_t	99.4	–	**99.3**	–	98.0	–

Table 2: System performance on the BCCWJ test (GEN), and the JCMS SCI and GOV domain data.

was regarded as the gold standard.

3 Experiments

3.1 Systems and Language Resources

In this section, we report the experimental results for the JCMS data with the SUW annotation. See Appendix F for the results for the SUW-SC data.

We evaluated popular morphological analysis systems and recent neural WS models: MeCab version 0.996[12] (Kudo et al., 2004), KyTea version 0.4.7[13] (Neubig et al., 2011), BiLSTM, BiLSTM with Lexicon Features (LF) (Higashiyama et al., 2020), and BERT (Devlin et al., 2019). Additionally, we evaluated two domain-adaptable neural models proposed for Japanese and Chinese WS: BiLSTM with Lexicon Word Prediction (LWP) (Higashiyama et al., 2020) and BERT with Wordhood Memory (WM)[14] (Tian et al., 2020). We used the off-the-shelf MeCab model based on UniDic,[15] "unidic-cwj-3.1.0" (Den, 2009), and trained the other systems on the corpora and lexicons described later. We used a pretrained Japanese BERT model[16] with character-level tokenization for the BERT-based models. The detailed settings are described in Appendix B.

As source domain labeled data, we split the BCCWJ core data into 51K/6K/3K sentences and used them as training, development, and test data, respectively, for the above systems. As target domain test data, we used all the sentences in each JCMS domain.

For lexicon-enhanced models, we used entries in UniDic as the source domain lexicon D_s and entries in the MeCab-IPADIC user dictionaries for science and technology terms[17] as the target domain lexicon D_t.[18] As target domain unlabeled data for BiLSTM-LWP and BERT-WM, we used 0.98M Japanese sentences in the ASPEC extracted from 20+ domains as single unlabeled data U_t shared for scientific target domains. Using these resources, we trained single domain-adapted model instances for SCI domains. We used no additional resources for the GOV and OTH domains.

3.2 Overall Results

Table 2 shows the WS and POS tagging (top-level POS) F1 scores for each system on the BCCWJ test data (GEN), and the JCMS SCI and GOV domain data; the scores in the SCI and GOV rows are the macro average F1 scores for 22 SCI domains and three GOV domains, respectively. The neural model scores are the mean F1 scores of three runs with random initialization.

For the GEN domain, MeCab, BiLSTM-LF, and BERT-based models achieved high performance: ≥99.4% and ≥98.8% F1 scores for WS and POS tagging, respectively.[19] For the SCI domains, for the two tasks, the systems with only source domain resources (except BERT) had a 0.6–1.8 F1 point degradation from the scores for the GEN domains. Training with target domain resources contributed to robust performance; for example, BiLSTM-LWP achieved a 0.9 F1 point improvement over BiLSTM for each task. BERT achieved the best performance

[12] https://taku910.github.io/mecab/

[13] http://www.phontron.com/kytea/

[14] https://github.com/SVAIGBA/WMSeg

[15] https://clrd.ninjal.ac.jp/unidic/back_number.html

[16] https://huggingface.co/cl-tohoku/bert-base-japanese-char-v2

[17] https://dbarchive.biosciencedbc.jp/en/mecab/download.html

[18] Because the dictionaries included many compound words, we split the original entries into substrings at the positions before and after continuous Japanese characters, continuous Latin characters, continuous Arabic numerals, and each symbol character, as preprocessing.

[19] Notably, the MeCab model was trained on the BCCWJ core data and other corpora (Den, 2009; Oka, 2017), which may have included the GEN test sentences.

Dom.	Unknown Tok/Type Ratio	MeCab D_s		BL-LWP D_s, D_t, U_t		BERT –	
		Seg	POS	Seg	POS	Seg	POS
GEN	2.7 / 16.1	99.6	99.0	98.9	98.3	99.4	99.1
ENE	2.5 / 15.4	99.3	98.9	99.6	99.2	99.7	99.4
TRA	3.0 / 18.2	98.8	98.4	99.4	98.9	99.6	99.2
ENV	3.2 / 15.1	98.8	98.1	99.3	98.7	99.5	99.2
MAN	3.3 / 19.5	98.6	98.2	99.4	99.0	99.6	99.3
CON	3.5 / 19.5	98.9	98.1	99.2	98.6	99.5	99.1
AGR	4.5 / 21.0	98.5	98.0	99.0	98.4	99.4	99.0
THM	4.5 / 24.0	98.4	97.7	99.1	98.3	99.4	98.8
INF	4.7 / 22.6	97.9	97.5	99.1	98.5	99.5	99.1
MEC	5.0 / 25.3	98.4	97.8	99.3	98.7	99.5	99.1
NUC	5.3 / 20.2	98.1	97.3	98.9	98.0	99.4	98.9
CHE-I	5.5 / 23.7	97.9	97.3	99.0	98.3	99.5	99.0
ETH	5.5 / 24.5	98.5	97.8	99.3	98.4	99.4	98.8
MED	5.6 / 27.0	97.1	96.6	99.1	98.6	99.5	99.1
SYS	5.6 / 24.8	98.4	97.7	98.9	98.0	99.4	98.7
ELC	5.8 / 29.4	97.4	97.0	99.0	98.5	99.5	99.1
PAT	6.0 / 26.8	97.0	96.8	99.1	98.7	99.4	99.2
CHE-E	6.1 / 23.7	97.9	97.0	99.0	98.0	99.2	98.7
MIN	6.6 / 22.6	98.0	97.4	98.8	98.1	99.0	98.6
BIO	6.7 / 30.2	96.7	96.0	98.8	98.0	99.3	98.7
PHY	7.5 / 29.6	97.1	96.4	98.5	97.7	99.2	98.8
CHE-B	8.1 / 35.4	97.0	96.1	98.5	97.4	99.1	98.4
EMR	11.2 / 30.2	95.4	91.9	95.6	92.5	97.1	94.0
DIE	0.9 / 7.5	98.0	97.6	97.7	97.0	97.9	97.4
LAW	2.1 / 11.0	97.4	97.0	97.6	97.4	97.9	97.8
PRM	2.8 / 11.1	98.7	98.1	97.7	96.8	98.3	97.8
TBK	4.4 / 19.0	99.0	97.0	97.7	95.5	98.7	96.8
VRS	19.7 / 47.4	87.3	82.3	81.8	75.1	87.1	83.0

Table 3: System performance for each domain. BL represents BiLSTM.

without explicit DA steps and demonstrated the strong effectiveness of PLMs. This may be because the BERT representations were pretrained on Wikipedia text, including articles on scientific topics. BERT-WM did not show salient improvements over BERT, even when we used U_t unlabeled data. For the GOV domains, MeCab and BERT achieved the best WS and POS tagging performance. Most systems achieved lower performance than that for the GEN and SCI domains, which may be because of the high proportions of unknown non-noun tokens, such as verbs, in the GOV domains, as shown in Appendix C.

3.3 Results for Each Domain

Table 3 shows the performance (F1 scores) of the three accurate systems for the GEN and each JCMS domain. For each domain group, the domains are shown in descending order of the unknown token ratio (UTR).[20] The performance of the systems for the two tasks tended to decrease as the UTR increased. However, BiLSTM-LWP and BERT achieved robust performance for SCI domains with higher UTR (scores $\geq$98% and $\geq$99% are shown with the light blue and blue background). As indicated by the high UTR and low system performance, EMR and VRS were two difficult domains.

In Appendices D, E, and G, we present additional experiments for domain-specific enhanced models for EMR and VRS, the evaluation of the differences between the JCMS annotation and original annotation for GOV and OTH, and segmentation examples output by the systems, respectively.

3.4 Discussion

The JCMS comprises well-formed written text from, for example, scientific papers and government documents. Because of this characteristic, systems trained only on source domain resources achieved reasonable performance (WS and POS tagging F1 scores of 96.6–98.5%, on average), and more sophisticated systems enhanced with DA techniques or PLMs, that is, BiLSTM-LWP and BERT, achieved more accurate performance (F1 scores of 97.1–99.3%), as shown in Table 2. Straightforward extensions include the introduction of POS tagging-oriented DA techniques and the integration of DA techniques into PLM-based models.

Furthermore, possible research directions include WS and POS tagging on more challenging text registers, such as speech and social media text on specialized topics. Another important text analysis task is chunking or recognizing multi-word terms because NLP applications in specialized domains can require term-level processing.

4 Related Work

Japanese Morphology Corpora The representative Japanese morphology corpora used in the 1990s and early 2000s include the EDR Japanese Corpus (Miyoshi et al., 1996) and RWCP Text Database (Toyoura et al., 1998), and those used from the 2000s to the present include the Kyoto University Text Corpus (Kurohashi and Nagao, 2003) and BCCWJ (Maekawa et al., 2014). These corpora mainly comprise newspaper articles and other written language text, such as magazines, books, and dictionary example sentences. These corpora have played a significant role in the development of many Japanese morphological analysis and WS systems (Takeuchi and Matsumoto, 1995; Asahara and Matsumoto, 2000; Kudo et al., 2004; Neubig et al., 2011; Tolmachev et al., 2020). Additionally, web corpora (Hashimoto et al., 2011; Hangyo et al., 2012) and transcribed speech corpora (Maekawa, 2003; Koiso et al., 2022) annotated with morphology information have been con-

[20]The unknown token (type) ratio is the percentage of word tokens (types) that did not occurr in the BCCWJ training sentences among all test word tokens (types).

structed and released. Efforts have also been made to construct and publish corpora of other specialized domain text: patent (Mori et al., 2014), shogi (Japanese chess) commentary (Mori et al., 2016), and recipes (Harashima and Hiramatsu, 2020).

Domain Adaptation Methods To improve Japanese morphological analysis and WS performance on target domains, domain-specific or domain-independent adaptation methods have been proposed. Fujita et al. (2014) explored data augmentation techniques to improve morphological analysis performance on picture book text. Kameko et al. (2015) enhanced a WS model for shogi commentary text using shogi game state information. Partially labeled data have been used to fine-tune general WS models to target domains; Tsuboi et al. (2008) adapted a CRF model to a medical domain and Neubig et al. (2011) adapted a pointwise prediction model to a web domain. Higashiyama et al. (2020) enhanced a BiLSTM-based WS model by introducing an auxiliary word prediction task and adapted the model to several Japanese and Chinese target domains.

5 Conclusion

We presented the JCMS, which is a Japanese corpus of 27 specialized domains annotated with word boundaries and POS tags. The experiments on the corpus demonstrated the robust WS and POS tagging performance of recent neural models on many out-of-domain datasets. Our corpus could be a useful benchmark for developing and evaluating cross-domain systems for WS and POS tagging.

Acknowledgements

We would like to thank the anonymous reviewers for their constructive comments. We used the Asian Scientific Paper Excerpt Corpus, NITCIR-9 PatentMT test collection, NTCIR-11 MedNLP-2 test collection, and Balanced Corpus of Contemporary Written Japanese to construct our corpus.

References

Eiji Aramaki, Mizuki Morita, Yoshinobu Kano, and Tomoko Ohkuma. 2014. Overview of the NTCIR-11 MedNLP-2 task. In *Proceedings of the 11th NTCIR Conference*, pages 147–155, Tokyo, Japan.

Masayuki Asahara and Yuji Matsumoto. 2000. Extended models and tools for high-performance part-of-speech. In *COLING 2000 Volume 1: The 18th International Conference on Computational Linguistics*.

Yasuharu Den. 2009. A multi-purpose electronic dictionary for morphological analyzers [in Japanese]. *Journal of the Japanese Society for Artificial Inteligence*, 34(5):640–646.

Jacob Devlin, Ming-Wei Chang, Kenton Lee, and Kristina Toutanova. 2019. BERT: Pre-training of deep bidirectional transformers for language understanding. In *Proceedings of the 2019 Conference of the North American Chapter of the Association for Computational Linguistics: Human Language Technologies, Volume 1 (Long and Short Papers)*, pages 4171–4186, Minneapolis, Minnesota, USA. Association for Computational Linguistics.

EDR. 2001. EDR denshika jisho shiyō setsumēsho (The EDR electronic dictionary specification manual) [in Japanese].

Atsushi Fujii, Masao Utiyama, Mikio Yamamoto, Takehiro Utsuro, Terumasa Ehara, and Sayori Shimohata. 2010. Overview of the patent translation task at the NTCIR-8 workshop. In *Proceedings of the 8th NTCIR Conference*, pages 371–376, Tokyo, Japan.

Sanae Fujita, Hirotoshi Taira, Tessei Kobayashi, and Takaaki Tanaka. 2014. Japanese morphological analysis of picture books. *Journal of Natural Language Processing*, 21(3):515–539.

Masatsugu Hangyo, Daisuke Kawahara, and Sadao Kurohashi. 2012. Building a diverse document leads corpus annotated with semantic relations. In *Proceedings of the 26th Pacific Asia Conference on Language, Information, and Computation*, pages 535–544, Bali, Indonesia. Faculty of Computer Science, Universitas Indonesia.

Jun Harashima and Makoto Hiramatsu. 2020. Cookpad parsed corpus: Linguistic annotations of Japanese recipes. In *Proceedings of the 14th Linguistic Annotation Workshop*, pages 87–92, Barcelona, Spain. Association for Computational Linguistics.

Chikara Hashimoto, Sadao Kurohashi, Daisuke Kawahara, Keiji Shinzato, and Masaaki Nagata. 2011. Construction of a blog corpus with syntactic, anaphoric, and sentiment annotations. *Journal of Natural Language Processing*, 18(2):175–201.

Shohei Higashiyama, Masao Utiyama, Yuji Matsumoto, Taro Watanabe, and Eiichiro Sumita. 2020. Auxiliary lexicon word prediction for cross-domain word segmentation. *Journal of Natural Language Processing*, 27(3):573–598.

Hirotaka Kameko, Shinsuke Mori, and Yoshimasa Tsuruoka. 2015. Can symbol grounding improve low-level NLP? word segmentation as a case study. In *Proceedings of the 2015 Conference on Empirical Methods in Natural Language Processing*, pages 2298–2303, Lisbon, Portugal. Association for Computational Linguistics.

Hanae Koiso, Haruka Amatani, Yasuharu Den, Yuriko Iseki, Yuichi Ishimoto, Wakako Kashino, Yoshiko Kawabata, Ken'ya Nishikawa, Yayoi Tanaka, Yasuyuki Usuda, and Yuka Watanabe. 2022. Design and evaluation of the corpus of everyday Japanese conversation. In *Proceedings of the Language Resources and Evaluation Conference*, pages 5587–5594, Marseille, France. European Language Resources Association.

Taku Kudo, Kaoru Yamamoto, and Yuji Matsumoto. 2004. Applying conditional random fields to Japanese morphological analysis. In *Proceedings of the 2004 Conference on Empirical Methods in Natural Language Processing*, pages 230–237, Barcelona, Spain. Association for Computational Linguistics.

Sadao Kurohashi and Makoto Nagao. 2003. Building a Japanese parsed corpus. In *Treebanks*, pages 249–260. Springer.

Kikuo Maekawa. 2003. Corpus of spontaneous Japanese: Its design and evaluation. In *Proceedings of the ISCA & IEEE Workshop on Spontaneous Speech Processing and Recognition*, pages 7–12.

Kikuo Maekawa, Makoto Yamazaki, Toshinobu Ogiso, Takehiko Maruyama, Hideki Ogura, Wakako Kashino, Hanae Koiso, Masaya Yamaguchi, Makiro Tanaka, and Yasuharu Den. 2014. Balanced corpus of contemporary written Japanese. *Language Resources and Evaluation*, 48(2):345–371.

Hideo Miyoshi, Kenji Sugiyama, Masahiro Kobayashi, and Takano Ogino. 1996. An overview of the EDR electronic dictionary and the current status of its utilization. In *COLING 1996 Volume 2: The 16th International Conference on Computational Linguistics*.

Shinsuke Mori, Hideki Ogura, and Tetsuro Sasada. 2014. A Japanese word dependency corpus. In *Proceedings of the 9th International Conference on Language Resources and Evaluation*, pages 753–758, Reykjavik, Iceland. European Language Resources Association.

Shinsuke Mori, John Richardson, Atsushi Ushiku, Tetsuro Sasada, Hirotaka Kameko, and Yoshimasa Tsuruoka. 2016. A Japanese chess commentary corpus. In *Proceedings of the Tenth International Conference on Language Resources and Evaluation*, pages 1415–1420, Portorož, Slovenia. European Language Resources Association.

Toshiaki Nakazawa, Manabu Yaguchi, Kiyotaka Uchimoto, Masao Utiyama, Eiichiro Sumita, Sadao Kurohashi, and Hitoshi Isahara. 2016. ASPEC: Asian scientific paper excerpt corpus. In *Proceedings of the Tenth International Conference on Language Resources and Evaluation*, pages 2204–2208, Portorož, Slovenia. European Language Resources Association.

Graham Neubig, Yosuke Nakata, and Shinsuke Mori. 2011. Pointwise prediction for robust, adaptable Japanese morphological analysis. In *Proceedings of the 49th Annual Meeting of the Association for Computational Linguistics: Human Language Technologies*, pages 529–533, Portland, Oregon, USA. Association for Computational Linguistics.

Toshinobu Ogiso, Mamoru Komachi, and Yuji Matsumoto. 2013. Morphological analysis of historical Japanese text [in Japanese]. *Journal of Natural Language Processing*, 20(5):727–748.

Hideki Ogura, Hanae Koiso, Yumi Fujiike, Sayaka Miyauchi, Hikari Konishi, and Yutaka Hara. 2011a. Gendai nihongo kakikotoba kinkō corpus kētairon kitēshū dai 4 ban ge (Regulations of morphological information for balanced corpus of contemporary written Japanese 4th edition volume 2) [in Japanese]. *NINJAL Internal Reports*.

Hideki Ogura, Hanae Koiso, Yumi Fujiike, Sayaka Miyauchi, Hikari Konishi, and Yutaka Hara. 2011b. Gendai nihongo kakikotoba kinkō corpus kētairon kitēshū dai 4 ban jō (Regulations of morphological information for balanced corpus of contemporary written Japanese 4th edition volume 1) [in Japanese]. *NINJAL Internal Reports*.

Teruaki Oka. 2017. UniDic for morphological analysis with reduced model size by review of CRF feature templates [in Japanese]. In *Language Resources Workshop*, pages 144–153. National Institute for Japanese Language and Linguistics.

Teruaki Oka, Yuichi Ishimoto, Yutaka Yagi, Takenori Nakamura, Masayuki Asahara, Kikuo Maekawa, Toshinobu Ogiso, Hanae Koiso, Kumiko Sakoda, and Nobuko Kibe. 2020. KOTONOHA: A corpus concordance system for skewer-searching NINJAL corpora. In *Proceedings of The 12th Language Resources and Evaluation Conference*, pages 7077–7083.

Katsuhito Sudoh, Masaaki Nagata, Shinsuke Mori, and Tatsuya Kawahara. 2014. Japanese-to-English patent translation system based on domain-adapted word segmentation and post-ordering. In *Proceedings of the 11th Conference of the Association for Machine Translation in the Americas: MT Researchers Track*, pages 234–248, Vancouver, Canada. Association for Machine Translation in the Americas.

Koichi Takeuchi and Yuji Matsumoto. 1995. HMM parameter learning for Japanese morphological analyzer. In *Proceedings of the 10th Pacific Asia Conference on Language, Information and Computation*, pages 163–172, Hong Kong. City University of Hong Kong.

Yuanhe Tian, Yan Song, Fei Xia, Tong Zhang, and Yonggang Wang. 2020. Improving Chinese word segmentation with wordhood memory networks. In *Proceedings of the 58th Annual Meeting of the Association for Computational Linguistics*, pages 8274–8285, Online. Association for Computational Linguistics.

Arseny Tolmachev, Daisuke Kawahara, and Sadao Kurohashi. 2020. Design and structure of the Juman++

morphological analyzer toolkit. *Journal of Natural Language Processing*, 27(1):89–132.

Jun Toyoura, Hitoshi Isahara, Shiho Ogino, Wakako Kuwahata, Hironobu Takahashi, Takenobu Tokunaga, Koichi Hashida, Minako Hashimoto, and Fumio Motoyoshi. 1998. RWCP niokeru kenkyūyō text database no kaihatsu (Development of the text database for research at RWCP) [in Japanese]. pages 454–455.

Yuta Tsuboi, Hisashi Kashima, Shinsuke Mori, Hiroki Oda, and Yuji Matsumoto. 2008. Training conditional random fields using incomplete annotations. In *Proceedings of the 22nd International Conference on Computational Linguistics*, pages 897–904, Manchester, UK. Coling 2008 Organizing Committee.

	SUW		SUW-SC		
	POS tag	Example	POS tag (stem)	POS tag (ending)	Example
V1	動詞-一般	ある	動詞-語幹-一般	活用語尾-動詞型	あ|る
V2	動詞-非自立可能	すぎる	動詞-語幹-非自立可能	活用語尾-動詞型	すぎ|る
V3	動詞-一般	有し	動詞-特殊型-一般	–	有し
V4	動詞-非自立可能	する	動詞-特殊型-非自立可能	–	する
A1	形容詞-一般	高い	形容詞-語幹-一般	活用語尾-形容詞型	高|い
A2	形容詞-非自立可能	欲しい	形容詞-語幹-非自立可能	活用語尾-形容詞型	欲し|い
A3	形容詞-非自立可能	ねえ	形容詞-特殊型	–	ねえ
S1	接尾辞-動詞的	(悪)ぶる	接尾辞-動詞型語幹	活用語尾-動詞型	(悪)ぶ|る
S2	接尾辞-形容詞的	っぽい	接尾辞-形容詞型語幹	活用語尾-形容詞型	っぽ|い
AV1	助動詞	させる	助動詞-動詞型語幹	活用語尾-動詞型	させ|る
AV2	助動詞	(行か)ない	助動詞-形容詞型語幹	活用語尾-形容詞型	(行か)な|い
AV3	助動詞	だろう	助動詞-特殊型	–	だろう

Table 4: POS tags and example words of the SUW and SUW-SC criteria

A SUW-SC POS Tags

Table 4 shows the SUW-SC POS tags that differ from the SUW POS tags. Characters in "()" indicate the preceding context and the symbol "|" presents a word boundary.

B Details for the Evaluated Systems

We used the default hyperparameters of KyTea. We used similar model architectures, hyperparameters, and training settings to Higashiyama et al. (2020) for BiLSTM, BiLSTM-LF, and BiLSTM-LWP, except we introduced an additional multi-layer perceptron with one hidden layer (300 hidden units) for POS tagging for each model. We used Tian et al. (2020)'s code for BERT and BERT-WM models with their hyperparameters and training settings for the MSR data, except we used softmax inference similarly to BiLSTM-based models and decreased the mini-batch size to 4 or 8 because of the memory limitation. The BERT model predicted joint segmentation and POS tags, such as B-名詞 (noun), using a single inference layer.

C POS Proportions of Unknown Tokens

Figure 1 shows the proportions of POS tags of unknown tokens for each domain in the JCMS SUW data. Nouns accounted for 95–99% of all unknown tokens for the SCI (AGR to PAT) domains, whereas non-noun tokens, such as verbs and symbols, accounted for 15–60% for the GOV and OTH domains.

D Performance of domain-specific models

The VRS data consisted of Japanese verse sentences written in historical literary styles. The EMR data consisted of medical history summaries

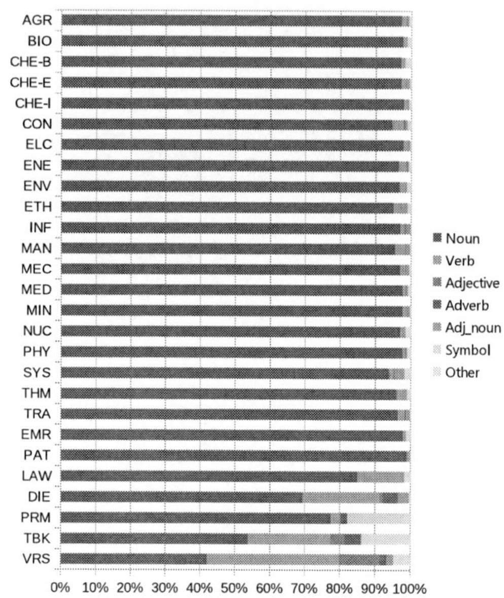

Figure 1: POS Proportions of Unknown Tokens in the SUW data

of imaginary patients. We additionally evaluated two domain-specific models for the VRS and EMR domains of the SUW data. One is the off-the-shelf MeCab model with the morphological analysis dictionary for historical literary style text: "UniDic-202203_65_novel" D_h (Ogiso et al., 2013). The other is a BiLSTM-LWP model trained with medical domain-specific lexicon D_m and unlabeled data U_m, which we describe later. As shown in Table 5, the improved performance of the MeCab model on the VRS domain indicates the alleviation of domain mismatch. The BiLSTM-LWP model adapted for the EMR domain achieved 1.2–1.3 F1 point improvement for WS and POS tagging over the model adapted for all scientific domains, and achieved competitive scores to BERT.

Domain	MeCab D_h Seg	MeCab D_h POS	BiLSTM-LWP D_s, D_m, U_m Seg	BiLSTM-LWP D_s, D_m, U_m POS
EMR	–	–	96.9	93.7
VRS	94.1	91.3	–	–

Table 5: Performance of domain-specific models for the EMR or VRS domain of the SUW data

Domain		F1 Seg	F1 POS	F1 FPOS	FP
GOV	DIE	98.2	98.1	97.9	544
	LAW	98.3	98.3	98.1	501
	PRM	98.6	98.1	96.8	637
OTH	TBK	99.7	99.6	99.3	100
	VRS	95.3	92.9	91.7	1,380

Table 6: Accuracy of original annotation in the BCCWJ non-core data evaluated on the JCMS SUW data

Regarding the resources for the EMR domain, we preprocessed and merged five medical dictionaries into a single lexicon D_m: MEDIS hyojun byomei master,[21] J-GLOBAL Mesh,[22] ComeJisyo,[23] Manbyo dictionary,[24] and Hyakuyaku dictionary.[25] We merged 400K sentences from the ASPEC medical domain and 137K sentences from the MedTxt[26] case report and radiography report corpus into a single unlabeled dataset U_m.

E Accuracy of the Original BCCWJ annotation

The original annotation of the BCCWJ non-core data was performed semi-automatically; hence, the average annotation accuracy was 98%.[27] We regarded the original annotation of the GOV and OTH domain data as system prediction and evaluated it using the SUW annotated sentences in the JCMS as the gold standard. Table 6 shows the WS and POS tagging (top-level POS as "POS" and full POS as "FPOS") F1 scores and the numbers of false positives (FP) based on the FPOS errors. All domain data contained annotation errors, which corresponded to 100–1380 FPs; however, the original annotation achieved higher F1 scores than the evaluated systems in §3.3 because of manual correction efforts by NINJAL.

[21] `http://www2.medis.or.jp/stdcd/byomei/index.html`

[22] `https://dbarchive.biosciencedbc.jp/en/mecab/data-2.html`

[23] `https://ja.osdn.net/projects/comedic/`

[24] `https://sociocom.naist.jp/manbyou-dic/`

[25] `https://sociocom.naist.jp/hyakuyaku-dic/`

[26] `https://sociocom.naist.jp/medtxt/`

[27] `https://clrd.ninjal.ac.jp/bccwj/doc/manual/BCCWJ_Manual_01.pdf`

Dom.	Unknown Tok/Type Ratio	MeCab D_s Seg	MeCab D_s POS	BL-LWP D_s, D_t, U_t Seg	BL-LWP D_s, D_t, U_t POS	BERT – Seg	BERT – POS
GEN	3.7 / 21.1	99.6	99.1	98.8	98.3	99.3	99.1
SCI Avg.		98.0	97.3	98.9	98.2	99.3	98.8
GOV Avg.		98.0	97.6	97.5	97.0	98.0	97.7
ENE	3.1 / 18.1	99.3	98.9	99.5	99.2	99.7	99.4
TRA	3.6 / 20.9	98.8	98.4	99.4	98.9	99.6	99.2
ENV	3.8 / 17.4	98.8	98.2	99.3	98.8	99.6	99.3
MAN	3.9 / 22.0	98.6	98.3	99.4	99.0	99.6	99.3
CON	4.0 / 22.2	98.9	98.2	99.3	98.7	99.5	99.1
THM	4.9 / 26.7	98.4	97.8	99.1	98.4	99.4	98.9
AGR	5.1 / 23.5	98.5	98.1	99.0	98.5	99.4	99.1
INF	5.1 / 25.2	98.0	97.6	99.1	98.6	99.5	99.1
MEC	5.5 / 27.8	98.4	97.9	99.2	98.7	99.5	99.2
NUC	5.7 / 22.6	98.2	97.5	98.9	98.1	99.4	99.0
CHE-I	5.9 / 26.2	98.0	97.4	99.0	98.4	99.5	99.2
ETH	6.0 / 27.1	98.6	97.9	99.4	98.5	99.4	98.9
MED	6.0 / 29.3	97.2	96.8	99.1	98.6	99.6	99.2
SYS	6.1 / 27.7	98.4	97.8	98.9	98.1	99.4	98.8
ELC	6.2 / 31.8	97.5	97.1	99.0	98.5	99.5	99.1
PAT	6.4 / 29.9	97.1	96.9	99.0	98.6	99.4	99.3
CHE-E	6.5 /26.5	97.9	97.1	98.9	98.1	99.3	98.8
MIN	6.9 / 24.9	98.0	97.5	98.8	98.1	99.1	98.7
BIO	7.2 / 32.6	96.8	96.2	98.8	98.1	99.3	98.8
PHY	8.0 / 32.2	97.2	96.6	98.7	97.9	99.2	98.8
CHE-B	8.6 / 38.2	97.1	96.3	98.6	97.5	99.2	98.6
EMR	11.1 / 32.4	95.5	92.1	95.9	92.5	97.3	94.3
LAW	2.7 / 12.4	97.4	97.0	97.6	97.3	98.1	97.9
DIE	3.4 / 12.0	98.1	97.8	97.7	97.1	98.0	97.5
PRM	3.7 / 14.3	98.5	97.9	97.3	96.6	98.1	97.7
TBK	5.5 / 23.6	98.9	97.2	97.6	95.7	98.6	97.0
VRS	18.1 / 47.6	88.6	81.4	80.0	72.9	85.0	81.1

Table 7: Performance of the three systems on the JCMS SUW-SC data. BL represents BiLSTM.

F Results for the SUW-SC POS Tag Set

Table 7 shows the performance of the three systems trained and evaluated on the SUW-SC annotation data. For MeCab, we applied the conversion rules mentioned in §2.3 to SUW results and obtained SUW-SC results. For BiLSTM-LWP and BERT, we trained new model instances with SUW-SC training data. Similar to the results of the SUW experiments, we observed that system performance tended to decrease as the UTR increased.

G Segmentation Examples

Table 8 shows the gold standard annotation and segmentation results of several JCMS sentence fragments[28] output by three systems: MeCab, BiLSTM-LWP, and BERT. Incorrect segmentation (including incorrect manual annotation) is highlighted in the gray background. System errors include oversegmentation of Latin characters (a–c), oversegmentation of English loanwords written

[28] The Japanese writing system uses multiple script types, including *kanji* (e.g., '漢字'), *hiragana* (e.g., 'ひらがな'), *katanaka* (e.g., 'カタカナ'), Arabic numerals (e.g., '012' or '０１２'), Latin characters (e.g., 'ABC' or 'ＡＢＣ'), and punctuation and auxiliary symbols.

	Domain	Gold	MeCab	BiLSTM-LWP	BERT
(a)	PHY	ＮａＣｌ(型)	Ｎａ|Ｃｌ	Ｎａ|Ｃｌ	ＮａＣｌ
(b)	INF	Ｂｌｕｅｔｏｏｔｈ	Ｂｌｕｅ|ｔｏｏｔｈ	Ｂｌｕｅ|ｔｏｏｔｈ	Ｂｌｕｅｔｏｏｔｈ
(c)	BIO	ＨＥＶ(の感染)	Ｈ|Ｅ|Ｖ	ＨＥＶ	ＨＥＶ
(d)	INF	サブルーチン(の効率)	サブルーチン	サブ|ルーチン	サブルーチン
(e)	INF	(ＴＣＰ)スループット	スルー|プット	スループット	スループット
(f)	CHE-B	クロマトグラフィー	クロマトグラフィー	クロマト|グラフィー	クロマト|グラフィー
(g)	LAW	(関係)市町村長	市町村長	市|町村長	市|町村長
(h)	PHY	(Ｂ)中間|子(物理)	中間|子	中間子	中間|子
(i)	PHY	希|土類|金属	希|土類|金属	希土|類|金属	希土|類|金属
(j)	LAW	ただし書(又は)	ただし書	ただし|書	ただし書
(k)	PHY	撹はん(する)	撹|はん	撹|はん	撹はん
(l)	PHY	り患(年数)	り患	り患	り|患
(m)	PHY	(パルス)静電|場	静電|場	静|電場	静電|場
(n)	EMR	右下|腹部|痛	右下|腹部|痛	右|下腹|部|痛	右下|腹部|痛
(o)	EMR	両下|肢	両|下肢	両|下肢	両|下肢

Table 8: Segmentation results of the JCMS sentence examples using the three systems. Characters in "()" indicate the surrounding context. The meanings of the examples are as follows: (a) 'NaCl (-type),' (b) 'Bluetooth,' (c) 'HEV (infection),' (d) '(efficiency of) the subroutine,' (e) '(TCP) throughput,' (f) 'chromatography,' (g) '(the relevant) municipal mayors,' (h) 'B-meson physics,' (i) 'rare earth metal,' (j) 'proviso (or),' (k) 'stir,' (l) '(duration years of) the disorder,' (m) '(pulse) electrostatic field,' (n) 'right lower quadrant pain,' and (o) 'both lower extremities.'

with katakana (often into English morphemes) (d–f), incorrect segmentation of kanji sequences (g–i), and incorrect segmentation of hiragana and kanji mixed sequences (j–l). We found words that were correctly segmented by the systems but were evaluated as errors because of the annotation errors (m–o).

Assessing Resource-Performance Trade-off of Natural Language Models using Data Envelopment Analysis

Zachary Zhou
Industrial and Systems Engineering
University of Wisconsin – Madison
1415 Engineering Drive
Madison, WI 53706
zzhou246@wisc.edu

Alisha Zachariah
Devin Conathan
Jeffery Kline
American Family Insurance
6000 American Parkway
Madison, WI 53783
{alisha044,dconathan,jeffery.kline}@gmail.com

Abstract

Natural language models are often summarized through a high-dimensional set of descriptive metrics including training corpus size, training time, the number of trainable parameters, inference times, and evaluation statistics that assess performance across tasks. The high dimensional nature of these metrics yields challenges with regard to objectively comparing models; in particular it is challenging to assess the trade-off models make between performance and resources (compute time, memory, etc.).

We apply Data Envelopment Analysis (DEA) to this problem of assessing the resource-performance trade-off. DEA is a nonparametric method that measures productive efficiency of abstract *units* that consume one or more *inputs* and yield at least one *output*. We recast natural language models as units suitable for DEA, and we show that DEA can be used to create an effective framework for quantifying model performance and efficiency. A central feature of DEA is that it identifies a subset of models that live on an *efficient frontier* of performance. DEA is also scalable, having been applied to problems with thousands of units. We report empirical results of DEA applied to 14 different language models that have a variety of architectures, and we show that DEA can be used to identify a subset of models that effectively balance resource demands against performance.

1 Introduction

A standard task in the machine learning lifecycle is to compare performance of many models; typically this process involves analyzing high-dimensional sets of summary statistics (hyperparameters, evaluation metrics, etc.). A common use case is quantifying the trade-off between performance and resource constraints; the goal being to achieve the best possible performance using minimal resources.

Meanwhile, multitask performance benchmarks (e.g., GLUE) have found widespread adoption in the natural language processing (NLP) community, with transformer-based models often leading in evaluation performance (Vaswani et al., 2017). While the performance of transformer-based language models is impressive, they are notoriously resource-intensive, and often smaller models can more efficiently leverage a limited resource budget. However, it is nontrivial to demonstrate this fact by formulating a rational and fair comparison among models of different sizes and architectures.

In this paper, we apply *data envelopment analysis* (DEA) to this challenge of assessing model resource-performance trade-off (Charnes et al., 1978; Banker et al., 1984). DEA is a technique that originated in the operations research community, and it has been applied to a wide range of settings over many decades. It is traditionally concerned with rigorously defining *decision making efficiency* for teams, departments, companies, and other types of people-oriented organizations. But DEA is a generic technique that is based on solving a series of linear programs that are constructed to analyze the relative efficiency of *decision making units* (DMUs). A DMU is an abstract object that converts a set of *inputs* or *resources* into a set of *outputs* or *benefits*.

Our adaptation of DEA to the NLP context begins by treating each model as a DMU. Example inputs for the analysis include training time, training corpus size, the number of trainable parameters, and total monetary cost to train. Typical outputs would be performance evaluation metrics, evaluation throughput, etc.

Our main contribution in this paper is that we apply DEA to the problem of assessing the resource-performance trade-off of machine learning models with an emphasis on evaluating the efficiency of language models. To our knowledge, this application of DEA to machine learning has not appeared in prior work. We do not assume familiarity with DEA, so in Section 4 we provide sufficient detail

Proceedings of the 3rd Workshop on Evaluation and Comparison of NLP Systems, pages 11 - 20
November 20, 2022

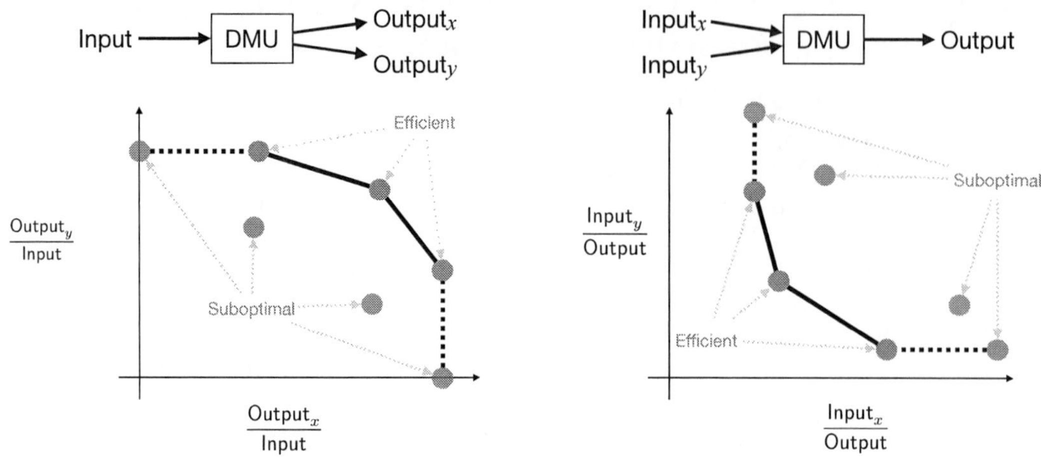

Figure 1: Two simple examples of DEA. *(Left)* Each DMU, represented by a blue dot, has two outputs and a single input. Efficient DMUs generally lie far from the origin, which corresponds to DMUs that have high output per unit of input. *(Right)* Each DMU ingests two inputs and yields a single output. The set of DMUs that lie close to either axis are more efficient, which has the interpretation of low unit input per unit of output. The Pareto fronts are indicated with the heavy black line segments. Note that the dashed lines segments are not considered part of the front. Suboptimal DMUs are said to be "enveloped" by efficient DMUs.

to interpret our empirical results, which apply DEA to a variety of models, in Section 5.

2 Background

DEA was developed to enable performance assessment of teams of people and organizations such as not-for-profits, governmental organizations, departments within larger organizations and meta-analyses of industries. Traditional inputs include organizational staff salary, operational costs, and time. Traditional outputs include revenue, sales volume, and other organizational goals. The Pareto front of DEA in this context is also known as the *best practice frontier*, with the name derived from the observation that if a decision making unit (DMU) is on this frontier, it is objectively more efficient at transforming its inputs into outputs.

DEA analysis is applied to the inputs and outputs of a population of DMUs, and it assigns a scalar value between 0 and 1 to each DMU which expresses its efficiency. A DMU that is more effective at transforming inputs into outputs is considered more efficient.

Figure 1 illustrates two simple scenarios where DEA-type efficiency can be endowed with an intuitive representation. On the left, several DMUs are represented as blue dots, and each DMU ingests a single input and yields two outputs. A process that generates more output for a given input is considered to have greater efficiency. In this scenario, processes that lie on the Pareto front are far from the origin. At right, a different set of DMUs is shown. In this example, each DMU ingests two inputs and performance is assessed through a single output. A DMU with low input or large output will live close to one of the axes, and DMUs close to the origin are more efficient.

We now illustrate how DEA quantifies model efficiency by briefly describing a hypothetical, and simple, example. Consider a language model trained on a small amount of data with high accuracy for some task. DEA classifies this model as *more efficient* than (1) a model that achieves the same accuracy with more training data or (2) a model that achieves a lower accuracy with the same amount of training data.

We describe the formal definition of DEA below in Section 4, but for now it suffices to understand that DEA is the result of solving a sequence of linear programs. In particular, global solutions are guaranteed to be found rapidly and with high numerical precision.

A DEA-based approach to model comparison has several advantages. Since it is based on linear programming, the DEA framework lends itself to detailed theoretical analysis, which extends to interpreting solutions and modifying the programs in a controlled way. Furthermore, DEA is extensible both in the number of models that one can consider as well as the metrics that are used to represent each model's inputs and outputs. Finally, DEA is a scalable technique, since it allows one to analyze model performance of tens of thousands of models.

DEA can be applied to almost arbitrary data that satisfies a small number of weak conditions, but this flexibility comes with some cost. In order to derive meaning from DEA, one must carefully choose the set of inputs and outputs. This process of selection is necessarily subjective. The specifics of our implementation are not meant to be universal prescriptions but rather a demonstration of the concept and useful starting point.

3 Related work

DEA was introduced to the operations research community as a tool to help organizations quantify efficiency, and to objectively identify suborganizations that perform especially well (Charnes et al., 1978). Since its introduction, DEA has been applied to a vast array of fields, including international banking, cloud computing operations, economic sustainability, police department operations, hospital operations, and logistical applications (Charnes et al., 1995; Emrouznejad et al., 2016; Sun, 2002; Thanassoulis, 1995; Tsaples et al., 2022). Recent work has applied DEA to the machine learning context to optimize generalization error of models (Guerrero et al., 2022); we are unaware of prior work that applies DEA to the purpose of assessing model efficiency as we do here.

The theory of DEA continues to be an active field of research, and there have been many developments over the years in an attempt to address perceived shortcomings. In addition to the relaxation of constant returns to scale, "cross-efficiency" was introduced to generate unique efficiency rankings, and "stochastic data envelopment analysis" was developed to account for noise and uncertainty in the measurements that are used to inform DEA (Banker et al., 1984; Doyle and Green, 1994; Olesen and Petersen, 2016).

DEA is parallelizable, and it has been applied to problems with tens of thousands of DMUs (Phillips et al., 1990; Khezrimotlagh et al., 2019). Reducing the required computation time of DEA has also been explored (Ali, 1990, 1993).

Assessment of natural language understanding requires models to execute a range of linguistic tasks across different domains. Recognizing this, the GLUE benchmarks were introduced (Wang et al., 2018). The GLUE benchmarks consist of nine English sentence understanding tasks, so the performance of a single model on the GLUE benchmark yields a nine-dimensional vector. Typically, this vector is summarized through an average and reported as a single score.

A challenge of modern transformer-based machine learning is the large number of different architectures that can be tested. A fairly comprehensive overview of recent performance results related to language models is reported in (Narang et al., 2021). The primary method of reporting the results is in tabular form (see, for example Tables 1 and 2 of that reference), and comparative analysis is challenging. Others propose rigorous scientific methods and experiment design to help manage these challenges (Ulmer et al., 2022), (Dror et al., 2019), (Dror et al., 2017); we believe DEA is another tool that can be leveraged for these analyses.

Multidimensional descriptions of models are an inescapable feature of machine learning, and scalarization of such descriptions are equally common. Several metrics commonly used to describe models include precision, recall, accuracy, model size, and a variety measures of performance including BLEU and the family of ROUGE scores (Lin, 2004; Papineni et al., 2002). Aside from DEA, other well-known examples of scalarization techniques used within the machine learning community include the F1 score, the Matthews correlation coefficient, and the Fowlkes–Mallows index, which summarizes the confusion matrix (Matthews, 1975; Yule, 1912; Fowlkes and Mallows, 1983).

4 Mathematical background

In this section, we provide sufficient background for one who is unfamiliar with DEA to interpret the results of Section 5.

When DEA was originally introduced, a technical requirement of the processes being assessed was that they exhibit *constant returns to scale*; for example this means that doubling the value of each input (e.g., sales staff) should cause the doubling of the value of all the outputs (e.g., monthly sales). DEA found widespread adoption despite this assumption almost never holding in practice. To address this perceived deficiency in DEA, the original formulation of DEA was modified to relax the constant returns to scale assumption. Several other extensions of DEA are now in common use, and we provide an overview below. More details can be found in (Cooper et al., 2007).

We introduce the setup and notation as follows. There are n DMUs, each of which consumes m inputs and produces s outputs. Concretely, DMU$_j$ consumes $x_{ij} \geq 0$ units of input and produces $y_{rj} \geq 0$ units of output, where $1 \leq i \leq m$, $1 \leq r \leq s$, and $1 \leq j \leq n$. The measurement units of the different inputs and outputs need not be congruent. For shorthand, we can express the data corresponding to DMU$_j$ with the pair $(x_j, y_j) \in \mathbb{R}^{m+s}$ where $x_j = (x_{ij})_{i=1}^{m}$ and $y_j = (y_{rj})_{r=1}^{s}$. We call the pair (x_j, y_j) an *activity*. We can additionally arrange the input data in an $m \times n$ matrix $X = (x_{ij})$ and the output data in an $s \times n$ matrix $Y = (y_{rj})$. All the vectors x_j and y_j are assumed to be *semipositive*, meaning their entries are nonnegative and at least one entry is strictly positive. Equivalently, this means DMU$_j$ consumes a positive amount of some input and produces a positive amount of some output.

4.1 CCR efficiency

We first introduce the (input-oriented) CCR model (Charnes et al., 1978), named as such after its creators Charnes, Cooper, and Rhodes. The CCR model is widely regarded as the first DEA model, and assumes constant returns to scale.

For each o, where $1 \leq o \leq n$, we evaluate DMU$_o$ against its peers. Let $v = (v_i)_{i=1}^{m} \in \mathbb{R}_{+}^{m}$ and $u = (u_r)_{r=1}^{s} \in \mathbb{R}_{+}^{s}$ denote the weights that are applied to all the inputs and all the outputs of DMU_o, respectively. For an arbitrary activity $(x, y) \in \mathbb{R}_{+}^{m+s}$, the ratio $u^\top y / v^\top x$ measures efficiency by reducing the multiple inputs (resp. outputs) to a single "virtual" input (resp. "virtual" output), then returning the ratio of virtual output to virtual input. The CCR model aims to solve the following fractional program, indexed by o, where $1 \leq o \leq n$:

$$\underset{v,u}{\text{maximize}} \quad \theta := \theta_o = \frac{u^\top y_o}{v^\top x_o} \tag{1a}$$

$$\text{subject to} \quad \frac{u^\top y_j}{v^\top x_j} \leq 1 \quad \text{for } j = 1, \ldots, n \tag{1b}$$

$$v \in \mathbb{R}_{+}^{m}, \; u \in \mathbb{R}_{+}^{s}. \tag{1c}$$

The constraints (1b) bound the efficiency ratio of each DMU above by 1. The objective (1a) aims to find multipliers v, u that maximize the efficiency ratio of target DMU$_o$; due to the constraints (1b), clearly the optimal value θ^* is at most 1. It can be shown that Eq. (1) is equivalent to the following linear program, called the CCR multiplier form:

$$\underset{v,u}{\text{maximize}} \quad \theta = u^\top y_o \tag{2a}$$

$$\text{subject to} \quad v^\top x_o = 1 \tag{2b}$$

$$-v^\top X + u^\top Y \leq 0^\top \tag{2c}$$

$$v \in \mathbb{R}_{+}^{m}, \; u \in \mathbb{R}_{+}^{s}. \tag{2d}$$

Equivalence of (1) and (2) can be verified through a simple exercise (Cooper et al., 2007). We call DMU$_o$ *CCR-efficient* if $\theta^* = 1$ and there exists an optimal (v^*, u^*) with $v^* > 0$ and $u^* > 0$. Otherwise we call DMU$_o$ *CCR-inefficient*.

It is possible for DMU$_o$ to achieve the maximal value $\theta^* = 1$ and still be CCR-inefficient; this occurs when some DMU$_j \neq$ DMU$_o$ consumes no more input than DMU$_o$, produces at least as much output as DMU$_o$, and either consumes strictly less of some input or produces strictly more of some output than DMU$_o$. In the literature, such CCR-inefficient DMUs are occasionally referred to as *weakly efficient*, whereas DMUs satisfying both $\theta^* = 1$ and $(v^*, u^*) > 0$ are called *strongly efficient* (Cooper et al., 2004). In Figure 1, the weakly inefficient points are the endpoints of the dashed line segments that are parallel to the axes, and they are labeled "suboptimal." For the most part, we will not use this terminology and simply refer to DMUs satisfying $\theta^* = 1$ and not $(v^*, u^*) > 0$ as inefficient.

Computationally, one typically does not work with the CCR multiplier form directly, but rather with its dual. The dual of (2) is referred to as the *CCR envelopment form*:

$$\underset{\theta,\lambda}{\text{minimize}} \quad \theta \tag{3a}$$

$$\text{subject to} \quad \theta x_o - X\lambda \geq 0 \tag{3b}$$

$$Y\lambda \geq y_o \tag{3c}$$

$$\theta \in \mathbb{R}, \; \lambda \in \mathbb{R}_{+}^{n}. \tag{3d}$$

We now describe the connection between the CCR model and the assumption of constant returns to scale with an alternative interpretation of the envelopment form. Recall that an arbitrary pair of vectors $(x, y) \in \mathbb{R}_{+}^{m+s}$ is called an *activity*. The CCR model assumes there is a set of feasible activities, called the *production possibility set*, denoted P_{CCR}, which is defined as the polytope

$$P_{CCR} := \{(x, y) \in \mathbb{R}_{+}^{m+s} : \; x \geq X\lambda, \; y \leq Y\lambda, \; \lambda \in \mathbb{R}_{+}^{n}\},$$

and which has the following properties:

1. We assume the observed activities $\{(x_j, y_j)\}_{j=1}^n$ are contained in P_{CCR}.

2. If $(x, y) \in P_{CCR}$, then $(\bar{x}, \bar{y}) \in P_{CCR}$ for any $\bar{x} \geq x$, $\bar{y} \geq y$. (In the economics literature, this is known as *free disposability* (Carter and Koopmans, 1952).)

3. Conic combinations of activities in P_{CCR} belong to P_{CCR}.

The last property implies constant returns to scale, as $(x, y) \in P_{CCR}$ implies $(tx, ty) \in P_{CCR}$ for any $t > 0$.

Eq. (3) can be viewed as finding the minimum θ such that $(\theta x_o, y_o) \in P_{CCR}$. More intuitively, Eq. (3) aims to synthesize a new activity using conic combinations of the observed activities $\{(x_j, y_j)\}_{j=1}^n$, i.e., $(X\lambda, Y\lambda)$ where $\lambda \in \mathbb{R}_+^n$. Eq. (3) tries to scale the inputs x_o as small as possible by the factor θ while ensuring that the synthesized activity $(X\lambda, Y\lambda)$ consumes no more inputs than θx_o and maintains output levels at least as high as y_o.

The envelopment form allows for an alternative characterization of CCR-efficiency: DMU$_o$ is CCR-efficient if for any optimal solution (θ^*, λ^*) to (3), $\theta^* = 1$ and the solution has zero slack, i.e., the constraints (3b) and (3c) hold at equality; DMU$_o$ is CCR-inefficient otherwise. If DMU$_o$ is CCR-inefficient, then there exists $\lambda \in \mathbb{R}_+^n$ such that $x_o \geq X\lambda$, $Y\lambda \geq y_o$ and at least one inequality in the system holds strictly; the synthesized activity $(X\lambda, Y\lambda)$ is thus strictly better than (x_o, y_o), and so DMU$_o$ is said to be *enveloped* by the observed activities $\{(x_j, y_j)\}_{j=1}^n$.

Solving (3) alone is not enough to determine whether DMU$_o$ is CCR-efficient; to determine whether every optimal solution to (3) has zero slack, one additionally solves the following linear program:

$$\begin{aligned}
\underset{\lambda, s^-, s^+}{\text{maximize}} \quad & 1^\top s^- + 1^\top s^+ && \text{(4a)}\\
\text{subject to} \quad & s^- = \theta^* x_o - X\lambda && \text{(4b)}\\
& s^+ = Y\lambda - y_o && \text{(4c)}\\
& \lambda \in \mathbb{R}_+^n,\ s^- \in \mathbb{R}_+^m,\ s^+ \in \mathbb{R}_+^s, && \text{(4d)}
\end{aligned}$$

where θ^* in (4) is the optimal value of (3). If DMU$_o$ is CCR-inefficient, we can additionally find its *reference set*, the set of CCR-efficient DMUs that envelop DMU$_o$ thus making it CCR-inefficient. The reference set is defined based on the max-slack solution $(\theta^*, \lambda^*, s^{-*}, s^{+*})$ of (3) and (4) to be

$$E_o^{CCR} = \{j \in \{1, \ldots, n\} : \lambda_j^* > 0\}.$$

4.2 BCC efficiency

The constant returns to scale assumption of the CCR model can be problematic when comparing language models, e.g., one typically expects diminishing returns from increased training time. Fortunately, this can be relaxed with a very simple modification to the CCR formulation (Banker et al., 1984). The so-called BCC model, named after its creators Banker, Charnes, and Cooper, addresses this shortcoming and allows for variable returns to scale by adding a single additional constraint, namely $1^\top \lambda = 1$, on the production possibility set. The BCC envelopment form, which is almost identical to Eq. (3), is as follows:

$$\begin{aligned}
\underset{\theta, \lambda}{\text{minimize}} \quad & \theta && \text{(5a)}\\
\text{subject to} \quad & \theta x_o - X\lambda \geq 0 && \text{(5b)}\\
& Y\lambda \geq y_o && \text{(5c)}\\
& 1^\top \lambda = 1 && \text{(5d)}\\
& \theta \in \mathbb{R},\ \lambda \in \mathbb{R}_+^n. && \text{(5e)}
\end{aligned}$$

The dual of (5) is the BCC multiplier form:

$$\begin{aligned}
\underset{v, u, u_0}{\text{maximize}} \quad & u^\top y_o - u_0 && \text{(6a)}\\
\text{subject to} \quad & v^\top x_o = 1 && \text{(6b)}\\
& -v^\top X + u^\top Y - u_0 1^\top \leq 0^\top && \text{(6c)}\\
& v \in \mathbb{R}_+^m,\ u \in \mathbb{R}_+^s,\ u_0 \in \mathbb{R}. && \text{(6d)}
\end{aligned}$$

The production possibility set P_{BCC} of the BCC model is defined as

$$\begin{aligned}
P_{BCC} = \{&(x, y) \in \mathbb{R}_+^{m+s} :\\
& x \geq X\lambda,\ y \leq Y\lambda,\ 1^\top \lambda = 1,\ \lambda \in \mathbb{R}_+^n\}.
\end{aligned}$$

The envelopment form (5) can be viewed as finding the minimum θ such that $(\theta x_o, y_o) \in P_{BCC}$. We call *DMU$_o$ BCC-efficient* if for any optimal solution (θ^*, λ^*) to (5), $\theta^* = 1$ and the solution has zero slack, i.e., the constraints (5b) and (5c) hold at equality; DMU$_o$ is *BCC-inefficient* otherwise. As in the case of the CCR model, one not only solves

(5) but also the following:

$$\begin{aligned} \underset{\lambda, s^-, s^+}{\text{maximize}} \quad & 1^\top s^- + 1^\top s^+ && \text{(7a)} \\ \text{subject to} \quad & s^- = \theta^* x_o - X\lambda && \text{(7b)} \\ & s^+ = Y\lambda - y_o && \text{(7c)} \\ & 1^\top \lambda = 1 && \text{(7d)} \\ & \lambda \in \mathbb{R}^n_+,\ s^- \in \mathbb{R}^m_+,\ s^+ \in \mathbb{R}^s_+, && \text{(7e)} \end{aligned}$$

where θ^* in (7) is the optimal value of (5).

If DMU$_o$ is BCC-inefficient, we are interested in finding its *reference set*, the set of BCC-efficient DMUs that envelop DMU$_o$ thus making it BCC-inefficient. The reference set is defined based on the max-slack solution (θ^*, λ^*, s^{-*}, s^{+*}) of (5) and (7) to be

$$E_o^{BCC} = \{j \in \{1, \ldots, n\} : \lambda_j^* > 0\}.$$

If DMU$_o$ is BCC-efficient, we can additionally determine returns to scale as follows:

1. Increasing returns to scale prevails at (x_o, y_o) iff $u_0^* < 0$ *for all* optimal solutions to (6).
2. Decreasing returns to scale prevails at (x_o, y_o) iff $u_0^* > 0$ *for all* optimal solutions to (6).
3. Constant returns to scale prevails at (x_o, y_o) iff $u_0^* = 0$ *for some* optimal solution to (6).

Suppose we solve (6) and obtain $u_0^* < 0$. We then solve the following modified program:

$$\begin{aligned} \underset{v, u, u_0}{\text{maximize}} \quad & u_0 && \text{(8a)} \\ \text{subject to} \quad & v^\top x_o = 1 && \text{(8b)} \\ & u^\top y_o - u_0 = 1 && \text{(8c)} \\ & -v^\top X + u^\top Y - u_0 1^\top \leq 0^\top && \text{(8d)} \\ & v \in \mathbb{R}^m_+,\ u \in \mathbb{R}^s_+,\ u_0 \leq 0. && \text{(8e)} \end{aligned}$$

If (8) yields an optimal solution with $u_0^* = 0$, then constant returns to scale prevails at (x_o, y_o), otherwise increasing returns to scale prevails. If on the other hand we solve (6) and obtain $u_0^* > 0$, (8) can be modified by replacing the constraint $u_0 \leq 0$ with $u_0 \geq 0$ and switching the optimization sense to minimize u_0.

Since the BCC envelopment form differs from the CCR envelopment form only in the addition of the convexity constraint $1^\top \lambda = 1$, if DMU$_o$ is CCR-efficient, it is also BCC-efficient, and constant returns to scale prevail at DMU$_o$.

The CCR score θ^*_{CCR} is called the *(global) technical efficiency* (TE) as the CCR model ignores the effects of scaling. The BCC score θ^*_{BCC} is called the *(local) pure technical efficiency* (PTE) as the BCC model accounts for variable returns to scale. The *scale efficiency* (SE) is defined as

$$SE = \frac{TE}{PTE} = \frac{\theta^*_{CCR}}{\theta^*_{BCC}}. \tag{9}$$

Note that $0 \leq SE \leq 1$. Eq. (9) implies a decomposition of technical efficiency into pure technical efficiency and scale efficiency; if technical efficiency TE is low, it is either because of inefficient operation (low PTE) or poor scaling of resources (low SE).

We remark that all of the CCR and BCC models we consider are *input-oriented*, as they attempt to reduce input consumption while maintaining the same if not higher level of output production. We do not consider *output-oriented* models which consider the opposite situation where output production is increased while maintaining the same or lower level of input consumption.

5 Results and analysis

In this section, we describe the results of applying DEA to compare a variety of NLP models. The input features and the output features were selected to incorporate aspects of training, evaluation and task performance. Since training is one part of our analysis, several identical versions of the same models are represented in the set of models considered but with different learning rates selected. We also incorporate several simpler models as baselines including TF-IDF and GloVe embeddings with linear classifiers (Pennington et al., 2014).

The transformer models are pretrained models that are sourced from the Hugging Face Model Hub (Hugging Face, 2022). Each transformer model appears three times: once for each of the learning rates 10^{-3}, 10^{-4}, and 10^{-5}. The base models are `bert-base-uncased`, `bert-large-uncased` (Devlin et al., 2019), `roberta-base` (Liu et al., 2019), and their distilled versions: `distilbert-base-uncased`, `distilroberta-base` (Sanh et al., 2019). The GloVe embeddings used are all trained on the Wikipedia 2014 and Gigaword 5 6B corpuses and vary in embedding dimension between 50, 100, 200 and 300 (Pennington et al., 2014). As our simplest baseline we use `scikit-learn`'s implementation of TF-IDF which varies in vocabulary size between 100, 500, 1000, 5000, 10000 and 15000 (Pedregosa et al., 2011).

The number of trainable parameters for the transformer and other deep network models is determined by the model architecture and is typically in the millions. For the simpler embedding-based models, the number of trainable parameters is determined by the embedding dimension or vocabulary size. The GLUE benchmarks were coalesced in the standard manner by applying an average of all the scores. This score was treated as an output.

We ran each model through the standard GLUE benchmark by training them on the `train` split of the dataset and evaluating them on the `eval` split; in doing so we generated several dozen metrics for each model. These metrics include standard metrics that capture model throughput, running time and performance; a condensed representative summary is presented in Table 1.

In practical applications of DEA, if the analysis uses far more inputs and outputs than the number of DMUs, then the typical outcome classifies all DMUs as Pareto efficient. There can still be value in analyses where this happens, this is atypical and we wish to avoid it. A rule of thumb advises that the number of DMUs should be at least twice the number of inputs and outputs considered (Cook et al., 2014; Golany and Roll, 1989). Following this advice, we run an analysis with just two inputs and two outputs. The inputs we use are log (# trainable params) and total train runtime. The outputs were average score across all GLUE tasks and average eval throughput (samples/second).

We nonlinearly transform the number of trainable parameters by applying log to it for two reasons. First, there is a large disparity between the number of trainable parameters that the simple models have, and the number of trainable parameters that the transformer models have. The result of this gap is that the feature effectively becomes a binary indicator of whether the model is a transformer or not, and this is not what we would like the feature to convey. The second reason is based on empirical observations about performance. Informally, we expect performance to be a sublinear function of model size. That is, model performance should improve as a function of model size, but with decreasing returns.

We ran our experiments via Google Cloud Platform's Vertex AI Pipelines. Transformer models were trained on `n1-highmem-8` instances (8 vCPUs, 52 GiB memory) and one NVIDIA T4 GPU with CUDA toolkit version 11.2. Non-transformer models were trained on `e2-standard-4` instances (4 vCPUs, 16 GiB memory). All experiments used Python 3.8 and, at the time of writing, the latest versions of major libraries[1]. Our experiment script was a modified version of the `run_glue.py` script included with Hugging Face's examples [2]. Runtimes for all tasks varied from minutes to hours depending on the task and model but all experiments were completed within 24 hours.

After generating the model metrics, we constructed the relevant linear programs described in Section 4, and we solved them using Gurobi version 9.5.2.

The results shown in Table 2 use the following definitions. The column headed "CCR score" reports the optimal objective value of the program in Eq. (3), and the "BCC score" reports the optimal objective value of the program in Eq. (5). The column headed "scale efficiency" reports the ratio of the two optimal values, and is defined explicitly in Eq. (9). The column "CCR eff." indicates whether the optimal solution to (3) has zero slack, and reports the result of solving Eq. (4). The column headed "BCC eff." indicates whether the optimal solution to Eq. (5) has zero slack and requires solving Eq. (7) to make the determination. Note that several models exhibit a BCC score of 1.000 while not being BCC-efficient, i.e., they are weakly efficient. Finally, the "ret. to scale" column containing either CRS or DRS (IRS does not occur here) reports the results of Eq. (6) and Eq. (8). CRS indicates constant returns to scale, which corresponds to item 3 in the list appearing just prior to Eq. (8). DRS indicates decreasing returns to scale. In this case, DRS corresponds to item 2 in that same list.

As a result, of this table, it is clear that the models `glove-50-linear`, `tfidf-1000-linear`, and `roberta-base` with `lr=1e-4` perform well overall. It is also clear that the BCC equations provide a view of model performance that benefits the more complex models. This confirms the general intuition that large changes in model size, complexity and

[1]The libraries and their versions are: (`torch`, 1.11.0), (`transformers`, 4.20.1), and (`scikit-learn`, 1.1.1).

[2]`https://github.com/huggingface/transformers/blob/v4.20.1/examples/pytorch/text-classification/run_glue.py`

other inputs yield incremental improvements in performance. Additionally, it shows that `bert-large-uncased` models are suboptimal, requiring a lot of time and space in exchange for performance that is similar to that of other models.

6 Conclusions and Future Work

We have applied Data Envelopment Analysis to the challenge of quantifying the trade-off that exists between model performance and resource demands. We base this analysis on standard high-dimensional summary statistics that describe each model. We apply DEA to the analysis of 14 natural language models, and from this analysis we identify both simple and transformer-based models that effectively balance the competing objectives.

We demonstrate that the method is feasible and scales well. Future work can refine the approach presented above in several directions. First, specifics of our analysis can be modified by selecting different sets of inputs and outputs, or by selecting different ways of normalizing the inputs and outputs. Although DEA is a quantitative framework, there is much subjectivity in how the analysis is set up and interpreted. Second, it would be interesting to consider a more principled approach to the normalization of inputs and output attributes used in the analysis. We take the log of the number of trainable parameters to amplify the difference between models where the number of parameters is small, as well as to capture diminishing resource cost once models are sufficiently large. For future work, one may apply exp to achieve the opposite effect. In addition, for attributes that take on negative values, since DEA assumes semipositive data, one may consider splitting the attribute into its positive and negative parts. Third, we have only considered input-oriented models, and so inherent in our approach is the goal of minimizing input consumption while maintaining best-in-class performance. An output-oriented approach is conversely interested in holding input resources constant while producing superior results. We leave investigation of these types of models to future work. Finally, it seems possible that DEA might be integrated into the training process, where the analysis is used to direct training time, parameter size, performance criteria. Due to the high-dimensional nature of language model descriptions, we believe that DEA is well-suited for language model assessment.

Acknowledgments

We thank the anonymous reviewers for their insightful comments and suggestions. This work was done while Zachary Zhou was an intern at American Family Insurance. American Family Insurance sponsored this work.

References

Agha Iqbal Ali. 1990. Data envelopment analysis: Computational issues. *Computers, Environment and Urban Systems*, 14(2):157–165.

Agha Iqbal Ali. 1993. Streamlined computation for data envelopment analysis. *European Journal of Operational Research*, 64(1):61–67.

R. D. Banker, A. Charnes, and W. W. Cooper. 1984. Some models for estimating technical and scale inefficiencies in data envelopment analysis. *Management Science*, 30(9):1078–1092.

C. F. Carter and T. C. Koopmans. 1952. Activity analysis of production and allocation. *The Economic Journal*, 62(247):625.

A. Charnes, W.W. Cooper, A.Y. Lewin, and L.M. Seiford. 1995. *Data Envelopment Analysis: Theory, Methodology, and Applications*. Springer Netherlands.

Abraham Charnes, William W Cooper, and Edwardo Rhodes. 1978. Measuring the efficiency of decision making units. *European journal of operational research*, 2(6):429–444.

Wade D. Cook, Kaoru Tone, and Joe Zhu. 2014. Data envelopment analysis: Prior to choosing a model. *Omega*, 44:1–4.

William W. Cooper, Lawrence M. Seiford, and Joe Zhu, editors. 2004. *Handbook on Data Envelopment Analysis*. Springer US.

W.W. Cooper, L.M. Seiford, and K. Tone. 2007. *Data Envelopment Analysis: A Comprehensive Text with Models, Applications, References and DEA-Solver Software*. Springer US.

Jacob Devlin, Ming-Wei Chang, Kenton Lee, and Kristina Toutanova. 2019. BERT: pre-training of deep bidirectional transformers for language understanding. In *Proceedings of the 2019 Conference of the North American Chapter of the Association for Computational Linguistics: Human Language Technologies, NAACL-HLT 2019, Minneapolis, MN, USA, June 2-7, 2019, Volume 1 (Long and Short Papers)*, pages 4171–4186. Association for Computational Linguistics.

John Doyle and Rodney Green. 1994. Efficiency and cross-efficiency in dea: Derivations, meanings and uses. *Journal of the operational research society*, 45(5):567–578.

Metric	Percentiles: 25	50	75
eval_steps_per_second	0.258	0.295	0.561
train_samples_per_second	70.223	101.606	143.307
num_trainable_params	82119169	109483009	124646401
eval_samples_per_second	129.03	147.476	280.338
eval_runtime	5.3507	10.1712	11.6252
train_runtime	4011.6	5658.1	8186.7
train_steps_per_second	0.828	1.148	1.674
eval_combined_score	0.867	0.880	0.894
eval_spearmanr	0.866	0.878	0.893
eval_pearson	0.868	0.881	0.895

Table 1: Representative data for the stsb tests. The five models tested are: bert-base-uncased, bert-large-uncased, distilbert-base-uncased, distilroberta-base, and roberta-base with three different learning rates 10^{-5}, 10^{-4} and 10^{-3}. In addition to stsb, the other tests are mrpc, qqp, wnli, rte, mnli, cola, sst2, and qnli. For each distinct model, each test, and each learning rate, similar metrics are generated, for a total of over 100 different metrics.

	θ^*_{CCR}	θ^*_{BCC}	SE	CCR eff.	BCC eff.	RTS	GLUE score
glove-50-linear	1.000	1.000	1.000	+	+	$\rightarrow$	0.408
tfidf-1000-linear	1.000	1.000	1.000	+	+	$\rightarrow$	0.591
roberta-base, lr=1e-4	0.501	1.000	0.501		+	$\downarrow$	0.830
distilroberta-base, lr=1e-5	0.499	1.000	0.499		+	$\downarrow$	0.815
tfidf-10000-linear	0.999	1.000	0.999				0.591
tfidf-5000-linear	0.999	1.000	0.999				0.591
tfidf-500-linear	0.999	1.000	0.999				0.610
tfidf-15000-linear	0.999	1.000	0.999				0.591
glove-100-linear	0.952	0.961	0.990				0.455
roberta-base, lr=1e-5	0.460	0.919	0.500				0.807
bert-base-uncased, lr=1e-4	0.486	0.913	0.533				0.799
distilroberta-base, lr=1e-4	0.479	0.863	0.555				0.782
glove-200-linear	0.841	0.845	0.996				0.446
distilbert-base-uncased, lr=1e-5	0.460	0.842	0.546				0.579
bert-base-uncased, lr=1e-5	0.437	0.841	0.519				0.789
bert-large-uncased, lr=1e-5	0.385	0.835	0.461				0.800
glove-300-linear	0.827	0.834	0.991				0.460
distilbert-base-uncased, lr=1e-3	0.466	0.819	0.569				0.740
distilbert-base-uncased, lr=1e-4	0.473	0.803	0.588				0.769
bert-large-uncased, lr=1e-4	0.411	0.741	0.554				0.772
distilroberta-base, lr=1e-3	0.452	0.679	0.665				0.729
roberta-base, lr=1e-3	0.436	0.654	0.666				0.729
bert-base-uncased, lr=1e-3	0.410	0.543	0.756				0.703
bert-large-uncased, lr=1e-3	0.225	0.312	0.721				0.378

Table 2: Efficiency scores, returns to scale characterizations of BCC-efficient models, and GLUE scores (average performance across tasks). Models are ranked first by their BCC score, then by their CCR score. Returns to scale characteristics (increasing = $\uparrow$, decreasing = $\downarrow$, constant = $\rightarrow$) indicated only for BCC-efficient models.

Rotem Dror, Gili Baumer, Marina Bogomolov, and Roi Reichart. 2017. Replicability analysis for natural language processing: Testing significance with multiple datasets. *Transactions of the Association for Computational Linguistics*, 5(0):471–486.

Rotem Dror, Segev Shlomov, and Roi Reichart. 2019. Deep dominance - how to properly compare deep neural models. In *Proceedings of the 57th Annual Meeting of the Association for Computational Linguistics*, pages 2773–2785, Florence, Italy. Association for Computational Linguistics.

Ali Emrouznejad, Rajiv Banker, Subhash Ray, and Lei Chen. 2016. *Recent Applications of Data Envelopment Analysis*. Proceedings of the 14th International Conference on Data Envelopment Analysis.

E. B. Fowlkes and C. L. Mallows. 1983. A method for comparing two hierarchical clusterings. *Journal of the American Statistical Association*, 78(383):553–569.

B Golany and Y Roll. 1989. An application procedure for dea. *Omega*, 17(3):237–250.

Nadia M. Guerrero, Juan Aparicio, and Daniel Valero-Carreras. 2022. Combining data envelopment analysis and machine learning. *Mathematics*, 10(6).

Hugging Face. 2022. Models – Hugging Face. `https://huggingface.co/models`. Accessed: 2022-08-05.

Dariush Khezrimotlagh, Joe Zhu, Wade D. Cook, and

Mehdi Toloo. 2019. Data envelopment analysis and big data. *European Journal of Operational Research*, 274(3):1047–1054.

Chin-Yew Lin. 2004. Rouge: A package for automatic evaluation of summaries. *Proceedings of the ACL Workshop: Text Summarization Braches Out 2004*, page 10.

Yinhan Liu, Myle Ott, Naman Goyal, Jingfei Du, Mandar Joshi, Danqi Chen, Omer Levy, Mike Lewis, Luke Zettlemoyer, and Veselin Stoyanov. 2019. Roberta: A robustly optimized BERT pretraining approach. *CoRR*, abs/1907.11692.

B.W. Matthews. 1975. Comparison of the predicted and observed secondary structure of t4 phage lysozyme. *Biochimica et Biophysica Acta (BBA) - Protein Structure*, 405(2):442–451.

Sharan Narang, Hyung Won Chung, Yi Tay, William Fedus, Thibault Fevry, Michael Matena, Karishma Malkan, Noah Fiedel, Noam Shazeer, Zhenzhong Lan, et al. 2021. Do transformer modifications transfer across implementations and applications? In *Conference on Empirical Methods in Natural Language Processing (EMNLP)*.

Ole B. Olesen and Niels Christian Petersen. 2016. Stochastic data envelopment analysis—a review. *European Journal of Operational Research*, 251(1):2–21.

Kishore Papineni, Salim Roukos, Todd Ward, and Wei-Jing Zhu. 2002. Bleu: a method for automatic evaluation of machine translation. In *Proceedings of the 40th annual meeting on association for computational linguistics*, pages 311–318. Association for Computational Linguistics.

F. Pedregosa, G. Varoquaux, A. Gramfort, V. Michel, B. Thirion, O. Grisel, M. Blondel, P. Prettenhofer, R. Weiss, V. Dubourg, J. Vanderplas, A. Passos, D. Cournapeau, M. Brucher, M. Perrot, and E. Duchesnay. 2011. Scikit-learn: Machine learning in Python. *Journal of Machine Learning Research*, 12:2825–2830.

Jeffrey Pennington, Richard Socher, and Christopher D. Manning. 2014. GloVe: Global Vectors for Word Representation. In *Empirical Methods in Natural Language Processing (EMNLP)*, pages 1532–1543.

Fred Phillips, Ronald G. Parsons, and Andrew Donoho. 1990. Parallel microcomputing for data envelopment analysis. *Computers, Environment and Urban Systems*, 14(2):167–170.

Victor Sanh, Lysandre Debut, Julien Chaumond, and Thomas Wolf. 2019. Distilbert, a distilled version of BERT: smaller, faster, cheaper and lighter. *CoRR*, abs/1910.01108.

Shinn Sun. 2002. Measuring the relative efficiency of police precincts using data envelopment analysis. *Socio-Economic Planning Sciences*, 36(1):51–71.

Emmanuel Thanassoulis. 1995. Assessing police forces in england and wales using data envelopment analysis. *European Journal of Operational Research*, 87(3):641–657. Operational Research in Europe.

Georgios Tsaples, Jason Papathanasiou, and Andreas C. Georgiou. 2022. An Exploratory DEA and Machine Learning Framework for the Evaluation and Analysis of Sustainability Composite Indicators in the EU. *Mathematics*, 10(13).

Dennis Thomas Ulmer, Elisa Bassignana, Max Müller-Eberstein, Daniel Varab, Mike Zhang, Christian Hardmeier, and Barbara Plank. 2022. Experimental standards for deep learning research: A natural language processing perspective.

Ashish Vaswani, Noam Shazeer, Niki Parmar, Jakob Uszkoreit, Llion Jones, Aidan N Gomez, Ł ukasz Kaiser, and Illia Polosukhin. 2017. Attention is all you need. In *Advances in Neural Information Processing Systems*, volume 30. Curran Associates, Inc.

Alex Wang, Amanpreet Singh, Julian Michael, Felix Hill, Omer Levy, and Samuel Bowman. 2018. GLUE: A multi-task benchmark and analysis platform for natural language understanding. In *Proceedings of the 2018 EMNLP Workshop BlackboxNLP: Analyzing and Interpreting Neural Networks for NLP*, pages 353–355, Brussels, Belgium. Association for Computational Linguistics.

G. Udny Yule. 1912. On the methods of measuring association between two attributes. *Journal of the Royal Statistical Society*, 75(6):579–652.

From COMET to COMES – Can Summary Evaluation Benefit from Translation Evaluation?

Mateusz Krubiński and **Pavel Pecina**
Charles University, Faculty of Mathematics and Physics, Institute of Formal and Applied Linguistics
{krubinski,pecina}@ufal.mff.cuni.cz

Abstract

COMET is a recently proposed trainable neural-based evaluation metric developed to assess the quality of Machine Translation systems. In this paper, we explore the usage of COMET for evaluating Text Summarization systems – despite being trained on multilingual MT outputs, it performs remarkably well in monolingual settings, when predicting summarization output quality. We introduce a variant of the model – COMES – trained on the annotated summarization outputs that uses MT data for pre-training. We examine its performance on several datasets with human judgments collected for different notions of summary quality, covering several domains and languages.

1 Introduction

Since manual annotation for any generative task is costly and time consuming, automatic metrics are commonly used to both measure the progress during training and compare outputs from independent systems. Thanks to the Metrics Shared Task (Freitag et al., 2021b; Mathur et al., 2020; Ma et al., 2019) collocated with the WMT workshop since 2008 (Callison-Burch et al., 2008), advances in the MT models performance are accompanied by a continuous development of new automatic metrics (Lo, 2019; Kepler et al., 2019; Rei et al., 2020; Sellam et al., 2020) that improve correlation with human judgment and are robust to both domain shifts and changes in annotation style (Freitag et al., 2021a).

In contrary, for the task of text summarization remarkable advances in modeling techniques (Koto et al., 2022) are not followed by corresponding research on evaluation methods – a number of recent studies (Lewis et al., 2020a; Li et al., 2020; Raffel et al., 2020) keep relying mostly on ROUGE (Lin, 2004), a string-overlap metric measuring the n-gram correspondence with the reference summary.

One of the issues making research on summary evaluation metrics difficult is lack of standardized framework for collecting human judgments. They are collected not only along several dimensions (Table 1) but also using different methods – based on Likert scale (Fabbri et al., 2021; Stiennon et al., 2020), Direct Assessment (Koto et al., 2021) or methods that output numerical score indirectly (Maynez et al., 2020; Bhandari et al., 2020) by e.g. counting number of spans highlighted in the model output by annotators. The other issue is the amount of available annotated data. Even the largest datasets (Fabbri et al., 2021; Bhandari et al., 2020; Maynez et al., 2020) have no more than tens of thousands of annotated instances. This is by far less than the amount of available data for machine translation, with roughly 800k ⟨⟨source, hypothesis, reference⟩⟩ annotated triplets available from the evaluation campaigns of the previous editions of WMT News Translation shared task[1].

The question we ask is: *Can we use this resource to improve summary evaluation?* While the tasks of Machine Translation and Text Summarization are different, we believe that the problem of evaluating the quality of generated output is closely related.

To address this question, we examine the applicability of the COMET metric by Rei et al. (2020) (Section 2.2) that is trained on the annotated MT data and capable of directly regressing a quality score. We propose (Section 3) a variant of the model – COMES[2] – that uses the annotated MT data for pre-training and is capable of predicting several aspects of summary quality. We evaluate our approach (Section 4) on selected datasets with various annotation styles.

2 Related Work

2.1 Automatic Summary Evaluation

Historically, the quality of summary was measured by comparing n-gram overlap between reference

[1] https://wmt-metrics-task.github.io/

[2] **C**rosslingual **O**ptimized **M**etric for **E**valuation of **S**ummarization

Proceedings of the 3rd Workshop on Evaluation and Comparison of NLP Systems, pages 21 - 31
November 20, 2022

	Coherence	Consistency	Fluency	Relevance	SCU	Accuracy	Coverage	Focus	Overall
SummEval (Fabbri et al., 2021)	✓	✓	✓	✓					
REALSumm (Bhandari et al., 2020)					✓				
Human Feedback (Stiennon et al., 2020)	✓					✓	✓		✓
Multi_SummEval (Koto et al., 2021)							✓	✓	

Table 1: Comparison of the types of annotations in the summary evaluation datasets used in our experiments. For a comprehensive survey on the summary evaluation resources see Koto et al. (2022).

and system output (Papineni et al., 2002; Lin, 2004). Over the years, a variety of metrics were proposed for this task – based on question answering (Eyal et al., 2019; Scialom et al., 2019; Durmus et al., 2020; Wang et al., 2020), similarity between summary and reference embeddings (Zhao et al., 2019; Zhang et al., 2020) or the usefulness of summary for language modeling on the source document (Colombo et al., 2022; Liu et al., 2022).

2.2 COMET

COMET is a trained metric that, based on semantic similarities between the translated and reference texts, learns to output a score that resembles the human perception of translation quality. In the default settings, input to the model is a ⟨⟨source, hypothesis, reference⟩⟩ triple, but a reference-less variant for Quality Estimation (COMET_QE) that operates on ⟨⟨source, hypothesis⟩⟩ pairs was also proposed.

On a high level, COMET uses a pre-trained multilingual language model to independently extract representations for each of the input sequences, which are then pooled and concatenated, before being processed with a stack of feed-forward layers that outputs a single numerical value. The choice of COMET for our experiments (as opposed to e.g. BLEURT (Sellam et al., 2020) or YiSi (Lo and Larkin, 2020)) is motivated by a recent metrics study by Kocmi et al. (2021) that shows it's superior performance compared to other (pretrained) metrics and the availability of a well-documented implementation[3].

2.3 SummEval

SummEval[4] (Fabbri et al., 2021) is a recently proposed dataset with human annotations for several dimensions of summary quality. It consists of 100 articles randomly sampled from the test split of the CNN/DailyMail corpus (Nallapati et al., 2016), each of them summarized by 17 systems. For each system output, the authors collected 3 expert judgments for *Coherence*, *Consistency*, *Fluency* and *Relevance* on a Likert scale of 1 to 5. In addition to the original reference, for each article, 10 alternative references were created by Kryscinski et al. (2020).

3 COMES

In the context of Machine Translation two frameworks for collecting human ratings were employed recently – MQM (Lommel et al., 2014) and DA (Bojar et al., 2017), both producing a single numerical score that indicated the overall translation quality. That is not the case for Text Summarization – content, fluency and clarity are all graded independently (Hardy et al., 2019; Koto et al., 2022). As a result, the COMET metric trained on MT data outputs a single overall score.

In our experiments, when reporting COMET performance, we compare this single overall score to all evaluation dimensions. To enable (independently) predicting several aspects of summary quality at once, we propose a modification that alters the number of outputs in the last feed-forward layer, see Figure 1. We experiment with both training from scratch (COMES) and pre-training on the annotated MT data by initializing the model weights from the COMET checkpoint (COMES_MT). See Appendix A.1 for the training details. In both scenarios, we examine the reference-less variant of the metric (COMES_QE and COMES_QE_MT, respectively).

4 Experiments

4.1 SummEval experiments

Since, to the best of our knowledge, SummEval is the largest resource for summary evaluation, we

[3]https://github.com/Unbabel/COMET/

[4]https://github.com/Yale-LILY/SummEval

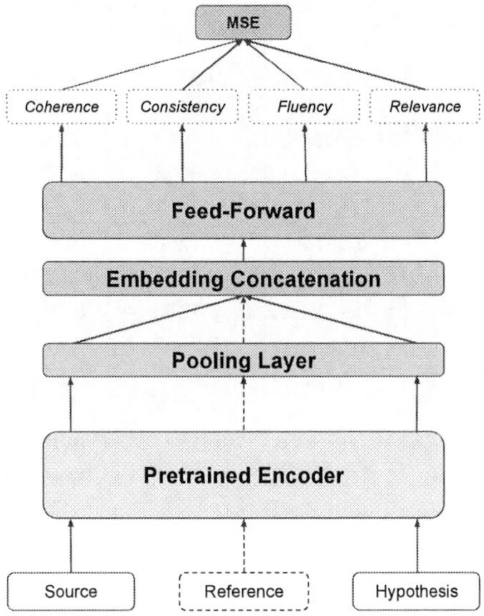

Figure 1: Estimator model architecture used in COMES. Source, reference and hypothesis are all independently encoded with a pre-trained encoder. Pooling layer is used to create sentence embeddings from sequences of token embeddings. In the COMES variant, the last feed-forward layer has 4 outputs, corresponding to different summary evaluation dimensions. Dashed lines are used to indicate the reference-less variant. For the full COMET description see Rei et al. (2020).

would like to use it both for training and evaluation. To achieve this, we rely on cross-validation. We split the data into 10 subsets of 10 articles each, using 80 articles for training, 10 for validation (early stopping) and evaluating on the remaining 10. We train 10 models, use each of them to score 10% of the available (unseen) data and merge the results. That way we can directly compare to other metrics that report correlation on the whole SummEval dataset. During training, we use each reference and each expert annotation[5] to create more training instances (80 articles $\times$ 11 references $\times$ 17 models $\times$ 3 annotations $= 44,880$ instances). During evaluation, we handle multiple references by scoring each reference independently and taking the maximum score.

The results of our experiments can be found in Table 2. We report the system-level Kendall's Tau correlations with (average) expert annotations. For comparison, we also include metrics which previously (Fabbri et al., 2021) achieved the highest correlation with each of the evaluation dimensions – ROUGE-1 and ROUGE-4, BERTScore (Zhang et al., 2020), CHRF (Popović, 2015) and METEOR (Lavie and Agarwal, 2007). Scoring system outputs with both out-of-the-box variants (COMET and COMET_QE) results in the highest correlation coefficients along all metrics analysed by Fabbri et al. (2021) for *Coherence* and *Relevance* dimensions. The reference-less variant has much higher correlation with the *Consistency* dimension (0.24 $\rightarrow$ 0.72). Both COMES and COMES_QE variants perform similarly, achieving higher correlations than both COMET (COMET_QE) and traditional metrics. However the effect of pre-training is ambiguous – on average it does not help, but the main cause is the poor performance on predicting the *Consistency* dimension.

4.2 Domain and Annotation Style shift

To get a better understanding of the metric performance, we apply it to several other annotated summarization datasets. Since we have trained 10 instances for each variant of the COMES models (Section 4.1), evaluating with each of them allows us to estimate the confidence intervals directly, not having to rely on e.g. bootstrapping (Deutsch et al., 2021).

To examine the performance on non-matching evaluation dimensions, we report results on data[6] from the same domain – subset of the CNN/DailyMail corpus. Bhandari et al. (2020) produced the numerical gold-standard scores by rating

[5]We have tried averaging human ratings during training, the results were comparable but slightly worse.

[6]`https://github.com/neulab/REALSumm`

Metric	Coherence	Consistency	Fluency	Relevance
ROUGE-3 f	0.2206	**0.7059**	0.5092	0.3529
ROUGE-4 f	0.3088	0.5882	0.5535	0.4118
BERTScore f	0.2059	0.0441	0.2435	0.4265
CHRF	0.3971	0.5294	0.4649	0.5882
METEOR	0.2353	0.6324	**0.6126**	0.4265
COMET	0.5735	0.2353	0.5240	0.6765
COMES	**0.6912**	**0.7206**	0.5830	**0.7206**
COMES_MT	0.6471	0.4412	**0.6273**	**0.7206**
COMET_QE	0.4118	**0.7206**	**0.7011**	0.5441
COMES_QE	**0.6618**	**0.7647**	**0.6126**	**0.7059**
COMES_MT_QE	**0.6912**	0.4853	**0.6126**	**0.6912**

Table 2: System-level Kendall's Tau correlations with (average) expert annotations for four evaluation dimensions annotated in the SummEval dataset. The three metrics with the highest correlation in each column are bolded. See Table 2 in Fabbri et al. (2021) for results of other metrics.

a system output based on a number of Semantic Content Units (SCUs) that can be inferred from it. LitePyramid (Shapira et al., 2019) method was used to obtain SCUs from reference summaries. On this dataset, the reference-less COMET_QE outperforms any other variant, almost doubling the correlation of COMET ($0.46 \rightarrow 0.75$). The *Consistency* head of COMES_QE comes in second (0.59). Considering the recall based nature of annotations, it is not surprising that the best correlation is obtained by the recall variant of ROUGE (0.85).

In an independent work[7], Stiennon et al. (2020) annotated a different subset of the CNN/DailyMail corpus by rating system outputs for *Accuracy*, *Coherence*, *Coverage* and *Overall Quality*. Again, the reference-less variant COMET_QE performs best, obtaining almost a perfect correlation with the *Overall* dimension (0.92). This is by far a better result than any traditional metric considered (0.65 by ROUGE-1 F-score). COMES trained from scratch out-performs the pre-trained variant COMES_MT which may indicate overfitting to the SummEval annotations. Surprisingly, the highest correlation with the *Coherence* dimension (present in the SummEval annotations used for training) is not obtained by the *Coherence* head of COMES. That is however the case for the variant pre-trained on MT data (COMES_MT). For the full, results see Table 5 and Table 6 in Appendix.

To validate the performance on a different domain, we evaluate on the subset of the TL;DR corpus (Völske et al., 2017) annotated in a similar manner by Stiennon et al. (2020), see Table 7 in Appendix. On this dataset COMET achieves the top correlation, with the COMES clearly lagging behind in performance compared to the pre-trained COMES_MT variant.

4.3 Non-English data

One of the strengths of the COMET metric is its multilinguality – the model has seen over 30 language pairs during training. To assess its quality as a summary evaluation tool for non-English data, we evaluated it on the Multi_SummEval dataset (Koto et al., 2021). With only two system outputs annotated (along the *Focus* and *Coverage* dimensions), the size of the resource is not sufficient for reporting system-level correlations. Thus, we report the summary-level (segment-level) Pearson correlations.

For a fair comparison, we wanted to train the COMES model variant using the multilingual data. Due to the lack of sufficient resources, we fall back on using automatic machine translation to translate the English annotated data. This approach has proven successful for e.g. Question Answering (Lewis et al., 2020b; Macková and Straka, 2020). We limit our analysis to the subset of languages from Multi_SummEval that originates from the MLSUM (Scialom et al., 2020) corpus. We have translated SummEval into German, French, Russian, Turkish and Spanish using the uni-directional models provided by the Helsinki-NLP group (Tiedemann, 2020) and used the data (together with the original SummEval) to train a multilingual COMES model (COMES_MT_ML).

Our findings indicate that in the summary-level evaluation, the original COMET metric is superior to any other variant considered, clearly outperforming the reference-less variant COMET_QE.

[7] https://github.com/openai/summarize-from-feedback

Metric	CV	Coherence	Consistency	Fluency	Relevance
COMES	✓	0.6912	0.7206	0.5830	0.7206
COMES	-	0.9412	0.9412	0.8340	0.9265
COMES_MT	✓	0.6471	0.4412	0.6273	0.7206
COMES_MT	-	0.8088	0.7941	0.6864	0.8676
COMES_QE	✓	0.6618	0.7647	0.6126	0.7059
COMES_QE	-	0.9706	0.9265	0.8782	0.9706
COMES_MT_QE	✓	0.6912	0.4853	0.6126	0.6912
COMES_MT_QE	-	0.8235	0.7794	0.6568	0.8676

Table 3: System-level Kendall's Tau correlations with (average) expert annotations for four evaluation dimensions annotated in the SummEval dataset. The *CV* variants correspond to the un-biased cross-validation settings (Section 4.1), the remaining ones are obtained with the over-fitted models, see Section 4.4.

Surprisingly, both the COMES_MT and the COMES variants perform better than the multilingual COMES_MT_ML variant. This is in line with recent findings by Braun et al. (2022), which indicate that summary evaluations do not survive translation. On this dataset, even the best performing COMET is still inferior to both ROUGE and BERTScore. Considering, however, the relatively small size of the dataset (270 instances per language, outputs from two systems) we believe that the question about COMET/COMES usefulness for multilingual and summary-level evaluation is still open. For the full results, see Table 8 in Appendix.

4.4 Ablation Study

In Section 4.1, we propose the usage of cross-validation to enable training and un-biased testing on the SummEval dataset – different articles are used for training, validation and testing. To show that the model can over-fit to the data, we have trained a model using all of the available annotations from the SummEval dataset and then applied it to the same articles, already seen during training. Table 3 (rows without the *CV* mark) presents the results. It is clear that the model is able to memorize the annotations proving that the cross-validation approach enables un-biased reporting on the whole SummEval dataset and thus is a fair way of comparing COMES to other metrics.

In Section 2.2 we mention that COMET (and COMES) uses a pre-trained multilingual language model to extract representations from input sequences. In our experiments, it is always the XLM-RoBERTa (Conneau et al., 2020) model. A major difference between Machine Translation and Text Summarization is the length of the typical input. By examining the lengths of the tokenized documents from SummEval, we have realized that only 48% of them fit completely within the model limit of 512 tokens. However, on average, 92% of input tokens are consumed (average input document length in tokens equals 502) so the information lost is hopefully not significant. We leave the detailed analysis for future works.

5 Conclusion

In this paper, we showed that the COMET metric trained on (multilingual) MT outputs can be successfully used to evaluate the quality of (monolingual) summaries. We proposed an adaptation that enables scoring several (independent) evaluation dimensions at once. Our results (Table 2) indicate, that the off-the-shelf COMET metric performs comparable to the variants fine-tuned on the annotated summarization outputs. Furthermore, the reference-less variants perform similar to the ones using references, making the metric applicable in settings when the gold-standard summary is not available.

Acknowledgements

This work was supported by the European Commission via its H2020 Program (contract no. 870930), the Czech Science Foundation (grant no. 19-26934X), and CELSA (project no. 19/018). In this work, we used data and tools provided by the LINDAT/CLARIAH-CZ Research Infrastructure (https://lindat.cz), supported by the Ministry of Education, Youth and Sports of the Czech Republic (project no. LM2018101).

References

Manik Bhandari, Pranav Narayan Gour, Atabak Ashfaq, Pengfei Liu, and Graham Neubig. 2020. Re-evaluating evaluation in text summarization. In *Proceedings of the 2020 Conference on Empirical*

Methods in Natural Language Processing (EMNLP), pages 9347–9359, Online. Association for Computational Linguistics.

Ondřej Bojar, Yvette Graham, and Amir Kamran. 2017. Results of the WMT17 metrics shared task. In *Proceedings of the Second Conference on Machine Translation*, pages 489–513, Copenhagen, Denmark. Association for Computational Linguistics.

Spencer Braun, Oleg Vasilyev, Neslihan Iskender, and John Bohannon. 2022. Does summary evaluation survive translation to other languages? In *Proceedings of the 2022 Conference of the North American Chapter of the Association for Computational Linguistics: Human Language Technologies*, pages 2425–2435, Seattle, United States. Association for Computational Linguistics.

Chris Callison-Burch, Cameron Fordyce, Philipp Koehn, Christof Monz, and Josh Schroeder. 2008. Further meta-evaluation of machine translation. In *Proceedings of the Third Workshop on Statistical Machine Translation*, pages 70–106, Columbus, Ohio. Association for Computational Linguistics.

Pierre Jean A. Colombo, Chloé Clavel, and Pablo Piantanida. 2022. Infolm: A new metric to evaluate summarization & data2text generation. In *Thirty-Sixth AAAI Conference on Artificial Intelligence, AAAI 2022, Thirty-Fourth Conference on Innovative Applications of Artificial Intelligence, IAAI 2022, The Twelveth Symposium on Educational Advances in Artificial Intelligence, EAAI 2022 Virtual Event, February 22 - March 1, 2022*, pages 10554–10562. AAAI Press.

Alexis Conneau, Kartikay Khandelwal, Naman Goyal, Vishrav Chaudhary, Guillaume Wenzek, Francisco Guzmán, Edouard Grave, Myle Ott, Luke Zettlemoyer, and Veselin Stoyanov. 2020. Unsupervised cross-lingual representation learning at scale. In *Proceedings of the 58th Annual Meeting of the Association for Computational Linguistics*, pages 8440–8451, Online. Association for Computational Linguistics.

Daniel Deutsch, Rotem Dror, and Dan Roth. 2021. A statistical analysis of summarization evaluation metrics using resampling methods. *Transactions of the Association for Computational Linguistics*, 9:1132–1146.

Esin Durmus, He He, and Mona Diab. 2020. FEQA: A question answering evaluation framework for faithfulness assessment in abstractive summarization. In *Proceedings of the 58th Annual Meeting of the Association for Computational Linguistics*, pages 5055–5070, Online. Association for Computational Linguistics.

Matan Eyal, Tal Baumel, and Michael Elhadad. 2019. Question answering as an automatic evaluation metric for news article summarization. In *Proceedings of the 2019 Conference of the North American Chapter of the Association for Computational Linguistics: Human Language Technologies, Volume 1 (Long and Short Papers)*, pages 3938–3948, Minneapolis, Minnesota. Association for Computational Linguistics.

Alexander R. Fabbri, Wojciech Kryściński, Bryan McCann, Caiming Xiong, Richard Socher, and Dragomir Radev. 2021. SummEval: Re-evaluating summarization evaluation. *Transactions of the Association for Computational Linguistics*, 9:391–409.

Markus Freitag, George Foster, David Grangier, Viresh Ratnakar, Qijun Tan, and Wolfgang Macherey. 2021a. Experts, errors, and context: A large-scale study of human evaluation for machine translation. *Transactions of the Association for Computational Linguistics*, 9:1460–1474.

Markus Freitag, Ricardo Rei, Nitika Mathur, Chi-kiu Lo, Craig Stewart, George Foster, Alon Lavie, and Ondřej Bojar. 2021b. Results of the WMT21 metrics shared task: Evaluating metrics with expert-based human evaluations on TED and news domain. In *Proceedings of the Sixth Conference on Machine Translation*, pages 733–774, Online. Association for Computational Linguistics.

Hardy Hardy, Shashi Narayan, and Andreas Vlachos. 2019. HighRES: Highlight-based reference-less evaluation of summarization. In *Proceedings of the 57th Annual Meeting of the Association for Computational Linguistics*, pages 3381–3392, Florence, Italy. Association for Computational Linguistics.

Fabio Kepler, Jonay Trénous, Marcos Treviso, Miguel Vera, and André F. T. Martins. 2019. OpenKiwi: An open source framework for quality estimation. In *Proceedings of the 57th Annual Meeting of the Association for Computational Linguistics: System Demonstrations*, pages 117–122, Florence, Italy. Association for Computational Linguistics.

Tom Kocmi, Christian Federmann, Roman Grundkiewicz, Marcin Junczys-Dowmunt, Hitokazu Matsushita, and Arul Menezes. 2021. To ship or not to ship: An extensive evaluation of automatic metrics for machine translation. In *Proceedings of the Sixth Conference on Machine Translation*, pages 478–494, Online. Association for Computational Linguistics.

Fajri Koto, Timothy Baldwin, and Jey Han Lau. 2022. Ffci: A framework for interpretable automatic evaluation of summarization. *J. Artif. Int. Res.*, 73.

Fajri Koto, Jey Han Lau, and Timothy Baldwin. 2021. Evaluating the efficacy of summarization evaluation across languages. In *Findings of the Association for Computational Linguistics: ACL-IJCNLP 2021*, pages 801–812, Online. Association for Computational Linguistics.

Wojciech Kryscinski, Bryan McCann, Caiming Xiong, and Richard Socher. 2020. Evaluating the factual consistency of abstractive text summarization. In *Proceedings of the 2020 Conference on Empirical Methods in Natural Language Processing (EMNLP)*, pages 9332–9346, Online. Association for Computational Linguistics.

Alon Lavie and Abhaya Agarwal. 2007. METEOR: An automatic metric for MT evaluation with high levels of correlation with human judgments. In *Proceedings of the Second Workshop on Statistical Machine Translation*, pages 228–231, Prague, Czech Republic. Association for Computational Linguistics.

Mike Lewis, Yinhan Liu, Naman Goyal, Marjan Ghazvininejad, Abdelrahman Mohamed, Omer Levy, Veselin Stoyanov, and Luke Zettlemoyer. 2020a. BART: Denoising sequence-to-sequence pre-training for natural language generation, translation, and comprehension. In *Proceedings of the 58th Annual Meeting of the Association for Computational Linguistics*, pages 7871–7880, Online. Association for Computational Linguistics.

Patrick Lewis, Barlas Oguz, Ruty Rinott, Sebastian Riedel, and Holger Schwenk. 2020b. MLQA: Evaluating cross-lingual extractive question answering. In *Proceedings of the 58th Annual Meeting of the Association for Computational Linguistics*, pages 7315–7330, Online. Association for Computational Linguistics.

Mingzhe Li, Xiuying Chen, Shen Gao, Zhangming Chan, Dongyan Zhao, and Rui Yan. 2020. VMSMO: Learning to generate multimodal summary for video-based news articles. In *Proceedings of the 2020 Conference on Empirical Methods in Natural Language Processing (EMNLP)*, pages 9360–9369, Online. Association for Computational Linguistics.

Chin-Yew Lin. 2004. ROUGE: A package for automatic evaluation of summaries. In *Text Summarization Branches Out*, pages 74–81, Barcelona, Spain. Association for Computational Linguistics.

Yu Lu Liu, Rachel Bawden, Thomas Scaliom, Benoît Sagot, and Jackie Chi Kit Cheung. 2022. Maskeval: Weighted mlm-based evaluation for text summarization and simplification. *CoRR*, abs/2205.12394.

Chi-kiu Lo. 2019. YiSi - a unified semantic MT quality evaluation and estimation metric for languages with different levels of available resources. In *Proceedings of the Fourth Conference on Machine Translation (Volume 2: Shared Task Papers, Day 1)*, pages 507–513, Florence, Italy. Association for Computational Linguistics.

Chi-kiu Lo and Samuel Larkin. 2020. Machine translation reference-less evaluation using YiSi-2 with bilingual mappings of massive multilingual language model. In *Proceedings of the Fifth Conference on Machine Translation*, pages 903–910, Online. Association for Computational Linguistics.

Arle Lommel, Aljoscha Burchardt, and Hans Uszkoreit. 2014. Multidimensional quality metrics (mqm): A framework for declaring and describing translation quality metrics. *Tradumàtica: tecnologies de la traducció*, 0:455–463.

Qingsong Ma, Johnny Wei, Ondřej Bojar, and Yvette Graham. 2019. Results of the WMT19 metrics shared task: Segment-level and strong MT systems pose big challenges. In *Proceedings of the Fourth Conference on Machine Translation (Volume 2: Shared Task Papers, Day 1)*, pages 62–90, Florence, Italy. Association for Computational Linguistics.

Kateřina Macková and Milan Straka. 2020. Reading comprehension in czech via machine translation and cross-lingual transfer. In *23rd International Conference on Text, Speech and Dialogue*, pages 171–179, Cham, Switzerland. Springer.

Christopher Manning, Mihai Surdeanu, John Bauer, Jenny Finkel, Steven Bethard, and David McClosky. 2014. The Stanford CoreNLP natural language processing toolkit. In *Proceedings of 52nd Annual Meeting of the Association for Computational Linguistics: System Demonstrations*, pages 55–60, Baltimore, Maryland. Association for Computational Linguistics.

Nitika Mathur, Johnny Wei, Markus Freitag, Qingsong Ma, and Ondřej Bojar. 2020. Results of the WMT20 metrics shared task. In *Proceedings of the Fifth Conference on Machine Translation*, pages 688–725, Online. Association for Computational Linguistics.

Joshua Maynez, Shashi Narayan, Bernd Bohnet, and Ryan McDonald. 2020. On faithfulness and factuality in abstractive summarization. In *Proceedings of the 58th Annual Meeting of the Association for Computational Linguistics*, pages 1906–1919, Online. Association for Computational Linguistics.

Ramesh Nallapati, Bowen Zhou, Cicero dos Santos, Çağlar Gulçehre, and Bing Xiang. 2016. Abstractive text summarization using sequence-to-sequence RNNs and beyond. In *Proceedings of The 20th SIGNLL Conference on Computational Natural Language Learning*, pages 280–290, Berlin, Germany. Association for Computational Linguistics.

Kishore Papineni, Salim Roukos, Todd Ward, and Wei-Jing Zhu. 2002. Bleu: a method for automatic evaluation of machine translation. In *Proceedings of the 40th Annual Meeting of the Association for Computational Linguistics*, pages 311–318, Philadelphia, Pennsylvania, USA. Association for Computational Linguistics.

Maja Popović. 2015. chrF: character n-gram F-score for automatic MT evaluation. In *Proceedings of the Tenth Workshop on Statistical Machine Translation*, pages 392–395, Lisbon, Portugal. Association for Computational Linguistics.

Colin Raffel, Noam Shazeer, Adam Roberts, Katherine Lee, Sharan Narang, Michael Matena, Yanqi Zhou, Wei Li, and Peter J. Liu. 2020. Exploring the limits of transfer learning with a unified text-to-text transformer. *Journal of Machine Learning Research*, 21(140):1–67.

Ricardo Rei, Ana C Farinha, Chrysoula Zerva, Daan van Stigt, Craig Stewart, Pedro Ramos, Taisiya Glushkova, André F. T. Martins, and Alon Lavie. 2021. Are references really needed? unbabel-IST 2021 submission for the metrics shared task. In *Proceedings of the Sixth Conference on Machine Translation*, pages 1030–1040, Online. Association for Computational Linguistics.

Ricardo Rei, Craig Stewart, Ana C Farinha, and Alon Lavie. 2020. COMET: A neural framework for MT evaluation. In *Proceedings of the 2020 Conference on Empirical Methods in Natural Language Processing (EMNLP)*, pages 2685–2702, Online. Association for Computational Linguistics.

Thomas Scialom, Paul-Alexis Dray, Sylvain Lamprier, Benjamin Piwowarski, and Jacopo Staiano. 2020. MLSUM: The multilingual summarization corpus. In *Proceedings of the 2020 Conference on Empirical Methods in Natural Language Processing (EMNLP)*, pages 8051–8067, Online. Association for Computational Linguistics.

Thomas Scialom, Sylvain Lamprier, Benjamin Piwowarski, and Jacopo Staiano. 2019. Answers unite! unsupervised metrics for reinforced summarization models. In *Proceedings of the 2019 Conference on Empirical Methods in Natural Language Processing and the 9th International Joint Conference on Natural Language Processing (EMNLP-IJCNLP)*, pages 3246–3256, Hong Kong, China. Association for Computational Linguistics.

Thibault Sellam, Dipanjan Das, and Ankur Parikh. 2020. BLEURT: Learning robust metrics for text generation. In *Proceedings of the 58th Annual Meeting of the Association for Computational Linguistics*, pages 7881–7892, Online. Association for Computational Linguistics.

Ori Shapira, David Gabay, Yang Gao, Hadar Ronen, Ramakanth Pasunuru, Mohit Bansal, Yael Amsterdamer, and Ido Dagan. 2019. Crowdsourcing lightweight pyramids for manual summary evaluation. In *Proceedings of the 2019 Conference of the North American Chapter of the Association for Computational Linguistics: Human Language Technologies, Volume 1 (Long and Short Papers)*, pages 682–687, Minneapolis, Minnesota. Association for Computational Linguistics.

Nisan Stiennon, Long Ouyang, Jeffrey Wu, Daniel Ziegler, Ryan Lowe, Chelsea Voss, Alec Radford, Dario Amodei, and Paul F Christiano. 2020. Learning to summarize with human feedback. In *Advances in Neural Information Processing Systems*, volume 33, pages 3008–3021. Curran Associates, Inc.

Jörg Tiedemann. 2020. The tatoeba translation challenge – realistic data sets for low resource and multilingual MT. In *Proceedings of the Fifth Conference on Machine Translation*, pages 1174–1182, Online. Association for Computational Linguistics.

Michael Völske, Martin Potthast, Shahbaz Syed, and Benno Stein. 2017. TL;DR: Mining Reddit to learn automatic summarization. In *Proceedings of the Workshop on New Frontiers in Summarization*, pages 59–63, Copenhagen, Denmark. Association for Computational Linguistics.

Alex Wang, Kyunghyun Cho, and Mike Lewis. 2020. Asking and answering questions to evaluate the factual consistency of summaries. In *Proceedings of the 58th Annual Meeting of the Association for Computational Linguistics*, pages 5008–5020, Online. Association for Computational Linguistics.

Tianyi Zhang, Varsha Kishore, Felix Wu, Kilian Q. Weinberger, and Yoav Artzi. 2020. Bertscore: Evaluating text generation with BERT. In *8th International Conference on Learning Representations, ICLR 2020, Addis Ababa, Ethiopia, April 26-30, 2020*. OpenReview.net.

Wei Zhao, Maxime Peyrard, Fei Liu, Yang Gao, Christian M. Meyer, and Steffen Eger. 2019. MoverScore: Text generation evaluating with contextualized embeddings and earth mover distance. In *Proceedings of the 2019 Conference on Empirical Methods in Natural Language Processing and the 9th International Joint Conference on Natural Language Processing (EMNLP-IJCNLP)*, pages 563–578, Hong Kong, China. Association for Computational Linguistics.

A Appendix

A.1 COMES Hyper-Parameters

During COMES training, we mostly follow the training/fine-tuning configuration of Rei et al. (2021), see Table 4. We monitor Pearson correlation on the validation set for early stopping. When fine-tuning the COMET model instead of training from scratch, we decrease the `learning_rate` to 1.0e-05 and load weights from the *wmt21-comet-da* checkpoint. In the reference-less variant, we set the `hidden_sizes` to [2048, 1024] and load weights from the *wmt21-comet-qe-da* checkpoint. We employ gradient accumulation to train with the effective batch size of 40. As a part of pre-processing, we de-tokenize and true-case system outputs with Stanford CoreNLP (Manning et al., 2014) tool.

nr_frozen_epochs	1.0
keep_embeddings_frozen	True
optimizer	AdamW
encoder_learning_rate	1.0e-0
learning_rate	3.1e-05
layerwise_decay	0.95
encoder	XLM-RoBERTa
pretrained_model	xlm-roberta-large
pool	avg
layer	mix
dropout	0.15
hidden_sizes	[3072, 1024]
epochs	5

Table 4: Hyper-parameters used for COMES training.

A.2 REALSumm results

In Table 5, we report the system-level Kendall's Tau correlations on the REALSumm corpus (100 articles × 25 models), annotated by Bhandari et al. (2020). „Score" column is used for metrics that output a single score, the following ones correspond to outputs from each of the COMES heads. From the analysis, we excluded 2 articles that appear in the SummEval dataset. For the COMES variants that we trained ourselves, we evaluate with models trained on each cross-validation fold, reporting mean and standard deviation, see Section 4.1 for details.

Metric	LitePyramid SCU				
	Score	Coherence	Consistency	Fluency	Relevance
ROUGE-1 r	**0.779**				
ROUGE-2 r	**0.853**				
ROUGE-L r	**0.746**				
BERTScore r	0.538				
JS-2	0.518				
MoverScore	0.264				
COMET	0.457				
COMES		0.242 ± 0.05	0.561 ± 0.07	0.290 ± 0.02	0.481 ± 0.05
COMES_MT		0.405 ± 0.03	0.423 ± 0.02	0.434 ± 0.02	0.409 ± 0.03
COMET_QE	0.745				
COMES_QE		0.264 ± 0.06	0.592 ± 0.04	0.309 ± 0.06	0.490 ± 0.06
COMES_MT_QE		0.457 ± 0.05	0.473 ± 0.04	0.472 ± 0.04	0.460 ± 0.05

Table 5: System-level Kendall's Tau correlations on the REALSumm corpus annotated by Bhandari et al. (2020). The three metrics with the highest correlation in each column are bolded.

A.3 Human Feedback data results

Table 6 presents the system-level Kendall's Tau correlations on the subset of the test split of the CNN/DailyMail corpus annotated by Stiennon et al. (2020). The columns indicate different evaluation dimensions in the annotated (test) data. In the rows, we include outputs from each of the COMES heads, that correspond to evaluation dimensions used in the training data. From the analysis, we excluded 6 articles that appear in the SummEval dataset. In Table 7, we present the corresponding numbers when evaluating on the subset of the TL;DR corpus annotated by Stiennon et al. (2020) in a similar manner. For the COMES variants that we trained ourselves we evaluate with models trained on each cross-validation fold, reporting mean and standard deviation, see Section 4.1 for details.

Metric		Overall	Accuracy	Coverage	Coherence
ROUGE-1 f		0.647	**0.752**	0.621	0.464
ROUGE-2 f		0.569	0.699	0.542	0.438
ROUGE-L f		0.595	0.699	0.569	0.412
BERTScore f		0.621	**0.725**	0.595	0.464
COMET		**0.843**	0.686	**0.817**	0.425
COMES	Coherence	−0.204 ± 0.05	−0.050 ± 0.04	−0.230 ± 0.05	0.264 ± 0.04
	Consistency	0.722 ± 0.12	0.630 ± 0.06	0.695 ± 0.12	0.565 ± 0.07
	Fluency	0.209 ± 0.10	0.340 ± 0.07	0.186 ± 0.09	0.625 ± 0.07
	Relevance	**0.774 ± 0.03**	**0.703 ± 0.04**	**0.750 ± 0.03**	0.627 ± 0.02
COMES_MT	Coherence	0.366 ± 0.16	0.403 ± 0.12	0.340 ± 0.16	**0.654 ± 0.07**
	Consistency	0.455 ± 0.11	0.418 ± 0.10	0.431 ± 0.12	0.604 ± 0.11
	Fluency	0.433 ± 0.12	0.414 ± 0.11	0.407 ± 0.12	0.634 ± 0.06
	Relevance	0.379 ± 0.16	0.403 ± 0.12	0.353 ± 0.16	**0.654 ± 0.06**
COMET_QE		**0.922**	0.660	**0.895**	0.477
COMES_QE	Coherence	−0.158 ± 0.1	−0.017 ± 0.09	−0.184 ± 0.10	0.305 ± 0.09
	Consistency	0.714 ± 0.05	0.630 ± 0.05	0.688 ± 0.05	0.544 ± 0.06
	Fluency	0.170 ± 0.13	0.272 ± 0.11	0.144 ± 0.13	0.559 ± 0.08
	Relevance	0.695 ± 0.07	0.648 ± 0.06	0.669 ± 0.07	0.646 ± 0.04
COMES_MT_QE	Coherence	0.480 ± 0.11	0.467 ± 0.09	0.454 ± 0.11	**0.668 ± 0.03**
	Consistency	0.528 ± 0.07	0.484 ± 0.08	0.502 ± 0.07	0.638 ± 0.06
	Fluency	0.519 ± 0.07	0.480 ± 0.08	0.493 ± 0.07	0.647 ± 0.05
	Relevance	0.493 ± 0.09	0.477 ± 0.08	0.467 ± 0.09	**0.678 ± 0.02**

Table 6: System-level Kendall's Tau correlations on the subset of CNN/DailyMail corpus annotated by Stiennon et al. (2020). The three metrics with the highest correlation in each column are bolded.

A.4 Multi_SummEval results

In Table 8, we report the summary-level (segment-level) Pearson correlations on the subset of Multi_SummEval corpus annotated by Koto et al. (2021). Koto et al. (2021) collected human judgments for *Focus* and *Coverage*, using the Direct Assessment method to collect scores on a continuous scale of 1 to 100. For other metrics, see Table 2 in Koto et al. (2021). For readability reasons, we report only the mean COMES scores and do not report variance, see Section 4.1 for details.

Metric		Overall	Accuracy	Coverage	Coherence
ROUGE-1 f		0.545	0.000	0.576	0.333
ROUGE-2 f		0.576	0.091	0.606	**0.424**
ROUGE-L f		0.606	0.061	0.636	**0.394**
BERTScore f		0.424	−0.121	0.455	0.212
COMET		**0.727**	−0.061	**0.758**	0.273
COMES	Coherence	−0.058 ± 0.19	**0.306 ± 0.15**	−0.052 ± 0.18	0.124 ± 0.09
	Consistency	0.239 ± 0.05	0.082 ± 0.01	0.209 ± 0.05	−0.003 ± 0.05
	Fluency	0.227 ± 0.09	−0.106 ± 0.04	0.258 ± 0.09	0.039 ± 0.04
	Relevance	0.600 ± 0.12	0.042 ± 0.08	0.630 ± 0.12	0.315 ± 0.08
COMES_MT	Coherence	**0.682 ± 0.02**	−0.100 ± 0.03	**0.712 ± 0.02**	0.294 ± 0.03
	Consistency	0.536 ± 0.14	−0.155 ± 0.05	0.567 ± 0.14	0.215 ± 0.09
	Fluency	0.561 ± 0.10	−0.161 ± 0.07	0.591 ± 0.10	0.233 ± 0.07
	Relevance	**0.676 ± 0.03**	−0.112 ± 0.03	**0.706 ± 0.03**	0.282 ± 0.03
COMET_QE		0.545	**0.121**	0.576	**0.394**
COMES_QE	Coherence	0.088 ± 0.27	**0.258 ± 0.14**	0.100 ± 0.27	0.173 ± 0.15
	Consistency	0.206 ± 0.11	0.085 ± 0.06	0.182 ± 0.11	0.012 ± 0.08
	Fluency	0.218 ± 0.11	−0.073 ± 0.06	0.248 ± 0.11	0.055 ± 0.06
	Relevance	0.533 ± 0.09	0.085 ± 0.07	0.564 ± 0.09	0.315 ± 0.07
COMES_MT_QE	Coherence	0.564 ± 0.04	0.048 ± 0.04	0.594 ± 0.04	**0.394 ± 0.02**
	Consistency	0.491 ± 0.11	0.012 ± 0.08	0.521 ± 0.11	0.321 ± 0.09
	Fluency	0.473 ± 0.11	0.000 ± 0.07	0.503 ± 0.11	0.297 ± 0.10
	Relevance	0.555 ± 0.05	0.058 ± 0.04	0.585 ± 0.05	0.385 ± 0.03

Table 7: System-level Kendall's Tau correlations on the subset of TL;DR corpus annotated by Stiennon et al. (2020). The three metrics with the highest correlation in each column are bolded.

		Focus					Coverage				
Metric		de	es	tr	fr	ru	de	es	tr	fr	ru
COMET		**0.82**	**0.51**	**0.64**	**0.47**	**0.42**	**0.82**	**0.54**	**0.72**	**0.40**	**0.45**
COMET_QE		0.29	0.06	0.03	0.01	0.10	0.31	0.09	0.27	−0.03	**0.24**
COMES	Coherence	0.21	0.03	0.07	**0.16**	−0.01	0.15	−0.01	−0.05	0.08	−0.07
	Consistency	0.33	0.11	**0.21**	0.10	**0.14**	0.35	0.13	0.30	0.07	0.22
	Fluency	0.36	0.05	0.10	0.11	0.08	0.33	0.06	0.10	0.05	0.15
	Relevance	**0.42**	**0.15**	**0.25**	**0.18**	**0.12**	**0.44**	**0.20**	**0.38**	**0.15**	**0.26**
COMES_MT	Coherence	**0.37**	0.13	**0.25**	0.15	0.08	0.36	0.09	**0.31**	0.11	0.14
	Consistency	0.31	0.10	0.20	0.14	0.09	0.30	0.09	0.24	0.09	0.16
	Fluency	0.31	0.10	**0.21**	0.14	0.09	0.30	0.09	0.25	0.09	0.16
	Relevance	0.36	0.12	**0.25**	0.15	0.09	0.35	0.09	0.30	0.10	0.15
COMES_MT_ML	Coherence	0.03	−0.01	−0.03	0.13	−0.09	−0.04	−0.04	−0.17	0.10	−0.14
	Consistency	0.10	0.02	0.01	0.00	0.01	0.10	0.00	0.01	−0.02	0.12
	Fluency	0.23	0.02	0.09	0.07	0.01	0.22	0.03	0.08	−0.01	0.01
	Relevance	0.36	**0.20**	0.16	0.15	0.06	**0.38**	**0.25**	0.27	**0.16**	0.23

Table 8: Summary-level Pearson correlations on the Multi_SummEval corpus annotated by Koto et al. (2021). The three metrics with the highest correlation in each column are bolded.

Better Smatch = Better Parser? AMR evaluation is not so simple anymore

Juri Opitz
Dept. of Computational Linguistics
Heidelberg University
69120 Heidelberg
opitz.sci@gmail.com

Anette Frank
Dept. of Computational Linguistics
Heidelberg University
69120 Heidelberg
frank@cl.uni-heidelberg.de

Abstract

Recently, astonishing advances have been observed in AMR parsing, as measured by the structural SMATCH metric. In fact, today's systems achieve performance levels that seem to surpass estimates of human inter annotator agreement (IAA). Therefore, it is unclear how well SMATCH (still) relates to human estimates of parse quality, as in this situation potentially fine-grained errors of similar weight may impact the AMR's meaning to different degrees.

We conduct an analysis of two popular and strong AMR parsers that – according to SMATCH– reach quality levels on par with human IAA, and assess how human quality ratings relate to SMATCH and other AMR metrics. Our main findings are: i) While high SMATCH scores indicate otherwise, we find that **AMR parsing is far from being solved**: we frequently find structurally small, but semantically unacceptable errors that substantially distort sentence meaning. ii) Considering high-performance parsers, **better SMATCH scores may not necessarily indicate consistently better parsing quality**. To obtain a meaningful and comprehensive assessment of quality differences of parse(r)s, we recommend augmenting evaluations with macro statistics, use of additional metrics, and more human analysis.

1 Introduction

Abstract Meaning Representation (AMR), proposed by Banarescu et al. (2013), aims at capturing the meaning of texts in an explicit graph format. Nodes describe *entities, events*, and *states*, while edges express key semantic relations, such as ARG_x (indicating semantic roles as in PropBank (Palmer et al., 2005)), or *instrument* and *cause*.

Albeit the development of parsers can be driven by multiple desiderata, better performance on benchmarks often serves as main criterion. For AMR, this goal is typically measured using SMATCH (Cai and Knight, 2013) against a reference corpus. The metric measures to what extent the reference has been reconstructed by the parser.

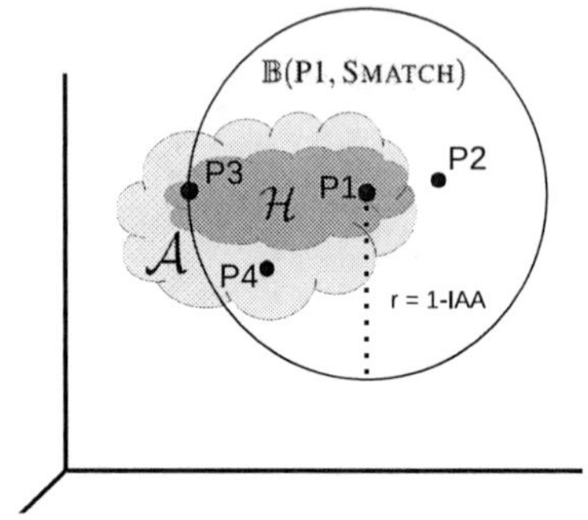

Figure 1: Sketch of AMR IAA ball. The center (P1) is a reference AMR, while P2, P3, P4 are candidates. Any AMR x from the ball has high structural SMATCH agreement with P1, i.e., SMATCH$(x, P1) \geq$ estimated human IAA. However, they may fall in different categories: $\mathcal{H}$ (green cloud) contains correct AMR alternatives. Its superset $\mathcal{A}$ (light cloud) contains acceptable AMRs that may misrepresent the sentence meaning up to a minor degree. Other parses from the ball, e.g., P2, mis-represent the sentence's meaning – despite possibly having higher SMATCH agreement with the reference than all other candidates.

However, thanks to astonishing recent advances in AMR parsing, mainly powered by the *language modeling and fine-tuning paradigm* (Bevilacqua et al., 2021), parsers now achieve benchmark scores that surpass IAA estimates.[1] Therefore, it is difficult to assess whether (fine) differences in SMATCH scores i) can be attributed to minor but valid divergences in interpretation or AMR structure, as they may also occur in human assessments, or ii) if they constitute significant meaning distorting errors.

This fundamental issue is outlined in Figure 1. Four parses are located in the ball $\mathbb{B}$(P1, SMATCH)

[1]Banarescu et al. (2013) find that an (optimistic) average annotator vs. consensus IAA (SMATCH) was 0.83 for newswire and 0.79 for web text. When newly trained annotators doubly annotated web text sentences, their annotator vs. annotator IAA was 0.71. Recent BART and T5 based models range between 0.82 and 0.84 SMATCH F1 scores.

Proceedings of the 3rd Workshop on Evaluation and Comparison of NLP Systems, pages 32 - 43
November 20, 2022 ©2022 Association for Computational Linguistics

of estimated IAA, (gold) parse P1 being the center. However, the true set of possible human candidates $\mathcal{H}$ is very likely much smaller than the ball and its shape is unknown.[2] Besides, a superset of $\mathcal{H}$ is a set of *acceptable* parses $\mathcal{A}$, i.e., parses that may have a small flaw which does not significantly distort the sentence meaning. Now, it can indeed happen that parse P2, as opposed to P3, has a lower distance to reference P1, i.e., to the center of $\mathbb{B}$(SMATCH) – but is not found in $\mathcal{A} \supseteq \mathcal{H}$, which marks it as an inaccurate candidate. On the other hand, P4 is contained in $\mathcal{A}$, but not in $\mathcal{H}$, which would make it acceptable, but less preferable than P3.

Research questions Triggered by these considerations, this paper tackles the key questions: *Do high-performance AMR parsers indeed deliver accurate semantic graphs, as suggested by high benchmark scores that surpass human IAA estimates*? *Does a higher* SMATCH *against a single reference necessarily indicate better overall parse quality*? And *what steps can we take to mitigate potential issues when assessing the true performance of high-performance parsers?*

Paper structure After discussing background and related work (Section 2), we describe our data setup and give a survey of AMR metrics (Section 3). We then evaluate the metrics with regard to scoring i) corpora (Section 5), ii) AMR pairs (Section 6) and iii) cross-metric differences in their ranking behavior (Section 7). We conclude by discussing limitations of our study (Section 8), give recommendations and outline future work (Section 9).[3]

2 Background and related work

AMR parsing and applications Over the years, we have observed a great diversity in approaches to AMR parsing, ranging from graph prediction with a pipeline (Flanigan et al., 2014), or a neural network (Lyu and Titov, 2018; Cai and Lam, 2020) to transition-based parsing (Wang et al., 2015) and sequence-to-sequence parsing, e.g., by exploiting large parallel corpora (Xu et al., 2020). A recent trend is to exploit the knowledge in large pre-trained sequence-to-sequence language models such as T5 (Raffel et al., 2019) or BART (Lewis et al., 2020), by fine-tuning them on AMR corpora, as show-cased, e.g., by Bevilacqua et al. (2021). Such models are on par or tend to surpass estimates for human AMR agreement (Banarescu et al., 2013), when measured in SMATCH points.

AMR, by virtue of its properties as a graph-based abstract meaning representation, is attractive for many key NLP tasks, such as machine translation (Song et al., 2019), summarization (Dohare et al., 2017; Liao et al., 2018), NLG evaluation (Opitz and Frank, 2021; Manning and Schneider, 2021; Ribeiro et al., 2022) and measuring semantic sentence similarity (Opitz and Frank, 2022).

Metric evaluation for MT evaluation Metric evaluation for machine translation (MT) has received much attention over the recent years (Ma et al., 2019; Mathur et al., 2020; Freitag et al., 2021). When evaluating metrics for MT evaluation, it seems generally agreed upon that the main goal of a MT metric is high correlation to human ratings, mainly with respect to rating adequacy of a candidate against one (or a set of) gold reference(s).

A recent shared task (Freitag et al., 2021) meta-evaluates popular metrics such as BLEU (Papineni et al., 2002) or BLEURT (Sellam et al., 2020), by comparing the metrics' scores to human scores for systems and individual segments. They find that the performance of each metric varies depending on the underlying domain (e.g., TED talks or news), and that most metrics struggle to penalize translations with errors in reversing negation or sentiment polarity, and show lower correlations for semantic phenomena including subordination, named entities and terminology. This indicates that there is potential for cross-pollination: clearly, AMR metric evaluation may profit from the vast amount of experience of metric evaluation for other tasks. On the other hand, MT evaluation may profit from relating semantic representations, to better differentiate semantic errors with respect to their type and severity. A first step in this direction may have been made by Zeidler et al. (2022), who assess the behaviour of MT metrics, AMR metrics, and hybrid metrics when analyzing sentence pairs that differ in only one linguistic phenomenon.

3 Study Setup: Data creation and AMR metric overview

In this Section, first we select data and two popular high-performance parsers for creating candidate AMRs. Then we describe the human quality annotation, and give an overview of automatic AMR

[2] Under the unrealistic assumptions of an omniscient annotator and AMR being the ideal way of meaning representation, one might require that $\mathcal{H}$ always has exactly one element.

[3] Code and data for our study are available at `https://github.com/Heidelberg-nlp/AMRParseEval`.

```
-----------------Reference AMR and Sentence------------------
(l / look-over-06                    ''Looking over to the flag''
     :ARG1 (f / flag))
---------------------Candidate parses------------------------
(l / look-01                     (z0 / look-01
     :direction (o / over)            :ARG2 (z1 / flag)
     :destination (f / flag))         :direction (z2 / over))
---------------------------Eval------------------------------
Smatch (ref, cand): both score 0.2 (indicates low quality)
Human (sent, cand): both are acceptable
Human (cand, cand): no preference
-------------------------------------------------------------
```

Figure 2: Data example: acceptable, low SMATCH. That is, $P \in \mathcal{H}$ but $P \notin \mathbb{B}(\text{SMATCH}, ref)$.

metrics that we consider in our subsequent studies.

Parsers and corpora We choose the AMR3 benchmark[4] and the literary texts from the freely available Little Prince corpus.[5] As parsers we choose T5- and BART-based systems, both on par with human IAA estimates, where BART achieves higher scores on AMR3.[6] We proceed as follows: we 1. parse the corpora with T5 and BART parsers and use SMATCH to select diverging parse candidate pairs, and 2. sample 200 of those pairs, both for AMR3, and for Little Prince (i.e., 800 AMR candidates in total).

3.1 Annotation dimensions

Annotation dimension I: pairwise ranking The annotator is presented the sentence and two candidate graphs, assigning one of three labels and a free-text rationale. The labels are either +1 (prefer first graph), -1 (prefer second graph), or 0 (both are of same or very similar quality).

Annotation dimension II: parse acceptability In addition, each graph is independently assigned a single label, considering only the sentence that it is supposed to represent. Here, the annotator makes a binary decision: +1, if the parse is acceptable, or 0, if the graph is not acceptable. A graph that is acceptable is fully valid, or may allow a very minor meaning deviation from the sentence, or a slightly weird but allowed interpretation that may differ from a normative interpretation. All other graphs are deemed not acceptable (0).

Example: Acceptable candidates, low SMATCH Figure 2 shows an example of two graphs that have very low structural overlap with the reference (SMATCH = 0.2), but are acceptable. Here, the candidate graphs both differ from the reference

```
----------------Reference AMR (excerpt)--------------------
(i2 / imagine-01
     :ARG0 (y / you)
     :ARG1 (a / amaze-01
          :ARG1 (i / i)))
          :time-of (w / wake-01
               :ARG0 (v / voice
                    :mod (o / odd)
                    :mod (l / little))
               :ARG1 i))))))
----------------Candidate parse (excerpt)-------------------
(ii / imagine-01
     :ARG0 (y / you)
     :ARG1 (a / amaze-01
          :ARG0 (v / voice
               :mod (l / little)
               :mod (o / odd))
          :ARG1 (ii2 / i)))

Means: (..) imagine my amazement (..) by an odd little voice
Should mean: (..) imagine my amazement (..) when I was
             awakened by an odd little voice
---------------------------Eval-----------------------------
Smatch (ref, cand): scores 0.88 (indicates high quality)
Human (sent, cand): not acceptable
------------------------------------------------------------
```

Figure 3: Data example excerpt that shows an unacceptable parse with high SMATCH. That is, $P \notin \mathcal{A} \supseteq \mathcal{H}$ but $P \in \mathbb{B}(\text{SMATCH}, ref)$

because they tend to a more conservative interpretation, using the more general *look-01* predicate instead of the *look-over-06* predicate in the human reference. In fact, the meaning of the reference can be considered, albeit valid, slightly weird, since *look-over-06* is defined in PropBank as *examining something idly*, which is a more 'specific' interpretation of the sentence in question. On the other hand, the candidate graphs differ from each other in the semantic role assigned to *flag*. In the first, *flag* is the destination of the *looking* action (which can be accepted), while in the second, we find a more questionable but still acceptable interpretation that *flag* is an *attribute of the thing that is looked at.*

Example: Candidate not acceptable, high SMATCH An inverse example (high SMATCH, unacceptable) is shown in Figure 3, where the parse omits *awaken*. Albeit the factuality of the sentence is not (much) changed, and the structural deviation may legitimately imply that the odd voice is the cause of amazement, it misses a relevant piece of meaning and is therefore rated unacceptable.

Label statistics will be discussed in Section 5, where the human annotations are also contrasted against parser rankings of automatic metrics.

3.2 Metric overview

We distinguish metrics targeting *monolingual AMR parsing evaluation* from *multi-purpose AMR metrics*. AMR metrics that are designed for evaluation of monolingual parsers typically have two features in common. First, they compare a candidate against

[4]LDC corpus LDC2020T02

[5]From https://amr.isi.edu/download.html

[6]See https://github.com/bjascob/amrlib-models for more benchmarking statistics.

a reference parse that both (try to) represent the *same sentence*. Second, they measure the amount of successfully reconstructed reference structure.[7]

We also consider multi-purpose AMR metrics that aim to extend to use cases where AMRs represent *different sentences*, such as evaluation of cross-lingual AMR parsing, natural language generation (NLG) or rating semantic sentence similarity.

3.2.1 Monolingual AMR parsing metrics

Triple matching strategies SMATCH (Cai and Knight, 2013) and SEMA (Anchiêta et al., 2019) consider graph triples as the elementary constituents of an AMR graph. Both compute a triple overlap score between candidate and reference parses. SMATCH computes an alignment between the variable nodes of two AMRs, which is accurate but slow. The SEMA metric achieves a large speed-up by removing AMR variables from the graphs, replacing them with concept labels.

Inspired by BLEU: SEMBLEU BLEU (Papineni et al., 2002) is a popular (but debated) metric for machine translation evaluation. It matches bags-of-k-grams from candidate and reference, with a geometric mean of the precision scores over the k different bags. Inspired by BLEU, and, similar to SEMA, driven by the goal to make AMR evaluation more fast and efficient, Song and Gildea (2019) propose the SEMBLEU metric for AMR graphs. It extracts bags-of-k-grams from graphs, collected via breadth-first traversal. A point of motivation, similarly to SEMA, is that the metric skips the costly graph alignment. Per default, SEMBLEU uses k=3. In this work we additionally use k=2, following Opitz et al. (2021) who find that k=2 better relates to human notions of sentence similarity.

3.2.2 Multi-purpose metrics

S²MATCH and WLK/WWLK Targeting AMR metric application cases beyond monolingual parsing evaluation, such as measuring AMR similarity of different sentences, or cross-lingual AMR parsing evaluation, Opitz et al. (2020, 2021); Uhrig et al. (2021) propose three metrics: i) **S²MATCH** is an adaption of SMATCH that computes graded concept similarity (reflecting that, e.g., *cat* is more similar to *kitten* than to *plant*). ii) **WLK** applies the Weisfeiler-Leman kernel (Shervashidze et al., 2011) to compute a similarity score over feature vectors that describe graph statistics in different iterations of node contextualization. iii) **WWLK** (Wasserstein WLK, Togninalli et al. (2019)) projects the nodes of the graphs to a latent space partitioned into different degrees of node contextualization. Wasserstein distance is then used to match the graphs, based on a pair-wise node distance matrix.

Setup of multi-purpose metrics For S²MATCH, WLK and WWLK we use the default setup, which consists of GloVe (Pennington et al., 2014) embeddings and k=2 in WLK and WWLK, where k indicates the depth of node contextualizations.

Default WWLK initializes parameters randomly, if tokens are out of vocabulary (a random embedding for each OOV token type). To achieve deterministic results, without fixing a random seed, we could initialize the OOV parameters to 0. However, with this we'd lose valuable discriminative information on graph similarity. We therefore adopt a slight adaptation for WWLK and calculate the *expected* distance matrix before Wasserstein metric calculation, making results more reproducible while keeping discriminative power.

We also introduce WWLK-**k3e2n**, a WWLK variant with *edge2node (e2n)* transforms, more tailored to monolingual AMR parsing evaluation, which is the focus of this paper. It increases the score impact of edge labels, motivated by the insight that edge labels are of particular importance in AMR parsing evaluation. It transforms an edge-labeled graph into an *equivalent* graph without edge-labels.[8] This is also known as 'Levi transform' (Levi, 1942), and has been previously advocated for AMR representation by Beck et al. (2018) and Ribeiro et al. (2019). Since due to the transform the distances in the graph will grow, we increase k by one (**k=3**). With this, we can set all edge weights to 1.

3.2.3 Simple baseline

To put the results into perspective, we introduce a very SIMPLE baseline: SIMPLE extracts bag-of-words (relation and concept labels) from two AMR graphs and computes the size of their intersection vs. the size of their union (aka *Jaccard Coefficient*).

4 Preliminaries

We denote an AMR metric m over AMRs as:

$$m : \mathcal{A} \times \mathcal{A} \rightarrow \mathbb{R}, \quad (1)$$

[7]The notion of *success* is mostly focused on structural matches, and can vary among metrics, usually depending on theoretical arguments of the developers of the metric.

[8]E.g., $(x, arg0, z) \rightarrow (x, y) \land (y, z) \land (y, arg0)$.

and a human metric h as

$$h : \mathcal{A} \times \mathcal{S} \rightarrow \mathbb{R}, \quad (2)$$

where $\mathcal{S}$ contains sentences.

5 Study I: System-level scoring

Research questions We focus on two questions:

1. How are the two parsers rated by humans?

2. How do metrics score our two parsers?

With 1. we aim to assess whether there is still room for AMR parser improvement, even though their SMATCH scores pass estimated human IAA. And for 2. we aim to know whether the metric rankings (still) appropriately reflect parser quality.

5.1 System scoring

Aggregation strategies: Micro vs. Macro We have defined a metric between two AMRs. For ranking systems, we need to aggregate the individual pair-wise assessments into a single score. At this point, it is important to note that most papers use (only) micro SMATCH for ranking parsers, i.e., counting triple matches of aligned AMR pairs over all AMR pairs (before a final F1 score calculation).

Naturally, such micro corpus statistics are *unbiased* w.r.t. to whatever is defined as a single evaluation instance (in SMATCH: triples), but the trade-off is that they are biased towards instance type frequency and sentence length, since longer sentences tend to yield substantially more triples. Hence, the influence of a longer sentence may marginalize the influence of a shorter sentence. This issue may be further aggravated by the fact that longer sentences tend to contain more named entity phrases, and entity phrases typically trigger large simple structures, that are mostly easy to project.[9] Therefore, micro corpus statistics alone *could* potentially yield an incomplete assessment of parser performance. To shed more light on this issue, we provide additional evaluation via macro aggregation.

Statistics for micro and macro system scoring We calculate two statistics. The first statistic shows the (micro/macro)-aggregated corpus score for a metric m, parsed corpus X and gold corpus G:

$$\mathbb{S}(m, X, G) \\ = AGGR(\{m(X_1, G_1), ..., m(X_n, G_n)\}),$$

For macro metrics, $AGGR$ is the mean of pairwise scores over all instances in a corpus X. In case of the human metric, this is the ratio of acceptable parses in X. For micro metrics, $AGGR$ computes overall matching triple F1 (SMATCH, SEMA) or overall k-gram BLEU (SEMBLEU). For WLK and WWLK, a micro variant is not implemented, hence we only show their macro scores.

The second statistic shows how often m prefers the parses in a parse corpus X over the these in Y:

$$\mathbb{P}(m, X, Y, G) = \sum_{i=1}^{n} \mathbb{I}[m(X_i, G_i) > m(Y_i, G_i)].$$

Here, $\mathbb{I}[c]$ denotes a function that returns 1 if the condition c is true, and zero in all other cases. For better comparability of numbers, we distribute cases where $m(X_i, G_i) = m(Y_i, G_i)$, which are frequent for the human metric, evenly over $\mathbb{P}(m, X, Y, G)$ and $\mathbb{P}(m, Y, X, G)$.

5.2 Results

Results are shown in Table 1. In view of our research questions, we make interesting observations.

AMR parsing is far from solved Considering the ratio of parses that were rated acceptable by the human (HUM, $\mathbb{S}$), they are surprisingly low, at only 0.58 (BART, Little Prince, Table 1); 0.69 (T5, Little Prince). Other parses have errors that substantially distort sentence meaning, even though major parts of the AMRs may structurally overlap.

Better SMATCH on AMR benchmark may not (always) imply a better parser On AMR3, when inspecting corpus-SMATCH (micro SMATCH, Table 1), BART is considered the better parser, in comparison to T5 (+2 points). However, when consulting macro statistics, a different picture emerges. Here, BART and T5 obtain the same scores: AMR3, 0.62 vs. 0.62, Table 1. On the literary texts (Little Prince), where the domain is different and sentences tend to be shorter, T5 significantly (binomial test, $p < 0.05$) outperforms BART, both in the ratio

[9] As a small example, consider *The bird sings* vs. *Jon Bon Jovi sings*. The first sentence yields 3 triples, while the second sentence yields 8 triples, where the *John Bon Jovi* named entitiy structure has added 6 triples, outweighing the key semantic event *x sings*. Micro score would assign 2.6 times more importance to the second sentence/AMR.

		Little Prince						AMR3					
		$\mathbb{P}$			$\mathbb{S}$			$\mathbb{P}$			$\mathbb{S}$		
		BART	T5	Δ	BART	T5	Δ	BART	T5	Δ	BART	T5	Δ
	HUM	87	113	-26	0.58	0.69	-0.11	100	100	0.0	0.62	0.62	0.00
	SIMPLE	87	113	-26	0.69	0.7	-0.01	82	118	-36	0.75	0.75	0.00
Macro	SEMA	84	116	-32	0.6	0.63	-0.03	89	111	-22	0.68	0.68	0.00
	SEMBLEU-k2	90	110	-20	0.61	0.63	-0.02	98	102	-4	0.70	0.69	0.01
	SEMBLEU-k3	90	110	-20	0.51	0.53	-0.02	103	97	6	0.58	0.58	0.00
	SMATCH	94	106	-12	0.73	0.74	-0.01	95	105	-10	0.77	0.77	0.00
	S^2MATCH	93	107	-14	0.75	0.76	-0.01	95	105	-10	0.79	0.79	0.00
	WLK-k2	92	108	-16	0.63	0.65	-0.02	96	104	-8	0.69	0.69	0.00
	WWLK-k2	91	109	-18	0.79	0.8	-0.01	102	98	4	0.84	0.84	0.00
	WWLK-k3e2n	97	103	-6	0.72	0.73	-0.01	94	106	-12	0.78	0.78	0.00
Micro	SEMA	-	-	-	0.62	0.64	-0.02	-	-	-	0.69	0.68	0.01
	SEMBLEU	-	-	-	0.53	0.54	-0.01	-	-	-	0.60	0.57	0.03
	SMATCH	-	-	-	0.74	0.74	-0.01	-	-	-	0.77	0.75	0.02
	S^2MATCH	-	-	-	0.76	0.76	0.00	-	-	-	0.80	0.77	0.03

Table 1: Corpus level scoring results. Negative Δ shows preference for T5, positive Δ shows preference for BART.

of acceptable sentences (BART: 0.58, T5: 0.69), and in number of preferred candidates (BART: 87, T5: 113). Note that this insight is independent from our human annotations.

All in all, this may suggest that BART tends to provide better performance for longer sentences, while T5 tends to provide better performance especially for shorter and medium-length sentences. Further analysis provides more evidence for this, cf. Appendix A.1: Figure 6 and Figure 7).

Metrics for system ranking Regarding our tested metrics, especially the macro metrics, a clear pattern is that they mostly agree with the human ranking. However, our current results for the different metrics do not tell much, yet, about their suitability for AMR assessment and ranking. Even if a metric ranks a parser more similarly to the human, this may be for the wrong reasons, since this statistic filters out pair-wise correspondences to the human. This is also indicated by results of the simplistic bag-of-structure metric SIMPLE, which achieves the same results as human (HUM) on Little Prince, with respect to the number of preferred parses ($\mathbb{P}$, Little Prince, Table 1, HUM vs. SIMPLE). In that respect, it is more important to assess the pair-wise metric accuracy and metric specificity, which we will visit next in Sections 6 and 7.

6 Study II: Metric accuracy on parse level

Research questions Now, we are interested in the metric accuracy, that is, agreement of AMR metrics with the human ratings. In particular, we would like to know, regarding:

- Pair-wise parse accuracy: How do metrics agree with human preferences when ranking two candidates?
- Individual parse accuracy: Can metrics tell apart acceptable from unacceptable parses?

Note that these are hard tasks for metrics, since both T5 and BART show performance levels on par or above estimated measurements for human IAA. Therefore, smaller structural divergences from the reference can potentially have a bigger impact on parse acceptability (or preference) than larger structural deviations, that could express different (but valid) interpretations or (near-)paraphrases.

6.1 Evaluation metrics

Pairwise accuracy Recall that the human assigned one of three ratings: 1, if AMR x is better, -1, if AMR y is better, and 0 if there is no considerable quality difference between two candidate graphs x and y. A metric assigns two real values, $m(x, g)$ and $m(y, g)$, where g is the reference graph. Mapping the score to -1 or 1 is simple and intuitive, prompting us to introduce pair-wise accuracy. Consider a data set SD that contains all graph triplets (x, y, g) with a human preference sign (label -1 or $+1$). Further, let $\delta^m(x, y, g) = m(x, g) - m(y, g)$ the (signed) quality difference between x and y when using m. Anal-

	Little Prince		AMR3	
	PA	$\mathbb{A}\Delta$	PA	$\mathbb{A}\Delta$
HUM	1.0	233	1.0	234
RAND	0.5	0.0	0.5	0.0
SIMPLE	0.66†	11.0	0.68†	39.5†
SEMA	0.66†	24.3	0.7†	35.3†
SEMBLEU-k2	0.67†	25.0	0.74†	28.0
SEMBLEU-k3	0.63†	32.0	0.68†	29.0
SMATCH	**0.72**†	42.0†	0.7†	35.0†
S^{2}MATCH	**0.72**†	35.3	0.7†	42.3†
WLK	0.66†	28.0	0.68†	41.5†
WWLK-k2	0.63†	20.5	0.73†	51.0†
WWLK-k3e2n	0.66†	**48.0**†	**0.76**†	**57.0**†

Table 2: Metric agreement with human. †: random baseline (RAND) not contained in 95% confidence interval.

ogously $\delta^h(x, y)$ is the human preference. Then, the pairwise accuracy is

$$PA = \frac{1}{|D|} \sum_{(x,y,g) \in D} \mathbb{I}[\delta^m(x, y, g) \cdot \delta^h(x, y) > 0] \tag{3}$$

This measures the ratio of candidate pairs where the metric has made the same signed decision as the human, in preferring one over the other parse.

Acceptability score When rating acceptability, the human rates a single parse (given its sentence), assigning 1 (acceptable) or 0 (no acceptable). The metrics make use of the reference graph to compute a score. Aiming at an evaluation metric that makes as few assumptions as possible, we formulate the following expectation for an AMR graph metric to fulfill: the average rank of the scores for parses that have been labeled acceptable by the human should surpass the average rank of the scores for parses labeled as being not acceptable. Let $\mathcal{I}^+$ ($\mathcal{I}^-$) be the set of indices for which the human has assigned a label that indicates (un-)acceptability. Let $S = \{m(X_1, G_1)...m(X_n, G_n)\}$ be the metric m's scores over all (x, g) parse/reference pairs, and R be the ranks of D. Let R^+ (and R^-) be the set of ranks indexed by $\mathcal{I}^+$ (and $\mathcal{I}^-$). Then

$$\mathbb{A}\Delta = avg(R^+) - avg(R^-) \tag{4}$$

To increase robustness, we use avg := median.

6.2 Results

The results are shown in Table 2. We conclude:

All metrics are suitable for pairwise-ranking of parses from high-performance parsers All metrics significantly outperform the random baseline with regard to the pair-wise ranking accuracy (PA). For Little Prince, SMATCH and S^{2}MATCH yield the best performance, while for AMR3, WWLK-k3e2n has the best performance (closely followed by SEMBLEU-k2). Among different metrics, however, the differences are not large enough to confidently recommend one metric over the other.

Parse acceptability rating is hard When tasked to rate parse acceptability ($\mathbb{A}\Delta$), all metrics show issues. For Little Prince, only SMATCH and WWLK-k3e2n significantly outperform the chance baseline, while for AMR3 all metrics are significantly above chance level, except SEMBLEU. Overall, however, the differences are not large enough to confidently recommend one metric over the other. On both corpora, best results are achieved with WWLK-k3e2n (Little Prince: 48.0, AMR3: 57.0).

Control experiment of metrics We additionally parse a subset of 50 sentences with an older parser (Flanigan et al., 2014) that scores more than 20 points lower SMATCH, when compared with IAA as estimated in Banarescu et al. (2013). All metrics (with the exception of SIMPLE for one pair) correctly figure out all rankings and acceptability (according to the human, BART and T5 are preferred in all cases, except two cases where all three systems deliver equally valid graphs). This indicates that metrics indeed can accurately tell apart quality differences, *if* they are large enough and do not lie beyond human IAA.

7 Metric specificity

We found little evidence that could help us giving recommendations on which metrics to prefer over others for monolingual parser evaluation in the high-performance regime. On the contrary, we found evidence that no metric can sufficiently assess parse acceptability. Therefore, it is interesting to see whether the metrics can provide *different* views on parse quality.

7.1 Correlation analysis

Statistics We compute Spearman's ρ over metric pairs. Spearman's ρ calculates Pearson's ρ on the ranked predictions, which increases robustness.

Results Results are plotted in Figures 4 and 5. For both datasets, we see that the Wasserstein metrics provide rankings that differ more from the rankings assigned by other metrics, suggesting that they

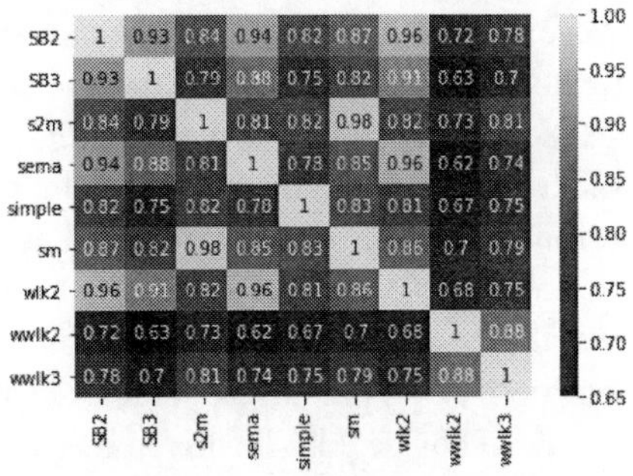

Figure 4: Inter-metric correlation on Little Prince.

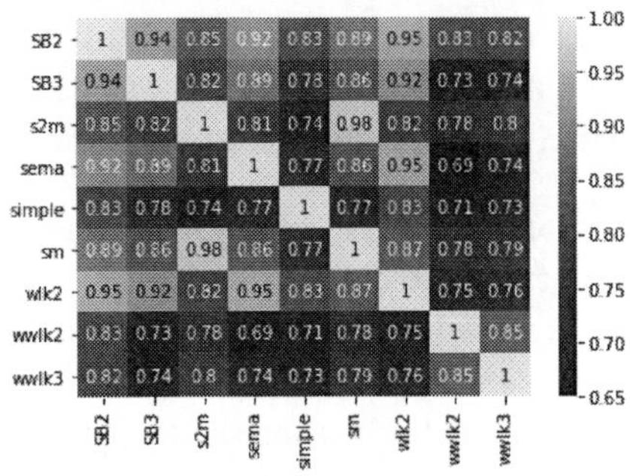

Figure 5: Inter-metric correlation on AMR3.

have unique features. On the other hand, the SEMBLEU metrics tend to agree the most with the rankings of the other metrics, suggesting that they share more features with other metrics. On a pair-wise level, the most similar metrics are SMATCH and S²MATCH, which is intuitive, since S²MATCH is an adaption of SMATCH that also targets the comparison of AMRs from different sentences. Indeed, synonyms and similar concepts are unlikely to often occur in monolingual parsing, where parses contain exactly matching concepts. Further, WLK very much agrees with SEMBLEU, which seems intuitive, since both aim at comparing larger AMR subgraphs. Lowest agreement is exhibited between SEMA and WWLK, perhaps because these metrics are of different complexity and share different goals: simple and fast match of structures vs. graded assessment for general AMR similarity.

8 Discussion of study limitations

There are limitations of our study:

Limitation I: *Single vs. Double annotation* While our quality annotations stem from an experienced human annotator, we would have liked to obtain annotations from a second annotator to measure IAA for AMR quality rating. This was partly precluded by the high costs of AMR annotation, which requires much time and experience. This is also reflected in the AMR benchmark corpora: the majority of graphs were created by a single annotator. Note, however, that some findings are independent of annotation (e.g., macro vs. micro metric corpus scoring, metric specificity).

Limitation II: *Assessing individual suitability of metrics for rating high-performance parsers* Our study reports relevant findings on (monolingual) AMR parsing evaluation in high-performance regimes, and on upper bounds of AMR parsing. But an important question we had to leave open is the individual suitability of the metrics for comparing high-performance parsers.

Limitation III: *Single-reference parses and ambiguity* Elaborating on *Limitation II* and recalling that AMR benchmarks have only single references, another caveat is that potentially correct metric behavior may be misinterpreted in our study. E.g., if a sentence allows two different interpretations, a metric might (correctly) yield a low score for the reference (different meaning), while the (reference-less) human rating may find the parse acceptable. This issue may also be mitigated by providing (costly) double annotation of AMR benchmark sentences.

To facilitate follow-up research, we release the annotated data. Our Little Prince annotations can be freely released, while AMR3 annotations require proof of LDC license.

9 Discussion and Conclusions

Main recommendations based on our study:

Recommendation I Besides micro aggregate scores we recommend using **a macro aggregate score** for parse evaluation (e.g., macro SMATCH, computed as an average over sentence scores): Commonly, only micro corpus statistics are used to compare and rank parsers. Yet, we found that macro (sentence-average) metrics can provide a valuable **complementary assessment** that can highlight important *additional* strengths of high-performance parsers.

Recommendation II We recommend conducting **more human evaluation of AMR parses**. With the available high-performance AMR parsers, it becomes more important to conduct manual analyses of parse quality. Our study provides evidence that AMR parsing still has large room for improvement, due to small but significant errors. Since this may not be noticeable for (current) metrics when given a single human reference, **future work on parsing may profit from careful human acceptability assessments**.

T5 vs. BART: which parser to prefer? Next to AMR parser developers, this question mainly concerns potential users of AMR parsers. Fine-tuned T5 and BART are both powerful AMR parsers. We observe a slight tendency that researchers prefer BART, possibly since it achieves slightly better SMATCH scores than T5 on the AMR3 benchmark. But our work shows that differences between the systems are often finer than what can be assessed with structural overlap metrics (SMATCH), and both systems are generally strong but struggle with small but significant meaning errors.

In our study we found that when choosing between T5 and BART based AMR systems, **the choice might depend on the target domain**. Indeed, our results on Little Prince and AMR3 (mainly news) could indicate that **T5 may have an edge over BART when parsing literary texts**, and shorter sentences in general, while **BART has an edge over T5 when parsing longer sentences, and sentences from news sources**, especially if they are longer. However, it must be clearly noted, that we do not know (yet) whether this insight carries over to other types of literary texts.

Perhaps, if we presume that performance is carried over to other types of literary texts, a possible explanation can be found in the data these two large models were trained on. BART uses the same training data as RoBERTa (Liu et al., 2019), e.g., Wikipedia, book corpora and news. T5 leverages the colossal common crawl corpus (C4), that contains all kinds of texts scraped from the web. This *could* make T5 more robust to AMR domain changes, but less suitable for analysing longer sentences, since these may occur more frequently in BART's corpora that seem more normative.

Which AMR metric to use? Our findings do not provide conclusive evidence on this question, partly due to insufficient data size, partly due to the general difficulty of the task. WWLK-k3e2n seems slightly more useful for detecting parse acceptability and pairwise ranking on news, while SMATCH yields best ranking on Little Prince.

However, our work shows that **it can be useful to calculate more than one metric to compare parsers**. In particular, we saw that predictions of structural matching metrics differ considerably from graded semantic similarity-based metrics, such as the WWLK metric variants. This suggests that these two types can provide complementary perspectives on parsing accuracy. Metric selection may, of course, also be driven by users' specific desiderata, such as speed (SEMA, SEMBLEU, WLK), 1-1 alignment (SMATCH), n:m alignment (WWLK), or graded matching (SMATCH, WWLK). Overall, we see much **profit to gain from more research into AMR metrics**, and will now outline a direction that we believe is very interesting.

A direction for future research: Reference-less AMR metrics Recall that for human quality assessments a candidate graph is compared to a *sentence*, in lieu of a reference AMR. If this process can be approximated by a metric, we gain an important mechanism for assessing the quality of high-performance parsers: a measure that is cheap and not biased towards a single reference.

To date, referenceless AMR parse quality rating has been attempted by Opitz and Frank (2019); Opitz (2020). However, an unsolved issue is that this approach does not approximate a human quality assessment, but instead tries to project SMATCH score without using a reference, and we saw that SMATCH cannot well assess the impact of fine errors of high-performing parsers.

A worthwhile solution could be found in the exploitation of indirect tools: E.g., our human annotation indicated that significant, but small structural errors are sometimes due to coreference, which is known to be a hard task in general (Levesque et al., 2012) and for AMR in particular (Anikina et al., 2020). Therefore, e.g., one may profit from matching parses from a high-performance parser against the structures predicted by a strong coreference system, possibly with the help of a predicted AMR-to-text alignment (Blodgett and Schneider, 2021). Another promising route to take may be to invert approaches of Opitz and Frank (2021); Manning and Schneider (2021) who evaluate AMR-to-text generation without reliance on a reference by using a strong parser for back-parsing. It may be beneficial to use strong AMR-to-text systems to generate from candidate AMRs, and to match the generations against the source sentence using strong automatic text-to-text metrics.

Acknowledgements

We are grateful to three anonymous reviewers for their valuable comments that have helped to improve this paper. We are also thankful to Julius Steen for valuable discussions.

References

Rafael Torres Anchiêta, Marco Antonio Sobrevilla Cabezudo, and Thiago Alexandre Salgueiro Pardo. 2019. Sema: an extended semantic evaluation for amr. In *(To appear) Proceedings of the 20th Computational Linguistics and Intelligent Text Processing*. Springer International Publishg.

Tatiana Anikina, Alexander Koller, and Michael Roth. 2020. Predicting coreference in Abstract Meaning Representations. In *Proceedings of the Third Workshop on Computational Models of Reference, Anaphora and Coreference*, pages 33–38, Barcelona, Spain (online). Association for Computational Linguistics.

Laura Banarescu, Claire Bonial, Shu Cai, Madalina Georgescu, Kira Griffitt, Ulf Hermjakob, Kevin Knight, Philipp Koehn, Martha Palmer, and Nathan Schneider. 2013. Abstract meaning representation for sembanking. In *Proceedings of the 7th Linguistic Annotation Workshop and Interoperability with Discourse*, pages 178–186, Sofia, Bulgaria. Association for Computational Linguistics.

Daniel Beck, Gholamreza Haffari, and Trevor Cohn. 2018. Graph-to-sequence learning using gated graph neural networks. In *Proceedings of the 56th Annual Meeting of the Association for Computational Linguistics (Volume 1: Long Papers)*, pages 273–283, Melbourne, Australia. Association for Computational Linguistics.

Michele Bevilacqua, Rexhina Blloshmi, and Roberto Navigli. 2021. One spring to rule them both: Symmetric amr semantic parsing and generation without a complex pipeline. In *Proceedings of the AAAI Conference on Artificial Intelligence*, volume 35, pages 12564–12573.

Austin Blodgett and Nathan Schneider. 2021. Probabilistic, structure-aware algorithms for improved variety, accuracy, and coverage of AMR alignments. In *Proceedings of the 59th Annual Meeting of the Association for Computational Linguistics and the 11th International Joint Conference on Natural Language Processing (Volume 1: Long Papers)*, pages 3310–3321, Online. Association for Computational Linguistics.

Deng Cai and Wai Lam. 2020. AMR parsing via graph-sequence iterative inference. In *Proceedings of the 58th Annual Meeting of the Association for Computational Linguistics*, pages 1290–1301, Online. Association for Computational Linguistics.

Shu Cai and Kevin Knight. 2013. Smatch: an evaluation metric for semantic feature structures. In *Proceedings of the 51st Annual Meeting of the Association for Computational Linguistics (Volume 2: Short Papers)*, pages 748–752, Sofia, Bulgaria. Association for Computational Linguistics.

Shibhansh Dohare, Harish Karnick, and Vivek Gupta. 2017. Text summarization using abstract meaning representation.

Jeffrey Flanigan, Sam Thomson, Jaime Carbonell, Chris Dyer, and Noah A. Smith. 2014. A discriminative graph-based parser for the Abstract Meaning Representation. In *Proceedings of the 52nd Annual Meeting of the Association for Computational Linguistics (Volume 1: Long Papers)*, pages 1426–1436, Baltimore, Maryland. Association for Computational Linguistics.

Markus Freitag, Ricardo Rei, Nitika Mathur, Chi-kiu Lo, Craig Stewart, George Foster, Alon Lavie, and Ondřej Bojar. 2021. Results of the WMT21 metrics shared task: Evaluating metrics with expert-based human evaluations on TED and news domain. In *Proceedings of the Sixth Conference on Machine Translation*, pages 733–774, Online. Association for Computational Linguistics.

Hector Levesque, Ernest Davis, and Leora Morgenstern. 2012. The winograd schema challenge. In *Thirteenth international conference on the principles of knowledge representation and reasoning*.

Friedrich Wilhelm Levi. 1942. *Finite geometrical systems: six public lectues delivered in February, 1940, at the University of Calcutta*. University of Calcutta.

Mike Lewis, Yinhan Liu, Naman Goyal, Marjan Ghazvininejad, Abdelrahman Mohamed, Omer Levy, Veselin Stoyanov, and Luke Zettlemoyer. 2020. BART: Denoising sequence-to-sequence pre-training for natural language generation, translation, and comprehension. In *Proceedings of the 58th Annual Meeting of the Association for Computational Linguistics*, pages 7871–7880, Online. Association for Computational Linguistics.

Kexin Liao, Logan Lebanoff, and Fei Liu. 2018. Abstract Meaning Representation for multi-document summarization. In *Proceedings of the 27th International Conference on Computational Linguistics*, pages 1178–1190, Santa Fe, New Mexico, USA. Association for Computational Linguistics.

Yinhan Liu, Myle Ott, Naman Goyal, Jingfei Du, Mandar Joshi, Danqi Chen, Omer Levy, Mike Lewis, Luke Zettlemoyer, and Veselin Stoyanov. 2019. Roberta: A robustly optimized bert pretraining approach. *arXiv preprint arXiv:1907.11692*.

Chunchuan Lyu and Ivan Titov. 2018. AMR parsing as graph prediction with latent alignment. In *Proceedings of the 56th Annual Meeting of the Association for Computational Linguistics (Volume 1: Long Papers)*, pages 397–407, Melbourne, Australia. Association for Computational Linguistics.

Qingsong Ma, Johnny Wei, Ondřej Bojar, and Yvette Graham. 2019. Results of the WMT19 metrics shared task: Segment-level and strong MT systems pose big challenges. In *Proceedings of the Fourth Conference on Machine Translation (Volume 2: Shared Task Papers, Day 1)*, pages 62–90, Florence, Italy. Association for Computational Linguistics.

Emma Manning and Nathan Schneider. 2021. Referenceless parsing-based evaluation of AMR-to-English generation. In *Proceedings of the 2nd Workshop on Evaluation and Comparison of NLP Systems*, pages 114–122, Punta Cana, Dominican Republic. Association for Computational Linguistics.

Nitika Mathur, Johnny Wei, Markus Freitag, Qingsong Ma, and Ondřej Bojar. 2020. Results of the WMT20 metrics shared task. In *Proceedings of the Fifth Conference on Machine Translation*, pages 688–725, Online. Association for Computational Linguistics.

Juri Opitz. 2020. AMR quality rating with a lightweight CNN. In *Proceedings of the 1st Conference of the Asia-Pacific Chapter of the Association for Computational Linguistics and the 10th International Joint Conference on Natural Language Processing*, pages 235–247, Suzhou, China. Association for Computational Linguistics.

Juri Opitz, Angel Daza, and Anette Frank. 2021. Weisfeiler-Leman in the Bamboo: Novel AMR Graph Metrics and a Benchmark for AMR Graph Similarity. *Transactions of the Association for Computational Linguistics*, 9:1425–1441.

Juri Opitz and Anette Frank. 2019. Automatic accuracy prediction for AMR parsing. In *Proceedings of the Eighth Joint Conference on Lexical and Computational Semantics (*SEM 2019)*, pages 212–223, Minneapolis, Minnesota. Association for Computational Linguistics.

Juri Opitz and Anette Frank. 2021. Towards a decomposable metric for explainable evaluation of text generation from AMR. In *Proceedings of the 16th Conference of the European Chapter of the Association for Computational Linguistics: Main Volume*, pages 1504–1518, Online. Association for Computational Linguistics.

Juri Opitz and Anette Frank. 2022. Sbert studies meaning representations: Decomposing sentence embeddings into explainable amr meaning features. *arXiv preprint arXiv:2206.07023*.

Juri Opitz, Letitia Parcalabescu, and Anette Frank. 2020. Amr similarity metrics from principles. *Transactions of the Association for Computational Linguistics*, 8:522–538.

Martha Palmer, Daniel Gildea, and Paul Kingsbury. 2005. The proposition bank: An annotated corpus of semantic roles. *Computational Linguistics*, 31(1):71–106.

Kishore Papineni, Salim Roukos, Todd Ward, and Wei-Jing Zhu. 2002. Bleu: a method for automatic evaluation of machine translation. In *Proceedings of the 40th Annual Meeting of the Association for Computational Linguistics*, pages 311–318, Philadelphia, Pennsylvania, USA. Association for Computational Linguistics.

Jeffrey Pennington, Richard Socher, and Christopher Manning. 2014. Glove: Global vectors for word representation. In *Proceedings of the 2014 Conference on Empirical Methods in Natural Language Processing (EMNLP)*, pages 1532–1543, Doha, Qatar. Association for Computational Linguistics.

Colin Raffel, Noam Shazeer, Adam Roberts, Katherine Lee, Sharan Narang, Michael Matena, Yanqi Zhou, Wei Li, and Peter J. Liu. 2019. Exploring the limits of transfer learning with a unified text-to-text transformer. *CoRR*, abs/1910.10683.

Leonardo Ribeiro, Mengwen Liu, Iryna Gurevych, Markus Dreyer, and Mohit Bansal. 2022. FactGraph: Evaluating factuality in summarization with semantic graph representations. In *Proceedings of the 2022 Conference of the North American Chapter of the Association for Computational Linguistics: Human Language Technologies*, pages 3238–3253, Seattle, United States. Association for Computational Linguistics.

Leonardo F. R. Ribeiro, Claire Gardent, and Iryna Gurevych. 2019. Enhancing AMR-to-text generation with dual graph representations. In *Proceedings of the 2019 Conference on Empirical Methods in Natural Language Processing and the 9th International Joint Conference on Natural Language Processing (EMNLP-IJCNLP)*, pages 3183–3194, Hong Kong, China. Association for Computational Linguistics.

Thibault Sellam, Dipanjan Das, and Ankur Parikh. 2020. BLEURT: Learning robust metrics for text generation. In *Proceedings of the 58th Annual Meeting of the Association for Computational Linguistics*, pages 7881–7892, Online. Association for Computational Linguistics.

Nino Shervashidze, Pascal Schweitzer, Erik Jan Van Leeuwen, Kurt Mehlhorn, and Karsten M Borgwardt. 2011. Weisfeiler-lehman graph kernels. *Journal of Machine Learning Research*, 12(9).

Linfeng Song and Daniel Gildea. 2019. SemBleu: A robust metric for AMR parsing evaluation. In *Proceedings of the 57th Annual Meeting of the Association for Computational Linguistics*, pages 4547–4552, Florence, Italy. Association for Computational Linguistics.

Linfeng Song, Daniel Gildea, Yue Zhang, Zhiguo Wang, and Jinsong Su. 2019. Semantic Neural Machine Translation Using AMR. *Transactions of the Association for Computational Linguistics*, 7:19–31.

Matteo Togninalli, Elisabetta Ghisu, Felipe Llinares-López, Bastian Rieck, and Karsten Borgwardt. 2019. Wasserstein weisfeiler-lehman graph kernels. In *Advances in Neural Information Processing Systems*, volume 32, pages 6436–6446. Curran Associates, Inc.

Sarah Uhrig, Yoalli Garcia, Juri Opitz, and Anette Frank. 2021. Translate, then parse! a strong baseline for cross-lingual AMR parsing. In *Proceedings of the 17th International Conference on Parsing Technologies and the IWPT 2021 Shared Task on Parsing into Enhanced Universal Dependencies (IWPT 2021)*, pages 58–64, Online. Association for Computational Linguistics.

Chuan Wang, Nianwen Xue, and Sameer Pradhan. 2015. A transition-based algorithm for AMR parsing. In *Proceedings of the 2015 Conference of the North American Chapter of the Association for Computational Linguistics: Human Language Technologies*, pages 366–375, Denver, Colorado. Association for Computational Linguistics.

Dongqin Xu, Junhui Li, Muhua Zhu, Min Zhang, and Guodong Zhou. 2020. Improving AMR parsing with sequence-to-sequence pre-training. In *Proceedings of the 2020 Conference on Empirical Methods in Natural Language Processing (EMNLP)*, pages 2501–2511, Online. Association for Computational Linguistics.

Laura Zeidler, Juri Opitz, and Anette Frank. 2022. A dynamic, interpreted CheckList for meaning-oriented NLG metric evaluation – through the lens of semantic similarity rating. In *Proceedings of the 11th Joint Conference on Lexical and Computational Semantics*, pages 157–172, Seattle, Washington. Association for Computational Linguistics.

A Appendix

A.1 Sentence length vs. score

See Figures 6, 7. For total sentence length distribution see Figure 8.

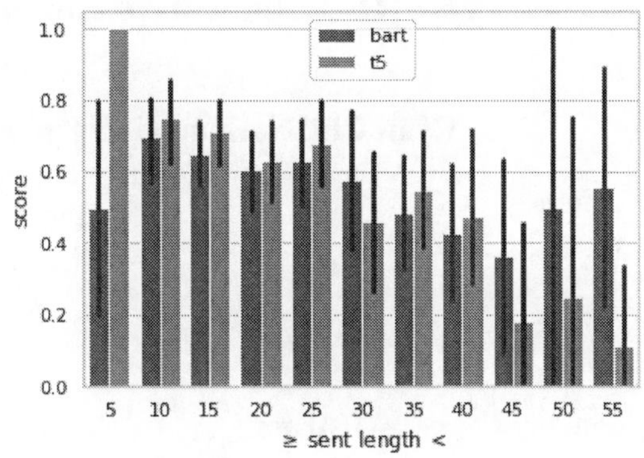

Figure 6: **Sentence length vs. human acceptability** on all annotated data. 55 includes all sentences longer than 55 tokens. See Figure 8 for occurences of different sentence lengths.

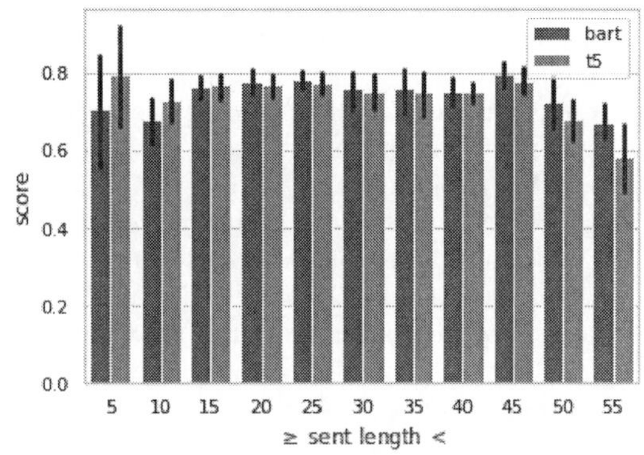

Figure 7: **Sentence length vs. Smatch** on all annotated data. 55 includes all sentences longer than 55 tokens. See Figure 8 for occurences of different sentence lengths. Other metrics look similar.

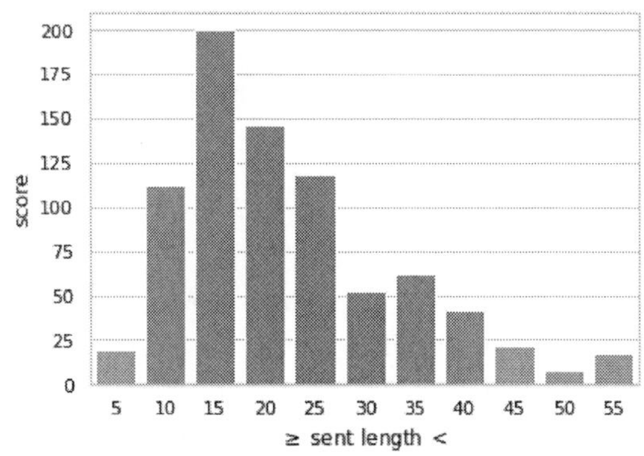

Figure 8: Sentence length occurrences. 55 includes all sentences longer than 55 tokens.

GLARE: Generative Left-to-right AdversaRial Examples

Ryan Chi, Nathan Kim,* Patrick Liu,* Zander Lack, Ethan A. Chi
Department of Computer Science
Stanford University
ryanchi@cs.stanford.edu

Abstract

Recently, transformer models (Vaswani et al., 2017) have been applied to adversarial example generation—word-level substitution models utilizing BERT (Devlin et al., 2018; Garg and Ramakrishnan, 2020; Li et al., 2020a,b) have outperformed previous state-of-the-art approaches. Extending the paradigm of transformer-based generation of adversarial examples, we propose a novel textual adversarial example generation framework based on transformer language models: our method (GLARE) generates word- and span-level perturbations of input examples using ILM (Donahue et al., 2020), a GPT-2 language model finetuned to fill in masked spans. We demonstrate that GLARE achieves a superior performance to CLARE (the current state-of-the-art model) in terms of attack success rate and semantic similarity between the perturbed and original examples.[1]

1 Introduction

A large body of evidence (Goodfellow et al., 2014; Chakraborty et al., 2018; Kurakin et al., 2016) has demonstrated that otherwise high-performing ML models can be deceived by "adversarial" examples—small perturbations of existing data points wrongly classified by the model. However, generating adversarial *textual* examples can be challenging due to text's discrete structure, which makes generating fluent, believable perturbations difficult (Jin et al., 2019b; Morris et al., 2020a). Recently, large pretrained Transformer language models (Devlin et al., 2018; Liu et al., 2019) have successfully been adapted to generate adversarial examples. Typically, such frameworks use a masked language model (Devlin et al., 2018)'s pretrained word substitution objective to generate word-level replacements; combining several such replacements allows the generation of perturbations that are both locally fluent and globally adversarial. However, this approach allows only one token to be substituted at a time, due to the pretraining objective of masked language models; although several `[MASK]` tokens can be inserted repeatedly, the overall result is that generating multi-word sequences of text is difficult (Wang and Cho, 2019).

In this work, we suggest instead applying *generative* language models (Radford et al., 2019) to produce adversarial examples. These models can easily generate multiple tokens at a time, enabling a larger space of possible attacks. Specifically, our framework, **GLARE**, applies GPT-2 (Radford et al., 2019) to generate adversarial examples, augmented by Donahue et al. (2020)'s *infilling*, which allows the LM access to rightwards context. Our approach, which can be easily used to substitute existing MLM attack methods, outperforms existing strong approaches as measured by attack success rate, semantic similarity between the perturbed and original examples, and modification rate of perturbed examples.

2 Background

2.1 Adversarial Example Generation

Adversarial example generation is focused on attacking a **victim** model f; in particular, we focus on *black-box* examples, where the attack method has access to model outputs given an arbitrarily large number of model inputs, but not its parameters. An adversarial example, then, is some perturbation $\text{Perturb}(x)$ of an original example x which triggers an error in the victim model, i.e. $f(\text{Perturb}(x)) \neq f(x)$, while being close semantically to the original x. Typically, one measures semantic similarity by computing the similarity between vector representations of the initial and modified sentence.

[1]Full source code for this project is available at `https://github.com/nathankim7/infilling-adversarial`.

Proceedings of the 3rd Workshop on Evaluation and Comparison of NLP Systems, pages 44 - 50
November 20, 2022 ©2022 Association for Computational Linguistics

2.2 Previous Approaches

Typically, an adversarial approach consists of some underlying set of perturbations; these can be at the subword level (e.g. typo introduction; Li et al., 2019), word level (e.g., word addition or deletion), or even sentence level (e.g., sentence paraphrasing; Iyyer et al., 2018). The iterated set of such perturbations represents the attack space from which an attack may be drawn, and an attack is considered "successful" for a particular example if a set of perturbations which flips the victim model's prediction can be found in the space. In practice, a standard search algorithm is typically applied to search through the space of perturbations for computational efficiency; these are typically implemented through a *framework*, such as TextAttack (Morris et al., 2020b) or OpenAttack (Zeng et al., 2021).

Modern adversarial methods typically apply a small set of perturbations computed via a masked language model. We can view most previous methods (Li et al., 2020b; Garg and Ramakrishnan, 2020; Li et al., 2020a) through the lens of the following broad operations (Li et al., 2020a):

- **Replace**: an existing token is masked and replaced with a new token.
- **Insert**: a [MASK] token is inserted, then to be replaced with a new token.
- **Delete**: a token is deleted.

Token replacement can be accomplished by computing vector similarity or manual dictionary lookups (Jin et al., 2019a); however, most competitive methods use masked language models (MLMs). BERTAttack (Li et al., 2020b) performs only **Replace** operations using BERT. BAE (Garg and Ramakrishnan, 2020) allows **Insert** operations simultaneously adjacent to substitutions. CLARE (Li et al., 2020a) allows all three operations. As all of these additions expand the attack space, their combination allows for an infinite space of new examples to be generated given enough exploration steps.

3 Methods

Like previous methods, GLARE utilizes the same fundamental **Replace** operation, where tokens from the input are replaced with neurally generated tokens. However, unlike previous approaches, we parameterize this replacement with a generative language model, allowing for the generation of arbitrarily large sequences. In particular, we apply *language-model infilling* (Donahue et al., 2020), which places both the leftwards and rightwards context of the original infill in the context window, allowing both sides to be considered during infilling (see Figure 1).

Specifically, GLARE entails the following steps, which closely follow previous approaches:

1. All possible replaceable **spans** are enumerated. Previous methods must limit spans to single tokens only due to the one-for-one nature of masked language model token replacement. Instead, GLARE defines a configurable hyperparameter c_{max} which controls the maximum number of contiguous tokens which may form a span.

2. The spans are **ranked** according to their Word Importance Ranking (Jin et al., 2019b): i.e. the difference between the score of the original example and the score after the span has been replaced by [MASK].

3. The top k candidates are selected and **infilled** using a GPT-2 model fine-tuned via Donahue et al. (2020)'s approach on the dataset itself. As the length of the infill is theoretically unlimited, we constrain its length during the decode; the final replacement for an original span of length n may between $[n - e_{\text{max}}, n + e_{\text{max}}]$, where e_{max} is a configurable hyperparameter. We rerank the candidates by likelihood under the infilling model, picking the top candidate.

Unlike CLARE, we do not use Delete and Insert operations, as the infilling process naturally allows the length of the resulting sequence to change.

Overall, GLARE dramatically increases the scope of the attack space by permitting more natural decoding of longer sequences. By allowing multiple words to be masked and for multiple tokens to be added at any given step, vastly fewer replacement steps are required. Additionally, the joint generation of multi-word replacements allow for greater flexibility; candidates of multiple different lengths can be compared rather than being constrained to utilizing multiple Insert operations.

3.1 Variants

We ablate two variants of our model:

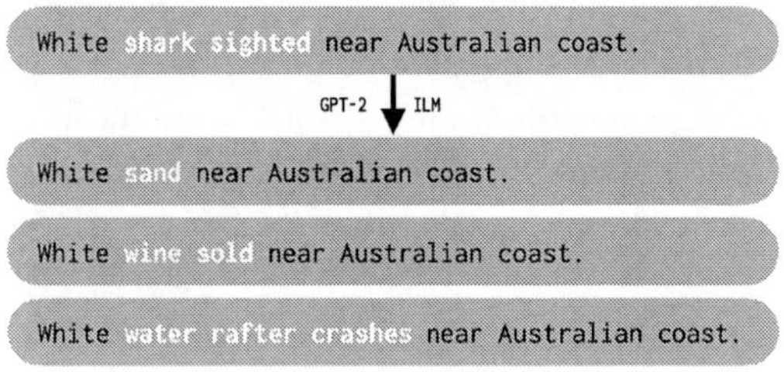

Figure 1: Illustrated example of infilling procedure.

- **GLARE$_{\text{single}}$** allows solely single-token replacements with no changes in length whatsoever—$c_{\max}$ is set to 1 and $e_{\max}$ is set to 0. Since GPT-2 is used solely for single-token replacement here, this approach is equivalent to a simple token-replacement strategy like BERTAttack (Li et al., 2020b), simply with a different model.
- **GLARE$_{\text{multi}}$** allows multi-word replacements: in our experiments, $c_{\max}$ is set to 3 and $e_{\max}$ is set to 3.

3.2 Framework

We implement GLARE as a recipe on TextAttack (Morris et al., 2020b). Specifically, the custom attack recipe consists of word-level replacements supplied by a fine-tuned version of an infilling GPT-2 model and constrained by the minimum sentence-wise cosine similarity score in a given example.

4 Experiments

Datasets We use the following datasets: Yelp Polarity (Zhang et al., 2015), AG News (Zhang et al., 2015), MultiNLI (Williams et al., 2018), and QNLI (Wang et al., 2018).

Victim Model We attack a BERT-base-uncased English model.

Metrics Evaluating adversarial attacks can be challenging, as attacks which achieve high success rate (successfully flipping a large fraction of model predictions) may be extremely obvious to a human reader due to a lack of fluency, coherency, or otherwise suspicious language (Morris et al., 2020a). We measure the following desiderata:

- **Attack success**: the percentage of model predictions successfully flipped, or Attack Success Rate (**A-rate**).
- **Distance from original example**: We measure modification rate (**Mod**), the mean fraction of words modified in each example, and (**Sim**), the cosine similarity between the original and perturbed text, as calculated by the Universal Sentence Encoder (Cer et al., 2018).
- **Fluency**: We measure perplexity (**PPL**) using a small (12-layer, 768-hidden, 12-heads, 117M parameters) non-finetuned GPT-2 model, as well as the average number of grammar errors (**GErr**) is the average number of grammatical errors introduced by each perturbed example.

Baselines We compare GLARE against prior attack methods: the non-neural TextFooler and the LLM-based BERT-Attack and CLARE (Section 2.2). Notably, CLARE is identical to our method except for the infilling method: fully generative rather than masked language modelling.[2]

5 Results

Overall, GLARE effectively attacks the victim model, achieving more fluent and grammatical attacks than baseline approaches (Table 1).

Notably, GLARE$_{\text{single}}$ achieves extremely strong performance as opposed to a method with an equivalent search space that uses BERT, BERTAttack, achieving an average of 8.3 points better on A-rate while achieving 0.04 higher Sim. Here, the search space is equivalent to BERTAttack; the advantage lies solely in using a better-parameterized GPT model.

GLARE$_{\text{multi}}$ generally performs better than GLARE$_{\text{single}}$. GLARE$_{\text{multi}}$ also achieves a 10.1 point better A-rate and 0.14 higher Sim than CLARE, another approach capable of changing token lengths – the GPT-2 infilling approach provides more flexibility and coherency to the attack.

6 Analysis

We are able to successfully outperform CLARE (the current SOTA) on a number of metrics: specifically, attack success rate, perplexity, and semantic similarity.

Effect of in-domain fine-tuning The infilling model used in our main experiments is fine-tuned

[2] Due to difficulties implementing the TEXTFOOLER and CLARE models with TEXTATTACK, the baseline values included in Table 2 were taken from (Li et al., 2020a).

	Yelp (PPL = 53.4)					AG News (PPL = 38.0)				
Model	**A-rate↑**	**Mod↓**	**PPL↓**	**GErr↓**	**Sim↑**	**A-rate↑**	**Mod↓**	**PPL↓**	**GErr↓**	**Sim↑**
TEXTFOOLER	77.0	16.6	163.3	1.23	0.70	81.7	23.6	177.5	1.27	0.83
BERTATTACK	71.8	10.7	90.8	0.27	0.72	63.4	**7.9**	90.6	**0.25**	0.71
CLARE	79.7	**10.3**	83.5	0.25	0.78	**84.7**	21.2	162.3	0.17	0.57
GLARE (single-word)	91.9	16.6	163.3	1.23	0.70	56.1	23.3	331.3	1.43	0.69
GLARE (variable-len)	**92.1**	56.7	**48.2**	**0.22**	**0.92**	79.0	69.77	**63.9**	1.69	**0.88**

	MNLI (PPL = 28.9)					QNLI (PPL = 37.9)				
Model	**A-rate↑**	**Mod↓**	**PPL↓**	**GErr↓**	**Sim↑**	**A-rate↑**	**Mod↓**	**PPL↓**	**GErr↓**	**Sim↑**
TEXTFOOLER	59.8	13.8	161.5	0.63	0.73	57.8	16.9	164.6	0.62	0.72
BERTATTACK	82.7	8.4	86.7	0.04	0.77	76.7	13.3	86.5	0.03	0.73
CLARE	88.1	7.5	82.7	**0.02**	0.82	83.8	11.8	76.7	**0.01**	0.78
GLARE (single-word)	**92.9**	**6.2**	77.9	0.23	**0.84**	**86.9**	**10.0**	72.9	0.22	0.87
GLARE (variable-len)	84.2	18.8	**60.2**	0.33	0.82	79.6	42.2	**55.6**	0.47	**0.89**

Table 1: Adversarial example performance compared on attack success rate (**A-rate**), modification rate (**Mod**), perplexity (**PPL**), number of increased grammar errors (**GErr**), and textual similarity (**Sim**) on four datasets. The perplexity of each dataset is marked in the header. ↑ (↓) represents which direction is more desirable. The best score per metric and dataset is bolded. Certain baseline results are drawn from Li et al. (2020a).

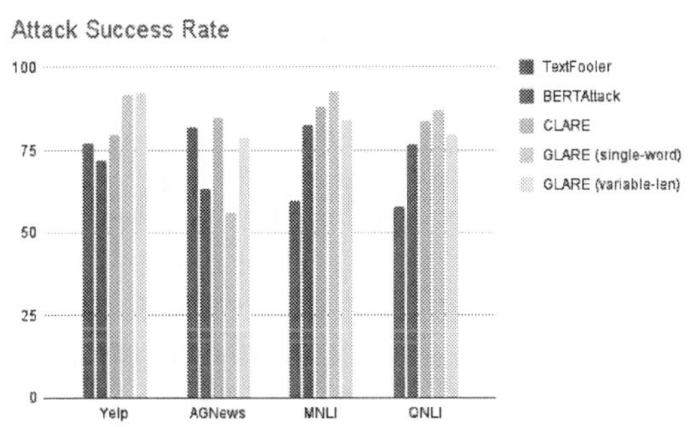

Figure 2: Comparison of attack success rates by different models.

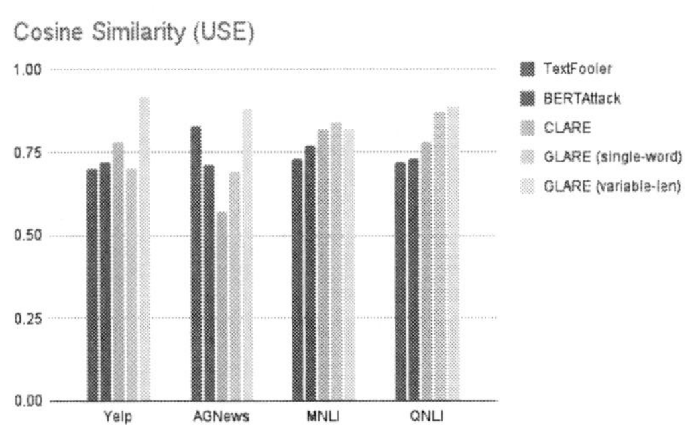

Figure 3: Comparison of cosine similarities between original and perturbed text by different models.

on in-domain data. To examine the impact of this fine-tuning on attack rates, we provide preliminary experiments on a GLARE model utilizing an OOD GPT-2 infilling model fine-tuned on the ROCStories corpus (Donahue et al., 2020). We use Donahue et al. (2020)'s fine-tuned checkpoints and otherwise use identical settings to $\text{GLARE}_{\text{single}}$. The results are inconclusive, though preliminary metrics suggest that fine-tuning the GPT-2 model does not appear to as successful as we would like, demonstrated by the fact that the ILM model fine-tuned on stories was able to often match or even outperform the corresponding model finetuned on the specific dataset (Table 2, Appendix).

Modification rate We note that our model suffers from a higher modification rate than CLARE. Although this is ostensibly undesirable, one benefit of a larger modification rate is that attacks are less likely to comprise simple polarity switches (e.g., "The food was delicious" → "The food was terrible"), which feature low modification rates but are not satisfactory adversarial examples as they necessitate a change in the example's gold label. A long-term goal is lower modification rate while maintaining the same fluent adversarial substitutions.

Example Length We note that longer inputs generally experience higher similarity scores when comparing their perturbed and original examples. We believe this is because the longer context gives the model a wider range of opportunities to perform an adversarial attack, as well as allowing the model a better glimpse into the semantic and syntactic structure of the example.

7 Conclusion

In this work we propose GLARE, a novel method for generating textual adversarial examples for use in adversarial attacks. GLARE operates by selecting spans in training examples to be masked out and then replaced with variable-length spans from a left-to-right generative model, bypassing restrictions on both the space of possible perturbations and the context available to each replacement step imposed by the single-token replacement strategy in existing methods. Our experiments show that GLARE outperforms contemporary methods in attack success, perplexity, grammatical correctness and semantic preservation when generating adversarial examples for a variety of classification benchmarks, and indicate that input text perturbation can be a promising application of left-to-right generative models for text infilling.

8 Acknowledgements

We would like to thank the anonymous reviewers for their insightful and thorough feedback, as well as Chris Donahue and Mina Lee for their assistance in adapting the ILM model to our system. Furthermore, we are grateful to Shikhar Murty and Akshay Smit for helpful discussions.

References

Daniel Cer, Yinfei Yang, Sheng yi Kong, Nan Hua, Nicole Limtiaco, Rhomni St. John, Noah Constant, Mario Guajardo-Cespedes, Steve Yuan, Chris Tar, Yun-Hsuan Sung, Brian Strope, and Ray Kurzweil. 2018. Universal sentence encoder.

Anirban Chakraborty, Manaar Alam, Vishal Dey, Anupam Chattopadhyay, and Debdeep Mukhopadhyay. 2018. Adversarial attacks and defences: A survey.

Jacob Devlin, Ming-Wei Chang, Kenton Lee, and Kristina Toutanova. 2018. Bert: Pre-training of deep bidirectional transformers for language understanding. *arXiv preprint arXiv:1810.04805*.

Chris Donahue, Mina Lee, and Percy Liang. 2020. Enabling language models to fill in the blanks. In *Proceedings of the 58th Annual Meeting of the Association for Computational Linguistics*.

Siddhant Garg and Goutham Ramakrishnan. 2020. Bae: Bert-based adversarial examples for text classification.

Ian J. Goodfellow, Jonathon Shlens, and Christian Szegedy. 2014. Explaining and harnessing adversarial examples.

Mohit Iyyer, John Wieting, Kevin Gimpel, and Luke Zettlemoyer. 2018. Adversarial example generation with syntactically controlled paraphrase networks. In *Proceedings of the 2018 Conference of the North American Chapter of the Association for Computational Linguistics: Human Language Technologies, Volume 1 (Long Papers)*, pages 1875–1885, New Orleans, Louisiana. Association for Computational Linguistics.

Di Jin, Zhijing Jin, Joey Tianyi Zhou, and Peter Szolovits. 2019a. Is bert really robust? a strong baseline for natural language attack on text classification and entailment.

Di Jin, Zhijing Jin, Joey Tianyi Zhou, and Peter Szolovits. 2019b. Is bert really robust? natural language attack on text classification and entailment. *arXiv preprint arXiv:1907.11932*.

Alexey Kurakin, Ian Goodfellow, and Samy Bengio. 2016. Adversarial examples in the physical world.

Dianqi Li, Yizhe Zhang, Hao Peng, Liqun Chen, Chris Brockett, Ming-Ting Sun, and Bill Dolan. 2020a. Contextualized perturbation for textual adversarial attack.

Jinfeng Li, Shouling Ji, Tianyu Du, Bo Li, and Ting Wang. 2019. Textbugger: Generating adversarial text against real-world applications. *Proceedings 2019 Network and Distributed System Security Symposium*.

Linyang Li, Ruotian Ma, Qipeng Guo, Xiangyang Xue, and Xipeng Qiu. 2020b. Bert-attack: Adversarial attack against bert using bert.

Yinhan Liu, Myle Ott, Naman Goyal, Jingfei Du, Mandar Joshi, Danqi Chen, Omer Levy, Mike Lewis, Luke Zettlemoyer, and Veselin Stoyanov. 2019. Roberta: A robustly optimized bert pretraining approach. *arXiv preprint arXiv:1907.11692*.

John X. Morris, Eli Lifland, Jack Lanchantin, Yangfeng Ji, and Yanjun Qi. 2020a. Reevaluating adversarial examples in natural language.

John X. Morris, Eli Lifland, Jin Yong Yoo, Jake Grigsby, Di Jin, and Yanjun Qi. 2020b. Textattack: A framework for adversarial attacks, data augmentation, and adversarial training in nlp.

Nasrin Mostafazadeh, Nathanael Chambers, Xiaodong He, Devi Parikh, Dhruv Batra, Lucy Vanderwende, Pushmeet Kohli, and James Allen. 2016. A corpus and cloze evaluation for deeper understanding of commonsense stories. In *Proceedings of the 2016 Conference of the North American Chapter of the Association for Computational Linguistics: Human Language Technologies*, pages 839–849, San Diego, California. Association for Computational Linguistics.

Alec Radford, Jeff Wu, Rewon Child, David Luan, Dario Amodei, and Ilya Sutskever. 2019. Language models are unsupervised multitask learners.

Ashish Vaswani, Noam Shazeer, Niki Parmar, Jakob Uszkoreit, Llion Jones, Aidan N Gomez, Ł ukasz Kaiser, and Illia Polosukhin. 2017. Attention is all you need. In *Advances in Neural Information Processing Systems*, volume 30. Curran Associates, Inc.

Alex Wang and Kyunghyun Cho. 2019. Bert has a mouth, and it must speak: Bert as a markov random field language model. *arXiv preprint arXiv:1902.04094*.

Alex Wang, Amanpreet Singh, Julian Michael, Felix Hill, Omer Levy, and Samuel R. Bowman. 2018. GLUE: A multi-task benchmark and analysis platform for natural language understanding. *CoRR*, abs/1804.07461.

Adina Williams, Nikita Nangia, and Samuel Bowman. 2018. A broad-coverage challenge corpus for sentence understanding through inference. In *Proceedings of the 2018 Conference of the North American Chapter of the Association for Computational Linguistics: Human Language Technologies, Volume 1 (Long Papers)*, pages 1112–1122. Association for Computational Linguistics.

Guoyang Zeng, Fanchao Qi, Qianrui Zhou, Tingji Zhang, Bairu Hou, Yuan Zang, Zhiyuan Liu, and Maosong Sun. 2021. Openattack: An open-source textual adversarial attack toolkit. In *Proceedings of the 59th Annual Meeting of the Association for Computational Linguistics and the 11th International Joint Conference on Natural Language Processing: System Demonstrations*, pages 363–371.

Xiang Zhang, Junbo Jake Zhao, and Yann LeCun. 2015. Character-level convolutional networks for text classification. *CoRR*, abs/1509.01626.

A GLARE Ablations

We perform a comparison of GLARE$_{\text{single}}$ with an out-of-domain version of the same attack. GLARE$_{\text{OOD}}$ uses an ILM model trained on the ROCStories short story corpus (Mostafazadeh et al., 2016), as provided by the authors, and performs single-token replacements like GLARE$_{\text{single}}$. We note that GLARE$_{\text{OOD}}$ outperforms GLARE$_{\text{single}}$ on almost all metrics across all of our datasets, as seen in Table 2.

	Yelp (PPL = 53.4)					**AG News** (PPL = 38.0)				
Model	**A-rate↑**	**Mod↓**	**PPL↓**	**GErr↓**	**Sim↑**	**A-rate↑**	**Mod↓**	**PPL↓**	**GErr↓**	**Sim↑**
GLARE (single-word)	91.9	16.6	163.3	1.23	0.70	56.1	23.3	331.3	1.43	0.69
GLARE (single, OOD)	**93.5**	**11.2**	**63.6**	**0.15**	**0.92**	**70.3**	**18.9**	**124.4**	**0.27**	**0.86**

	MNLI (PPL = 28.9)					**QNLI** (PPL = 37.9)				
Model	**A-rate↑**	**Mod↓**	**PPL↓**	**GErr↓**	**Sim↑**	**A-rate↑**	**Mod↓**	**PPL↓**	**GErr↓**	**Sim↑**
GLARE (single-word)	92.9	6.2	77.9	0.23	**0.84**	86.9	10.0	**72.9**	0.22	**0.87**
GLARE (single, OOD)	**93.6**	**5.8**	**64.6**	**0.15**	**0.84**	**91.1**	**9.7**	77.3	**0.18**	**0.87**

Table 2: Adversarial example performance of $\text{GLARE}_{\text{single}}$ and $\text{GLARE}_{\text{OOD}}$.

Random Text Perturbations Work, but not Always

Zhengxiang Wang
Department of Linguistics, Stony Brook University
zhengxiang.wang@stonybrook.edu

Abstract

We present three large-scale experiments on binary text matching classification task both in Chinese and English to evaluate the effectiveness and generalizability of random text perturbations as a data augmentation approach for NLP. It is found that the augmentation can bring both negative and positive effects to the test set performance of three neural classification models, depending on whether the models train on enough original training examples. This remains true no matter whether five random text editing operations, used to augment text, are applied together or separately. Our study demonstrates with strong implication that the effectiveness of random text perturbations is task specific and not generally positive.

1 Introduction

Data augmentation (DA) is a common strategy to generate novel label-preserving data to remedy data scarcity and imbalance problems (Xie et al., 2020), which has been applied with noteworthy success in image and speech recognition (Iwana and Uchida, 2021; Park et al., 2019; Shorten and Khoshgoftaar, 2019). In the field of natural language processing (NLP), there have also been a number of studies that use various DA techniques to boost the trained models' performance (Feng et al., 2021; Liu et al., 2020), ranging from word replacement (Wang and Yang, 2015; Wang et al., 2018; Zhang et al., 2015), to predictive neural language models (Hou et al., 2018; Kobayashi, 2018; Kurata et al., 2016). However, an evident and critical difference between text and image/speech is that text cannot be treated as purely physical. For any given sequence of words, both the word order and the semantic compatibility among words affect the meaning, and possibly the label of the sequence. This complex nature raises the question as to whether there exists some generally effective DA approach for NLP because automatic strict paraphrasing barely exists (Bhagat and Hovy, 2013).

Operation	Text
None	A sad, superior human comedy played out on the back roads of life.
SR	A sad, superior ***homo funniness*** played out on the back roads of life.
RI	A sad, superior human comedy played ***man*** out on the back ***stunned*** roads of life.
RS	***the*** sad, superior human comedy played out on ***roads back A*** of life.
RD	A superior human comedy played out on back roads life.

Table 1: Text augmented with two edits each DA technique by EDA. The original text is from Wei and Zou (2019). SR: Synonym Replacement; RI: Random Insertion; RS: Random Swap; RD: Random Deletion.

This study is a preliminary examination of the effectiveness and generalizability of random text perturbations as a DA approach, exemplified by Easy Data Augmentation (EDA)[1], which has been proposed to be a universal DA approach for NLP (Wei and Zou, 2019). This approach consists of four commonly used token-level editing operations (Wei et al., 2021; Wei and Zou, 2019), i.e., Synonym Replacement (SR), Random Insertion (RI), Random Swap (RS), and Random Deletion (RD). SR randomly replaces synonyms for eligible words, while RS randomly swap word pairs. RI inserts random synonyms, if any, instead of random words, whereas RD deletes words at random. Simple as these operations may seem, they have shown general success in various sentiment-related and sentence type classification tasks (Wei and Zou, 2019).

To do the examination, we first present a linguistically informed hypothesis and propose a relevant method of evaluation in section 2. We then introduce the experimental settings and results in section 3 and section 4, respectively. The paper ends with some discussions and conclusions in section 5.

The major contributions of this study are threefold. First, it reveals the possible inherent limitations of random text perturbations used as a DA

[1] https://github.com/jasonwei20/eda_nlp

Proceedings of the 3rd Workshop on Evaluation and Comparison of NLP Systems, pages 51 - 57
November 20, 2022 ©2022 Association for Computational Linguistics

approach for NLP with cross-lingual evidence. Second, the paper provides a critical angle and possibly a general way to evaluate the effectiveness and generalizability of a DA approach or technique for NLP. Third, we present an EDA-like Python program that refines EDA's functionalities, contains a novel DA technique, and can be easily employed for text augmentation in other languages. The source code for this program can be found at `https://github.com/jaaack-wang/reda`.

2 Hypothesis and evaluation method

From a linguistic point of view, the success of EDA defies understanding, as the augmented texts produced by EDA can often be unnatural, ungrammatical, or meaningless, such as examples shown in Table 1. However, it is also not surprising that these imperfect augmented texts may help models generalize better on test sets for some simple text classification tasks, as they introduce certain noise to the training examples that reduces overfitting while not damaging key information, which can easily lead to label change. For example, for sentence-level sentiment analysis, the sentiment of a sentence is often captured by only few keywords (Liu, 2012). It follows, as long as an augmented text keeps these few keywords or similar replaced words, it still reasonably preserves the sentiment label of the original text even if it is a problematic sentence. That explains the decline in models' performance in the ablation experiments by Wei and Zou (2019), where SR and RD were applied with 30% or larger editing rate, making the key lexical features more likely to be replaced or deleted. In contrast, RS and RI were overall harmless no matter how large proportion of a text was edited. This is simply because unlike SR and RD, RS and RI do not remove any lexical items in the original texts.

Therefore, we hypothesize that the effectiveness of random text perturbations is task specific and thus may not constitute a generally effective DA approach for NLP, especially if the task requires stricter semantic equivalence of the augmented text to the original text. To verify this hypothesis, we conduct experiments on binary text matching classification task both in Chinese and in English to see if five simple text editing operations, adapted from EDA, can improve the performance of three commonly used deep learning models. Since text matching classification involves prediction of whether a text pair match in meaning, it is inherently a more reliable way to test if a certain level of semantic changes, caused by text perturbations, can remain useful for training NLP models.

Split	LCQMC (Matched & Mismatched)	QQQD (Matched & Mismatched)
Train	238,766 (138,574 & 100,192)	260,000 (130,000 & 130,000)
Dev	8,802 (4,402 & 4,400)	20,000 (10,000 & 10,000)
Test	12,500 (6,250 & 6,250)	18,526 (9,263 & 9,263)

Table 2: Statistics of the LCQMAC & QQQD data sets.

3 Experimental settings

3.1 Datasets

We used two large-scale benchmark datasets, the Large-scale Chinese Question Matching Corpus (LCQMC) compiled by Liu et al. (2018) and the Quora Question Pairs Dataset (QQQD)[2], to represent binary text matching task in Chinese and in English, respectively. Both datasets contain a large collection of question pairs manually annotated with a label, 0 or 1, to indicate whether a pair match or not in terms of the expressed intents.

For LCQMC, we reused the original train, development, and test sets as provided by the authors (Liu et al., 2018). For QQQD, we created three label-balanced data sets based on its train set since the test set is made unlabeled for online competition. The basic statistics about these two datasets are given in Table 2.

3.2 Augmentation Setup

We created REDA (i.e., Revised EDA), a Python program adapted from EDA, to perform text augmentation in this study. REDA comes with the four text editing operations as in EDA, but also presents a novel technique called Random Mix (RM), which randomly selects 2-4 of the other four operations to further diversify the augmented texts. Besides, the rationales for REDA over EDA are as follows: unlike EDA, (1) REDA has a mechanism to prevent deduplicates, which can occur when there are no synonyms to replace (SR) or insert (RS) for words in the original text, or when the same words are replaced or swapped back during SR and RS operations. (2) REDA does not preprocess the input text (e.g., removing punctuations and stop words), which we believe are more in line with the basic

[2] `https://quoradata.quora.com/First-Quora-Dataset-Release-Question-Pairs`

Model	5k	10k	50k	100k	Full set
CBOW	59.4%	60.4%	65.4%	67.8%	73.8%
+ REDA	58.1%	60.9%	**68.2%**	**72.2%**	**76.4%**
CNN	59.3%	**63.4%**	67.2%	69.0%	72.9%
+ REDA	59.8%	62.6%	66.8%	69.8%	74.9%
LSTM	**60.0%**	62.1%	66.2%	69.6%	74.8%
+ REDA	58.9%	61.5%	67.7%	71.8%	**76.4%**
Average	59.6%	62.0%	66.3%	68.8%	73.8%
+ REDA	58.9%	61.7%	67.6%	71.3%	75.9%

Table 3: Test set accuracy scores of the three models trained on LCQMC's train sets of varying size with and without augmentation.

Metric	5k	10k	50k	100k	Full set
Precision	57.2%	59.2%	62.4%	64.1%	68.2%
+ REDA	56.9%	59.7%	63.9%	66.5%	70.2%
Recall	75.5%	77.3%	82.0%	85.5%	89.2%
+ REDA	73.6%	72.1%	80.7%	85.5%	90.0%

Table 4: Average test set precision and recall scores of the three models trained on LCQMC's train sets of varying size with and without augmentation.

Model	10k	50k	100k	150k	Full set
CBOW	64.4%	69.9%	72.1%	74.2%	77.7%
+ REDA	62.5%	68.5%	71.6%	74.8%	78.0%
CNN	**66.1%**	71.1%	72.6%	73.4%	75.9%
+ REDA	63.7%	69.9%	72.7%	**75.3%**	77.6%
LSTM	65.7%	**71.6%**	**72.9%**	75.0%	77.9%
+ REDA	64.0%	69.8%	72.5%	75.1%	**78.1%**
Average	65.4%	70.9%	72.5%	74.2%	77.2%
+ REDA	63.4%	69.4%	72.3%	75.1%	77.9%

Table 5: Test set accuracy scores of the three models trained on QQQD's train sets of varying size with and without augmentation.

Metric	10k	50k	100k	150k	Full set
Precision	63.8%	70.2%	71.1%	72.4%	75.6%
+ REDA	61.8%	67.6%	70.5%	74.2%	76.4%
Recall	71.4%	72.5%	76.1%	78.3%	80.2%
+ REDA	70.4%	74.3%	76.7%	76.9%	80.9%

Table 6: Average test set precision and recall scores of the three models trained on QQQD's train sets of varying size with and without augmentation.

idea of random text perturbations, the focus of this study. (3) REDA only replaces one word with its synonym at a given position at a time, instead of all its occurrences, which we see as extra edits. (4) REDA supports Chinese text augmentation in addition to English text augmentation.

Due to costs of doing experiments at this scale, we are unable to evaluate the effects of different initializations of REDA (e.g., editing rate) on the trained models' performance. Therefore, we initialized REDA with small editing rates, among others, based on our hypothesis and Wei and Zou (2019), which we believe is reasonably informed to reveal the effectiveness of random text perturbations for our experiments in general. Please refer to Appendix A for details.

3.3 Classification Models

We chose three common neural models, including Continuous Bag of Word (CBOW) model, Convolutional Neural Network (CNN) model, and Long Short-Term Memory (LSTM) model, as the classification models. The models were trained with a 64 batch size, a fixed .0005 learning rate, and constantly 3 epochs. We used Adaptive Moment Estimation (Adam) as the optimizer and cross entropy as the loss function. Also, unlike Wei and Zou (2019), we did not utilize pretrained word embeddings for our models, which will make the effects of text perturbations complicated and less interpretable. Plus, we believe for a DA approach to be generally effective, it should also work in a setting where resources for pretrained word embeddings are limited or unavailable.

The details of the model configurations and the training settings are provided in Appendix B.

4 Results

This section reports the test set performance of the three classification models trained on train sets of varying size with and without augmentation for the binary text matching task in Chinese and in English. We used accuracy as the main metric to evaluate the effectiveness of random text perturbations. The average precision and recall scores of the three models are taken as secondary metrics for more nuanced analyses. Due to the experimental costs, we only did ablation study on LCQMC to examine the effectiveness of the five DA techniques applied separately. The classification results on the original train sets are seen as baselines. Please refer to Appendix C for the size of augmented train sets.

4.1 For Chinese

As can be seen in Table 3, the size of the train set affects whether models trained on the augmented train sets outperform the baselines, with the threshold being near 50k (about 21% of the original full train set). Table 4 shows that the gains in the test set accuracy scores are mainly driven by two factors: (1) the leading precision scores of the REDA-led models after the 10k training size; (2) the narrowing gap in the recall scores after the 50k training size. That implies, the classification models learn to make less false positives with sufficient original training examples augmented. But before the threshold, augmentation is nevertheless detrimental to the models' performance even with the drastic increase of the training examples.

4.2 For English

Table 5 resembles Table 4 in data patterns, reaffirming the need of sufficient training examples for random text perturbations to work for the binary text matching task. The threshold, however, is much larger this time, nearing the 150k training size (about 57% of the original full train set), which may be dataset specific. Moreover, the REDA-led models only outperform the baselines by a small margin on average (i.e., less than 1%) on the test set, smaller than the previous section. Table 6 also shows that the increasing test set precision and recall scores, particularly the former, account for the performance gains of the REDA-led models.

4.3 Ablation Study: each DA technique

With random text perturbations requiring ample original training examples to be effective as presented above, a natural question becomes: what if the five DA techniques were applied separately? To get a more nuanced and reliable observation, we augmented train sets of 11 different sizes, instead of 5 as in the previous sections. These 11 training sizes roughly correspond to 2%, 4%, 10%, 21%, 31%, 42%, 52%, 63%, 73%, 84%, and 100% of the LCQMC's train set, respectively.

Figure 1 shows the average accuracy scores of the three classification models trained across these 11 training sizes and under different text editing conditions. Again, it confirms that there is a threshold of training size that needs to be satisfied so that each text editing operation can boost the performance of the models. Noticeably, the threshold here appears to be the 100k training size or so, instead of 50k as in Table 3, which may have to do with the separation of these DA techniques.

To explore the possible causes for the improvement in the test set accuracy scores, we also plotted the average precision and recall scores in the same way. It turns out that the rising accuracy scores are highly correlated with the increasing precision scores, as displayed in Figure 2, whereas such trend does not exist for the recall scores, as shown in Figure 3, which shows more complicated patterns.

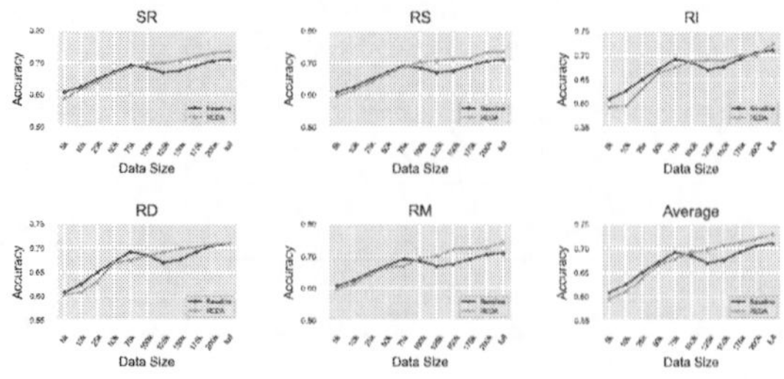

Figure 1: Average test set accuracy scores of the three models under different conditions (i.e., text editing type, training data size) for the two types of LCQMC's train sets. The sixth plot averages the statistics of the previous five plots.

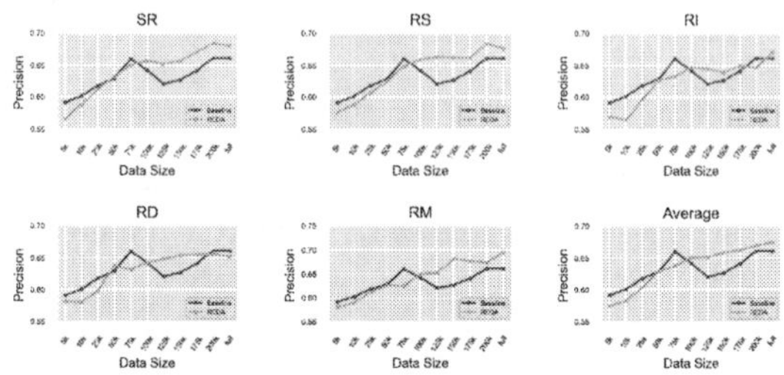

Figure 2: Average test set precision scores of the three models under different conditions (i.e., text editing type, training data size) for the two types of LCQMC's train sets. The sixth plot averages the statistics of the previous five plots.

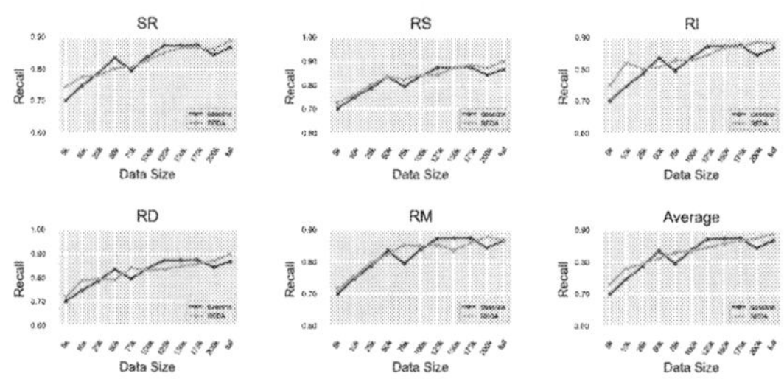

Figure 3: Average test set recall scores of the three models under different conditions (i.e., text editing type, training data size) for the two types of LCQMC's train sets. The sixth plot averages the statistics of the previous five plots.

5 Discussion and Conclusion

In this study, we evaluate the effectiveness and generalizability of random text perturbations as a DA approach for NLP. Our experiments on binary text matching classification task in Chinese and English indicate strongly that the effectiveness of the five random text editing operations, both applied together and separately, is task specific and not generally positive. Compared to Wei and Zou (2019) who show general success of text perturbations in simpler one-text-one-label NLP tasks across varying training sizes, we find that test set performance gains are only possible for the binary text matching task when a large amount of original training examples are seen by the models. This makes random text perturbations a less practical DA approach for text pair classification tasks, where having sufficiently large labeled data is usually expensive.

As expected, since text matching involves classification of text pairs, the task is by nature more sensitive to the semantic changes caused by text augmentation and thus represents a more reliable way to evaluate a DA approach for NLP. The failure of random text perturbations with small train sets may imply that the classification models are misguided by the negative effects of the augmented examples, possibly related to the augmented false matching pairs, which hamper their test set performance. However, with enough original training examples supplied, the models learn to mediate these negative effects and turn them somewhat into a means of regularizations, which help the models generalize better with improving precision on the test sets.

In relation to Wei and Zou (2019), another possible cause for the failure of augmentation on small train sets may have to do with the fact that REDA does not allow deduplicates to be in the augmented texts. That means, given comparably small editing rates, REDA tends to produce more diverse and yet non-paraphrastic augmented texts than EDA, which enlarges the negative effects of random text perturbations and thus demand more original training examples to mediate such effects. However, the exact theoretical reasons behind are worth further studying in the future.

Thoroughly evaluating a DA approach for NLP is not easy. There certainly remains a lot to be done so that we can better understand and leverage the effective sides of random text perturbations, or any other DA approaches/techniques for NLP. For example, future experiments may want to examine how a model's configurations (e.g., whether initialized with pretrained word embeddings, model architecture, hyperparameters) or the initialization of REDA may affect the test set performance for NLP tasks of various natures, e.g., classification or non-classification, binary or multi-class etc. In addition, since language is a complex discrete system, a fair evaluation also requires a large enough test set, either from one domain or across domains such that the evaluation results are more reliable and revealing. We hope this study will inspire more in-depth experiments to contribute to text augmentation, or more broadly, the empirical (evaluation) methods for NLP.

References

Rahul Bhagat and Eduard Hovy. 2013. Squibs: What is a paraphrase? *Computational Linguistics*, 39(3):463–472.

Steven Y. Feng, Varun Gangal, Jason Wei, Sarath Chandar, Soroush Vosoughi, Teruko Mitamura, and Eduard Hovy. 2021. A survey of data augmentation approaches for NLP. In *Findings of the Association for Computational Linguistics: ACL-IJCNLP 2021*, pages 968–988, Online. Association for Computational Linguistics.

Yutai Hou, Yijia Liu, Wanxiang Che, and Ting Liu. 2018. Sequence-to-sequence data augmentation for dialogue language understanding.

Brian Kenji Iwana and Seiichi Uchida. 2021. An empirical survey of data augmentation for time series classification with neural networks. *PLOS ONE*, 16(7):1–32.

Sosuke Kobayashi. 2018. Contextual augmentation: Data augmentation by words with paradigmatic relations. In *Proceedings of the 2018 Conference of the North American Chapter of the Association for Computational Linguistics: Human Language Technologies, Volume 2 (Short Papers)*, pages 452–457, New Orleans, Louisiana. Association for Computational Linguistics.

Gakuto Kurata, Bing Xiang, and Bowen Zhou. 2016. Labeled data generation with encoder-decoder lstm for semantic slot filling. In *INTERSPEECH*.

Bing Liu. 2012. *Sentiment Analysis and Opinion Mining*. Morgan & Claypool.

Pei Liu, Xuemin Wang, Chao Xiang, and Weiye Meng. 2020. A survey of text data augmentation. In *2020 International Conference on Computer Communication and Network Security (CCNS)*, pages 191–195.

Xin Liu, Qingcai Chen, Chong Deng, Huajun Zeng, Jing Chen, Dongfang Li, and Buzhou Tang. 2018. LCQMC:a large-scale Chinese question matching corpus. In *Proceedings of the 27th International Conference on Computational Linguistics*, pages 1952–1962, Santa Fe, New Mexico, USA. Association for Computational Linguistics.

Daniel S. Park, William Chan, Yu Zhang, Chung-Cheng Chiu, Barret Zoph, Ekin D. Cubuk, and Quoc V. Le. 2019. Specaugment: A simple data augmentation method for automatic speech recognition. *Interspeech 2019*.

Connor Shorten and Taghi M. Khoshgoftaar. 2019. A survey on image data augmentation for deep learning. *Journal of Big Data*, 6:1–48.

William Yang Wang and Diyi Yang. 2015. That's so annoying!!!: A lexical and frame-semantic embedding based data augmentation approach to automatic categorization of annoying behaviors using #petpeeve tweets. In *Proceedings of the 2015 Conference on Empirical Methods in Natural Language Processing*, pages 2557–2563, Lisbon, Portugal. Association for Computational Linguistics.

Xinyi Wang, Hieu Pham, Zihang Dai, and Graham Neubig. 2018. SwitchOut: an efficient data augmentation algorithm for neural machine translation. In *Proceedings of the 2018 Conference on Empirical Methods in Natural Language Processing*, pages 856–861, Brussels, Belgium. Association for Computational Linguistics.

Jason Wei, Chengyu Huang, Shiqi Xu, and Soroush Vosoughi. 2021. Text augmentation in a multi-task view. In *Proceedings of the 16th Conference of the European Chapter of the Association for Computational Linguistics: Main Volume*, pages 2888–2894, Online. Association for Computational Linguistics.

Jason Wei and Kai Zou. 2019. EDA: Easy data augmentation techniques for boosting performance on text classification tasks. In *Proceedings of the 2019 Conference on Empirical Methods in Natural Language Processing and the 9th International Joint Conference on Natural Language Processing (EMNLP-IJCNLP)*, pages 6382–6388, Hong Kong, China. Association for Computational Linguistics.

Qizhe Xie, Zihang Dai, Eduard Hovy, Minh-Thang Luong, and Quoc V. Le. 2020. Unsupervised data augmentation for consistency training.

Xiang Zhang, Junbo Zhao, and Yann LeCun. 2015. Character-level convolutional networks for text classification. In *Advances in Neural Information Processing Systems*, volume 28. Curran Associates, Inc.

Appendix

A. Initialization of REDA

We initialized REDA with the following editing rate for SR, RS, RI, and RD, respectively: 0.2, 0.2, 0.1, and 0.1. We applied Python rounding rule to calculate and perform the number of edits needed for each operation. That means, if the number of edits is less than or equal to 0.5, it will be rounded down to 0 and thus no editing operation will apply. To make our experiments more controlled and doable, (1) we made RM only randomly perform two of the other four editing operations with one edit each; (2) and every editing operation will produce up to 2 non-duplicated augmented texts, if the train set size is less than 50k; otherwise, there will only be one augmented text instead. Every augmented text was crossed paired with the other text that was the pair to the text being augmented with the original label kept for the augmented text pair. That means, the augmented text pairs double the number of augmented texts set for each text. These settings also apply for the ablation study.

The synonym dictionary for English comes from WordNet[3]. The synonym dictionary for Chinese comes from multiple reputable sources through web scraping[4].

B. Model Training

Training Settings. We reused the three simple models already constructed using Baidu's deep learning framework paddle[5]. We trained all the models in Baidu Machine Learning CodeLab on its AI Studio[6] with Tesla V100 GPU and 32G RAM, which the author could use up to 70 hours per week.

Basic Architecture. All the models begin with an Embedding layer that outputs 128-dimensional word embeddings. Then, the word embeddings for the text pairs each go through an encoder so that the encoded embeddings for the text pairs have same output dimensions and can be concatenated along the last axis. The concatenated embeddings run through a Linear layer, a Tanh activation function, and another Linear layer that outputs two dimensional logits. The details of the encoder configurations used for the CBOW, CNN, and LSTM models can be found at the footnote.[7]

Other. We did not use EarlyStopping or other similar callbacks, because that might increase the experimental costs to a point that obstructs training. Also, the effect of such a callback should be trivial as most of our models overfitted within 3 epochs.

C. Size of augmented train sets

Table 7 and Table 8 contain size of the train sets for the first two experiments on LCQMC and QQQD and the ablation experiment on LCQMC, respectively. Please note that, for simplicity, 240k is used to refer to the full size of LCQMC, which is 238,766 to be exact. Also, due to deduplication, different text editing operations may result in augmented train sets with non-trivial difference in size, as discernible in Table 8. The reason that the ratio of the augmented train sets to the corresponding original train sets in size is different is explained in Appendix A.

LCQMC	Augmented	QQQD	Augmented
5k	66,267	10k	148,341
10k	132,513	50k	543,066
50k	563,228	100k	1,086,063
100k	929,176	150k	1,629,178
240k	2,218,512	260k	2,823,733

Table 7: Size of augmented train sets for the first two experiments on LCQMC and QQQD.

Size	SR	RS	RI	RD	RM
5k	24,402	24,758	16,733	16,780	24,859
10k	48,807	49,575	33,090	33,208	49,652
25k	122,358	124,040	83,329	83,592	124,237
50k	244,577	248,074	166,839	167,296	248,539
75k	220,843	223,497	162,563	162,972	224,026
100k	294,516	297,987	216,540	217,012	298,620
125k	368,078	372,536	270,957	271,552	373,266
150k	441,643	446,941	325,027	325,738	447,838
175k	515,229	521,484	379,352	380,214	522,535
200k	588,901	595,977	433,521	434,469	597,084
240k	703,077	711,631	517,492	518,664	712,852

Table 8: Size of augmented train sets for the ablation experiment on LCQMC.

[3] https://wordnet.princeton.edu

[4] https://github.com/jaaack-wang/Chinese-Synonyms

[5] https://github.com/PaddlePaddle/PaddleNLP/blob/develop/examples/text_matching/simnet

[6] https://aistudio.baidu.com/aistudio/index

[7] https://github.com/PaddlePaddle/PaddleNLP/blob/develop/paddlenlp/seq2vec/encoder.py

A Comparative Analysis of Stance Detection Approaches and Datasets

Parush Gera and **Tempestt Neal**
Department of Computer Science and Engineering
University of South Florida
parush@usf.edu, tjneal@usf.edu

Abstract

Various approaches have been proposed for automated stance detection, including those that use machine and deep learning models and natural language processing techniques. However, their cross-dataset performance, the impact of sample size on performance, and experimental aspects such as runtime have yet to be compared, limiting what is known about the generalizability of prominent approaches. This paper presents a replication study of stance detection approaches on current benchmark datasets. Specifically, we compare six existing machine and deep learning stance detection models on three publicly available datasets. We investigate performance as a function of the number of samples, length of samples (word count), representation across targets, type of text data, and the stance detection models themselves. We identify the current limitations of these approaches and categorize their utility for stance detection under varying circumstances (e.g., size of text samples), which provides valuable insight for future research in stance detection.

1 Introduction

The task of detecting stance from a text sample, i.e., determining if the author of the text is in favor, against, or has a neutral attitude towards an entity or proposition in the text (Mohammad et al., 2016; Zhou et al., 2017), has not only contributed to increased understanding of how users behave and interact on these platforms (Küçük and Can, 2020), but it has also complemented sentiment and semantic analyses (Stieglitz and Dang-Xuan, 2013). In stance detection, the entity or proposition, which is often referred to as the *target*, can be a place, person, product, situation, policy, organization, etc. (Mohammad et al., 2016).

Many machine and deep learning and natural language processing (NLP) techniques have been proposed for automated stance detection (Zhou et al., 2017; Mohtarami et al., 2018; Mohammad et al., 2016; Augenstein et al., 2016). However, substantial advancements thus far have depended on publicly available datasets (Sobhani et al., 2017; Mohammad et al., 2017), which, at the time of their writing, were not large nor diverse in comparison to datasets for other NLP tasks like sentiment analysis (Socher et al., 2013; Ni et al., 2019; Neal et al., 2017). Most stance detection approaches have been trained and tested on the benchmark dataset used in the SemEval 2016 workshop (SemEval, 2016; Mohammad et al., 2017), limiting the analysis of stance detection on varying text types (blogs, social media posts, news articles, etc.).

Due to the nature of the datasets on which current stance detection models are trained, their ability to generalize to larger datasets is not well-studied. This includes a comparative analysis of their runtime, performance depending on the size of the dataset, and their application to cross-dataset stance detection, in which subtasks like cross-target stance detection are receiving increasing attention (Wei and Mao, 2019; Zhang et al., 2020; Liang et al., 2021; Conforti et al., 2021; Ji et al., 2022; Xu et al., 2018). Thus, we present a comparative analysis of stance detection models as a means of benchmarking existing approaches such that future research can address gaps identified in this work.

This paper presents an analyses of six commonly used stance detection classification approaches, each trained and tested on three publicly available datasets (Mohammad et al., 2017; Sen et al., 2018; Somasundaran and Wiebe, 2010). The text samples in these datasets cover three types of data sources (i.e., Twitter posts, responses to questions, and online debates), and are annotated with the target (e.g., gun rights, atheism, e-cigarettes, etc.) and the author's stance (`FAVOR`, `AGAINST`, or `NEUTRAL`) towards the target. In prior work, Ghosh et al. (2019) also compared the reproducibility of different stance detection models on two datasets (Sen et al., 2018; Mohammad et al., 2017). While

Proceedings of the 3rd Workshop on Evaluation and Comparison of NLP Systems, pages 58 - 69
November 20, 2022

their work studied stance detection within a single dataset, they observed that "no single method [was] able to give very high metric value over all datasets" (Ghosh et al., 2019). However, a comparative analysis of other parameters that could play a role in stance detection accuracy, alongside studying existing models in more demanding scenarios, such as their application across datasets, has yet to be explored. That is, prior work compares the merits and limitations of stance detection models in terms of stance detection accuracy alone, while we contribute novel insight concerning other metrics (e.g., runtime) and use cases (e.g., cross-dataset stance detection). Specific contributions include:

1. We examine the generalizability of stance detection models across text types by using three publicly available datasets, each representing three different text domains (i.e., Twitter data, query responses, and long debates).
2. We conduct cross-dataset stance detection to determine if current stance detection models can accurately identify stance on datasets unseen during training, furthering the analysis of generalizability.
3. We explore the impacts of different characteristics of the datasets, including sample size, sentence length, semantic context, and runtime, on stance detection accuracy.

2 Background

Initial work in stance detection focused on determining the stance of political and parliamentary debates (Somasundaran and Wiebe, 2010). Lately, this interest has shifted towards social media platforms due to the diversity of opinions shared on these applications (Mohammad et al., 2016). Many tasks have been proposed in the past owing to the diverse applications of stance analysis on social media like multi-target stance detection (Wei et al., 2018; Sobhani et al., 2017), cross-target stance detection (Zhang et al., 2020; Conforti et al., 2021; Wei and Mao, 2019), rumour stance classification (Zubiaga et al., 2018; Lukasik et al., 2019), and fake news stance detection (Ghanem et al., 2018; Umer et al., 2020).

To date, there have been numerous efforts for stance detection using traditional machine learning algorithms and deep learning techniques (Mohammad et al., 2016; Zhou et al., 2017; Ghosh et al., 2019; Mohtarami et al., 2018; Somasundaran and Wiebe, 2010; Zhang et al., 2020; Augenstein et al., 2016; Al-Ghadir et al., 2021), while the 2016 SemEval workshop's task on detecting stance in tweets (SemEval, 2016) generated various stance detection approaches which used traditional sentiment and sentence classification features like n-grams and embedded vectors (Zarrella and Marsh, 2016; Wei et al., 2016). Workshop submissions showed significant improvement in performance when using support vector machines (SVM), even in comparison to the top three submissions which leveraged transfer learning and recurrent neural networks (RNNs) (Mohammad et al., 2016). For instance, the method proposed by Zarrella and Marsh used transfer learning on features extracted from two large unlabeled datasets via distant supervision (Zarrella and Marsh, 2016), although their method failed to outperform the SVM-derived baseline.

On the other hand, RNN models also show promising results. Zhou et al. extended two RNN models (biGRU and biGRU-CNN) to incorporate target information via a token-level (AT-biGRU) and semantic-level attention (AS-biGRU) mechanism for detecting stance in tweets (Zhou et al., 2017). Similarly, Ghosh et al. (2019) reproduced a few competitive Convolutional Neural Network (CNN) and RNN based methods, and compared them with Google's Bidirectional Encoder Representations from Transformers (BERT) model.

3 Methodology

3.1 Dataset Descriptions

The chosen datasets were selected due to their diversity in text type, number of text samples, and size of each sample. Only datasets with samples written in English were considered.

The SemEval-2016 Task 6A Stance Dataset The SemEval-2016 Stance Dataset (Mohammad et al., 2017) was used in the task of stance detection at SemEval-2016 (SemEval, 2016). It contains 4,870 manually annotated (stance and target) tweets. Tweets in the dataset are divided among five targets: "Atheism"; "Climate Change is Real Concern"; "Feminist Movement"; "Hillary Clinton"; and "Legalization of Abortion." Each tweet is labeled with the author's stance (`FAVOR`, `AGAINST` or `NEITHER`) towards the target. An example is shown below:

Target	Tweet	Stance
Feminist movement	"Whether you label yourself a feminist or not I think it's important that we address equal rights."	`FAVOR`

Multi-Perspective Consumer Health Query Data (MPCHI) The MPCHI dataset (Sen et al., 2018) consists of responses to five different queries: "Are e-cigarettes safe?"; "Does the MMR vaccine lead to autism in children?"; "Does sunlight exposure lead to skin cancer?"; "Does vitamin C prevent the common cold?"; and "Should women take HRT post-menopause?" This dataset was created by retrieving the top 50 links corresponding to each query on the web, and then using crowd-sourcing to retrieve query relevant sentences. Each sentence has a polarized stance, i.e., `FAVOR` or `AGAINST`. An example is shown below:

Target	Response	Stance
Does sunlight exposure lead to skin cancer?	The UV explanation for melanoma is not adequate.	`AGAINST`

Ideological Online Debates The Ideological Online Debates dataset (Somasundaran and Wiebe, 2010) consists of political and ideological online debates on "Existence of God"; "Healthcare"; "Gun Rights"; "Gay Rights"; and "Abortion and Creationism." Debates for each topic are labeled as `FOR` or `AGAINST`; we converted the label `FOR` to `FAVOR` for consistency across datasets. An example is shown below:

Target	Response	Stance
Gun Rights	"The statement of 'Guns kill people, Guns kill children' is false guns don't kill people, people kill people. Guns should be allowed everywhere GUNS ARE GOOD."	`FAVOR`

3.2 Stance Detection Approaches

Approach #1: Support Vector Machines and N-grams Application of SVMs for stance detection were proposed by Mohammad et al. (2016), and used as the baseline method in the SemEval (Mohammad et al., 2016) and in other stance detection approaches (Zhou et al., 2017; Ghosh et al., 2019; Augenstein et al., 2016; Mohtarami et al., 2018). A SVM is a classification algorithm which finds a hyperplane having a maximum margin, or distance, between data points of different classes, in an n-dimensional space. We refer the reader to (Noble, 2006) for more details on SVMs.

We were unable to find publicly available code by the authors to replicate these experiments, and thus wrote the code from scratch using the details provided in the article (Mohammad et al., 2016). We note that the article does not mention which feature extraction method was used to extract n-grams (i.e., CountVectorizer or TfidfVectorizer). A CountVectorizer captures the frequency of tokens in a text sample, while a TfidfVectorizer (Term Frequency - Inverse Document Frequency) provides both the frequency of tokens and their importance by penalizing those that occur too frequently or not often enough. Here, we have implemented TfidfVectorizer as it performed better. We tuned the SVM's parameters (kernel, γ, C) using a grid search and five-fold cross-validation. Following the work of Mohammad et al. (2016), our experimental approach consisted of two tasks:

1. SVM-ngrams: Multiple SVMs (one per target) trained on n-grams, where $n = 1, 2, 3$ and $n = 2, 3, 4, 5$ for word and character n-grams, respectively.
2. SVM-ngram - comb (overall): A single classifier trained on all targets using the same features as SVM-ngram.

Approach #2: Bi-directional Gated Recurrent Units Gated Recurrent Units (GRUs) are very similar to basic RNNs except that they have a *update* and *relevance* gate which are capable of updating only relevant information, making them useful for stance detection (Zhou et al., 2017). A GRU maps the input sequence of length N, $[x^{<t_1>}, x^{<t_2>}, x^{<t_3>} \ldots . x^{<t_N>}]$ into a set of hidden states $[h^{<t_1>}, h^{<t_2>}, h^{<t_3>}, \ldots\ldots . h^{<t_N>}]$ as follows:

$$\Gamma_u = \sigma(W_u[h^{<t_0>}, x^{<t_1>}] + b_u)$$
$$\Gamma_r = \sigma(W_r[h^{<t_0>}, x^{<t_1>}] + b_r)$$
$$\mathrm{h}'^{<t_1>} = \tanh(W_h[\Gamma_r * h^{<t_0>}, x^{<t_1>}] + b_h)$$
$$\mathrm{h}^{<t_1>} = \Gamma_u * h^{<t_0>} + (1 - \Gamma_u) * h'^{<t_1>}$$

where Γ_u corresponds to the update gate and Γ_r to the reset gate; $\sigma(.)$ is a sigmoid function; $W_u, W_r, W_h \in R^{d_1 \times d_0}$ represent the weight matrices; $h'^{<t_1>} \in R^{d_1}$ corresponds to the generated *candidate* hidden state and $h^{<t_1>} \in R^{d_1}$ to the real updated hidden state; $b_u, b_r \in R^{d_1}$ are bias terms; and $x^{<t_n>} \in R^{d_0}$ represents a word embedding of tokenized and pre-processed text.

Bi-directional GRUs (bi-GRUs) process a sequence in forward and backward directions, i.e., the same gated mechanism is applied from both directions to the sequence. The final hidden state output is the concatenation of both outputs, capturing information from past and future sequences. For a text, X, the final vector representation is

$$X = \overrightarrow{h^{<t_N>}} \parallel \overleftarrow{h^{<t_1>}}$$

where $\parallel$ represents the concatenation of two vectors.

Dataset	Target	Train				Test				
		%Favor	*%Against*	*%Neutral*	*#Total Train*	*%Favor*	*%Against*	*%Neutral*	*#Total Test*	*Sentence Length - Mean*
SemEval 2016 Stance Dataset - Task A										
	Athesim (AT)	17.93	59.26	22.81	513	14.55	72.73	12.73	220	102.77
	Climate Change is Real Concern (CC)	53.67	3.80	42.53	395	72.78	6.51	20.71	169	101.2
	Feminist Movement (FM)	31.63	49.40	18.98	664	20.35	64.21	15.44	285	103.4
	Hillary Clinton (HC)	17.13	57.04	25.83	689	15.25	58.31	26.44	295	102.7
	Legalization of Abortion (LA)	18.53	54.36	27.11	653	16.43	67.50	16.07	280	103.9
	Total	**25.84**	**47.87**	**26.29**	**2914**	**24.34**	**57.25**	**18.41**	**1249**	**102.95 (Overall Mean)**
MPC Query Data										
	E-Cigarettes (EC)	20.76	40.83	38.41	289	26.61	37.90	35.48	124	144.58
	MMR Vaccine (MV)	26.52	33.70	39.78	181	30.77	42.31	26.92	78	157.83
	Sunlight Cancer (SC)	29.24	22.03	48.73	236	33.98	25.24	40.78	103	124.09
	Vitamin C (VC)	38.14	26.80	35.05	194	44.05	19.05	36.90	84	145.74
	HRT (HT)	19.19	55.23	25.58	172	12.16	55.41	32.43	74	148.83
	Total	**26.49**	**35.26**	**38.25**	**1072**	**29.81**	**35.21**	**34.99**	**463**	**143.18 (Overall Mean)**
Ideological Online Debates										
	Existence of God (EG)	48.28	51.72	NA	667	48.60	51.40	NA	286	678.59
	Healthcare (HC)	50.00	50.00	NA	466	56.22	43.78	NA	201	715
	Gun Rights (Gu R)	72.19	27.81	NA	748	72.90	27.10	NA	321	720
	Gay Rights (Ga R)	64.40	35.60	NA	1444	63.06	36.94	NA	620	807.5
	Abortion (AB)	54.04	45.96	NA	805	56.65	43.35	NA	346	746.13
	Creationism (CR)	33.91	66.09	NA	861	37.67	62.33	NA	369	958.43
	Total	**55.14**	**44.86**	**0.00**	**4991**	**56.56**	**43.44**	**0.00**	**2143**	**784.68 (Overall Mean)**

Table 1: Distribution of examples in all three datasets.

Approach #3: Bi-directional Gated Recurrent Unit - Convolutional Neural Network (Zhou et al., 2017) BiGRUs are powerful in capturing dependencies in sequential data, but its gated mechanism is highly dependent on the length of a text sequence. If the length of the sequence becomes very large, it can suffer from vanishing gradients, resulting in information loss from initial sequences. Because the Online Debate Dataset (Somasundaran and Wiebe, 2010) has an average text length that is much higher compared to the other datasets used in our experiments, we replicated the Bi-directional Gated Recurrent Unit - Convolutional Neural Network (biGRU-CNN) model. Using the approach proposed by Tan et al. (2015) and used by Zhou et al. (2017) for stance detection on Twitter data, each value of feature map, $c^{<i>}$, is obtained by applying filter, W_g, on k concatenated consecutive hidden states $h^{<i:i+k-1>}$ of the biGRU model. This calculation also includes the addition of a bias term, b_g, as given in the equation below:

$$c^{<i>} = g(W_g^T h^{<i:i+k-1>} + b_g)$$

where g is a rectified linear unit function. To capture the most important semantic features, c', max pooling is applied over the generated feature map $C = [c^{<1>}, c^{<2>}, c^{<3>} ... c^{<N-k+1>}]$, where N is the input sequence length. Multiple features are generated using different values of sliding windows (i.e., $k = 3, 4, 5$), which are concatenated to obtain a vector representation of a text sample. We refer the reader to (Zhou et al., 2017) for more details on the biGRU and biGRU-CNN models.

Approach #4: Bi-directional Long Short Term Memory Models Long Short Term Memory models (LSTMs) allow a deep network to forget irrelevant information. LSTMs have shown promising results in many applications like image captioning, speech recognition, chatbots, next-character prediction and music composition, and stance detection (Su et al., 2017; Wang et al., 2016; Eck and Schmidhuber, 2002; Graves et al., 2013; Sundermeyer et al., 2012; Augenstein et al., 2016). LSTMs map an input sequence of length N, $[x^{<t_1>}, x^{<t_2>}, x^{<t_3>} .... x^{<t_N>}]$ into a set of hidden states $[h^{<t_1>}, h^{<t_2>}, h^{<t_3>}, ... h^{<t_N>}]$ as follows:

$$\begin{aligned}
\Gamma_f &= \sigma(W_f[h^{<t-1>}, x^{<t_1>}] + b_f) \\
\Gamma_i &= \sigma(W_i[h^{<t-1>}, x^{<t>}] + b_i) \\
\widehat{c_t} &= \tanh(W_c[h^{<t-1>}, x^{<t>}] + b_c) \\
\mathrm{c}_t &= \Gamma_f \odot c_{t-1} + \Gamma_i \odot \widehat{c_t} \\
\Gamma_o &= \sigma(W_o[h^{<t-1>}, x^{<t>}] + b_o) \\
\mathrm{h}^{<t_1>} &= \Gamma_o \tanh(c_t)
\end{aligned}$$

where $\Gamma_f, \Gamma_i, \Gamma_o$ represent the *forget*, *input* and *output* gates, respectively; W_f, W_i, W_c, W_o are the weight matrices, b_f, b_i, b_c, b_o are the biases; $\widehat{c_t}$ and c_t are the candidate cell state and final cell state, respectively; $\sigma(.)$ is the sigmoid function; $\odot$ represents the Hadmard product or element wise multiplication; and $h^{<t_1>} \in R^{d_1}$ the real updated hidden state.

Similar to the biGRU, a biLSTM processes a given sequence forward and backward; the same gated mechanism is applied from both directions to the sequence. The final hidden state output is the concatenation of both outputs. This allows the capture of information from past and future sequences. For a text, X, the final vector representation is $X = \overrightarrow{h^{<t_N>}} \parallel \overleftarrow{h^{<t_1>}}$.

Approach #5: Bi-directional Long Short Term Memory - Convolutional Neural Network The architecture of a bi-directional LSTM-CNN is similar to biGRU-CNNs, except the outputs of consecutive hidden layers of the LSTM are fed into the same CNN architecture as discussed in Approach #3.

Approach #6: Bidirectional Encoder Representations from Transformers (BERT) BERT was developed by Google AI Language as a language representation model (Devlin et al., 2018a). It is a masked language model which generates contextual embeddings for each token in the raw text by incorporating context in both left and right directions in the sentence. It has also been used for next sentence prediction (Devlin et al., 2018b). We fine-tuned the BERT base model (uncased) for stance detection with 50 epochs, a batch size of 32, and a maximum sequence length of 128. We used 512 tokens per sequence and a learning rate of 2e-5. We used the pooled output from the final layer of BERT model and applied a dropout of 0.1 followed by a Dense layer with a sigmoid activation function. We note that BERT was trained in an early stopping fashion.

3.3 Experimental Setup

Data Preprocessing In line with Mohammad et al. (2016), for all other models except the SVM, the text was preprocessed as follows. Each text sample was converted to lowercase characters. Retweets, URLs, and hashtags were removed when applicable. Stop words and punctuation were removed to then create an array of tokens. To create a vocabulary dictionary, all unique words (i.e., keys) in the dataset were assigned a unique number (i.e., value) corresponding with its index in the dictionary. Indices 0, 1, and 2 were reserved for padding (`_PAD_`), end of sentence (`_</e>_`), and unknown tokens (`_UNK_`), respectively. Each text sample was then transformed into a numerical array, which consisted of the value corresponding to each key (i.e., word in the sentence) in the vocabulary dictionary. The resulting array was padded to the maximum sentence length.

Training and Testing Like Mohammad et al. (2016), all models were trained on all three classes for the SemEval and MPCHI datasets, and the `NEUTRAL/NEITHER` class was not considered during testing. Further, because the Ideological dataset only consist of two classes, all models were trained on these two classes for this dataset.

We considered several experiments: one model trained per target, a model trained on all targets, and a model trained on one dataset and tested on the others. For all models except BERT, we performed five-fold cross-validation with 50 epochs per fold. We used the same hyperparameters as Zhou et al. (2017) for all neural network models, along with using GLOVE (Global Vectors for Word Representation) Wikipedia embeddings (Pennington et al., 2014). These hyperparameters were obtained by using a grid search on the biGRU model. For BERT, we used the same hyperparameters as Ghosh et al. (2019). All hyperparameters are listed in Table 4.

3.4 Evaluation

In line with the evaluation metric used in the SemEval-2016 Task 6A and other studies, we employ the macro-average of the F_1 score of detecting `FAVOR` and `AGAINST` stance.

$$F_{favor} = \frac{2P_{favor}R_{favor}}{P_{favor} + R_{favor}}$$

$$F_{against} = \frac{2P_{against}R_{against}}{P_{against} + R_{against}}$$

$$F_{avg} = \frac{F_{favor} + F_{against}}{2}$$

4 Results

4.1 Performance Per Dataset

SemEval 2016 Stance Dataset According to Table 2, BERT outperforms all models across all targets, excluding LA, for the SemEval dataset. We note that the BERT model learns contextual dependencies in a sentence, while sequence learning models, biLSTM and biGRU, are based on GLOVE embeddings which do not take context into account. We also observe some merit (6 of 10 experiments showed increased accuracy with the added CNN layer) with adding the CNN layer for other models; biGRU-CNN outperformed biGRU for targets AT, CC, FM, LA by an average of 4.8%. biLSTM-CNN outperformed biLSTM with an average increase of 1.95% on targets FM and HC.

Dataset	Target	Models					
		SVM	*biGRU*	*biGRU-CNN*	*biLSTM*	*biLSTM-CNN*	*BERT*
SemEval-2016 TaskA	AT	58.72	54.33	60.21	54.67	56.35	**69.41**
	CC	43.01	40.57	43.22	42.11	42.00	**44.21**
	FM	58.18	52.30	53.75	57.06	56.58	**58.72**
	HC	58.04	53.35	44.77	54.05	54.68	**69.78**
	LA	**64.55**	59.22	63.40	61.83	57.73	59.30
	Overall	62.11	57.45	56.19	54.67	54.54	**66.24**
MPCHI	EC	60.96	52.89	59.29	57.89	**60.99**	60.21
	MV	**75.38**	56.75	62.79	59.42	66.93	44.50
	SC	59.97	50.13	57.99	60.79	57.88	**67.57**
	VC	61.64	56.91	49.87	40.80	48.56	**67.13**
	HT	55.13	59.00	47.57	44.26	**60.56**	41.38
	Overall	58.51	54.92	**60.72**	57.46	59.44	58.22
Ideological Online Debates	EG	**65.58**	54.57	59.70	53.49	59.31	54.73
	HC	63.75	60.21	61.00	59.27	59.38	**64.88**
	Gu R	**68.85**	58.10	62.55	64.35	64.76	42.30
	Ga R	**66.73**	57.67	64.69	60.92	65.97	61.24
	AB	**65.91**	58.21	62.30	58.09	61.86	57.69
	CR	54.91	51.33	52.24	53.45	**57.63**	47.92
	Overall	58.20	58.35	58.54	57.51	60.38	**61.84**

Table 2: F_1 *macro score for each model when trained and tested on the same target.*

However, an interesting observation is that, with the exception of BERT, the deep sequence models did not consistently outperform the SVM (the biGRU-CNN outperformed the SVM for AT and LA targets). We attribute the poor performance of deep learning models to their need for a large number of examples, which is not available in the SemEval dataset. We suspect that the BERT model outperformed SVM in most cases because it is a pre-trained model which is fine-tuned on the data corresponding to targets. Nonetheless, we posit that in the case smaller datasets, a SVM with a Tf-Idf vector captures more stance expressing features than deep learning sequence models.

MPCHI Dataset As shown in Table 2, we again observe that the SVM outperforms all models in most cases (EC, MV, HT). For biLSTM-CNN, the performance was increased by adding the CNN layer to biLSTM by an average of 8.85% for targets EC, MV, VC, and HT. Adding the CNN layer to biGRU boosted its performance by an average of 6.76% for targets EC, MV, and SC.

Further, the biLSTM-CNN's performance was improved by an average of 7.2% compared to biGRU's performance. We suspect this is due to the ability of these models to forget and the text sample size. The number of examples in the MPCHI dataset is one-third of the number of examples in the SemEval dataset, although the MPCHI has a greater average sentence length. Sequence models like biGRU and biLSTM can automatically extract stance expressing features from a sentence of adequate length, which should not be too short or too long. However, the biLSTM may be a more optimal model than biGRU since the biLSTM can forget irrelevant information while biGRU does not. Also, since sentences with high length will result in larger sequences to classify, the problem of vanishing gradient descent might arise.

Ideological Online Debates Dataset From Table 2, it can be observed that the SVM outperformed other models for targets EG, Gu R, Ga R, and AB. The biLSTM-CNN outperformed biLSTM for all targets by an average of 3.68%. The biGRU-CNN outperformed biGRU for all targets by an average of 3.41%. It is important to note that BERT's performance was generally poorer than previously observed for the other datasets. We attribute this to its limitation of the maximum processing sequence length of 512 for this dataset, whereas the actual average sentence length is greater than 512. Therefore, truncating the rest of the text leads to a loss of information.

We note that the Ideological dataset has the highest sentence average length (see Table 1). An interesting observation here is that given an adequate sequence length, both biLSTM-CNN and biGRU-CNN outperformed their non-CNN added version for all targets. However, for the SemEval and MPCHI datasets, where the sequence length is relatively small, these CNN-added models were only able to outperform on some targets. We attribute this to feeding the output of the bidirectional layers to a CNN, which further enables the model to capture most stance semantic features from the feature map.

4.2 Performance Per Stance Detection Model

biGRU and biGRU-CNN For the biGRU and biGRU-CNN models, Table 2 shows that adding a

Tested On	Trained on SemEval 2016 Task 6A					
	SVM_TFIDF	*biGRU*	*biGRU-CNN*	*biLSTM*	*biLSTM-CNN*	*BERT*
SemEval 2016 Task 6A	72.00	65.38	66.53	63.85	67.37	66.18
MPCHI	46.52	56.79	54.73	54.26	56.9	36.80
Ideological Online Debates	45.19	45.95	46.25	46.22	44.46	52.51
Tested On	**Trained on MPCHI**					
	SVM_TFIDF	*biGRU*	*biGRU-CNN*	*biLSTM*	*biLSTM-CNN*	*BERT*
SemEval 2016 Task 6A	55.15	49.81	48.50	45.34	48.55	50.06
MPCHI	74.00	65.05	73.69	67.73	72.03	77.77
Ideological Online Debates	48.89	52.66	51.54	51.57	52.91	38.90
Tested On	**Trained on Ideological Online Debates**					
	SVM_TFIDF	*biGRU*	*biGRU-CNN*	*biLSTM*	*biLSTM-CNN*	*BERT*
SemEval 2016 Task 6A	50.73	47.03	49.19	47.19	43.52	39.96
MPCHI	35.97	51.80	47.56	51.34	47.57	49.61
Ideological Online Debates	59.00	58.35	58.54	57.61	60.38	60.28

Table 3: F_1 *macro score for each model when trained on one dataset and tested on another dataset.*

CNN layer to the hidden layer outputs of biGRU generally provides improved F_1 macro scores in the SemEval and MPCHI datasets. We suspect that feeding the output of the bidirectional layers of the biGRU, which contains information about dependencies in a text sequence, into CNN layers with different filter sizes, enables the model to better capture important semantic features. A further possible explanation for the lower accuracy of the biGRU could be the lower average sentence length (after pre-processing) of 9 tokens in the SemEval dataset and 15 tokens in the MPCHI dataset, causing the biGRU to fail to recognize dependencies in the sequence; the CNN layer enabled the biGRU to better capture dependencies. This claim is supported by the fact that the biGRU-CNN performed better than SVM for targets AT, CC, and LA. On the other hand, the poor performance of biGRU for the Ideological Debates dataset can be attributed to longer sequences, which may be difficult to process and identify within sentence dependencies.

biLSTM and biLSTM-CNN Table 2 also shows the F_1 macro score of the biLSTM and biLSTM-CNN models. First, when trained and tested on the SemEval dataset, the biLSTM did not outperform the SVM. Further, adding a CNN layer did not improve the performance of biLSTM except for target AT and slightly for FM and HC. This is attributed to the lower sequence length. This claim is supported by the performance of biLSTM-CNN on MPCHI targets, where it outperformed the biLSTM along with biGRU and biGRU-CNN models in most cases, possibly because the LSTM is capable of forgetting irrelevant information, which enables it to capture more accurate dependencies in the text sequence than the biGRU.

BERT The BERT model is capable of capturing contextual information for each token in a text sequence, both in the left and right directions. Being an attention model, it also directs attention towards the desired word in the sequence. One interesting observation is that while the BERT model performs best in SemEval, except for target LA, it does not perform well on EC, MV, HT, and overall in the MPCHI dataset. Similarly, for the Ideological Debates dataset, it does not perform better than SVM and other sequence models. We attribute this to the following observations. First, the number of training examples in the SemEval dataset is three times the number of examples in the MPCHI dataset. Further, the F_1 macro score is computed for the `Favor` and `Against` classes only; the percentage of training examples is larger for the SemEval dataset (73.71%) compared to the MPCHI dataset (61.75%). For the Ideological Debates dataset, the mean sentence length is 784.68, whereas BERT can be trained on a maximum of 512 tokens. It is important to observe that the mean sentence length in the SemEval dataset is smaller (102.95) than the MPCHI dataset (143.18). However, BERT performed better on the former given the higher number of training examples.

4.3 Cross-Dataset Stance Detection

We investigated the performance across datasets (trained on one dataset and tested on the others) to determine the generalizability of each model. Our datasets are diverse in size and text types, thus motivating this analysis. Specifically, in SemEval, the average sentence length is 102.95 words. In MPCHI, the average sentence length is 143.18 words. In Ideological Online Debates, the average sentence length is 784.68 words. Detailed results are given in Table 3.

Overall, we find that each model generalizes poorly, highlighting the need for more robust algorithmic solutions to stance detection, especially for cross-dataset stance detection. Performance degradation could be attributed to many factors, including diversity of topics across datasets, diversity in sample sizes, and the failure of models to capture sequential information as the dataset sizes change. Specifically, the datasets used in this work comprise of contextually diverse targets and domains. There is some domain overlap in SemEval and Ideological Debates (e.g., (AT, EG) and (FM, LA, AB)), but the number of training examples in these datasets vary. Therefore, a model trained on less training data might under perform due to low and imbalanced learning. Since deep learning models are capable of capturing relevant information from the data automatically, they fail to generalize over datasets when trained on fewer data and significantly varying text lengths. Therefore, while using deep learning models, a large number of examples per target with adequate text length contributes highly towards training on prediction performance.

The common use of GLOVE embeddings could also play role in poor generalization across datasets. GLOVE embeddings in sequence models do not take context into account. Unlike sentiment analysis, where the positive, negative and neutral words are similar across datasets, stance analysis is dependent on the revolving context around the target. Cross-dataset stance detection might be improved by using contextual embeddings for training.

4.4 Runtime Performance Comparison

Table 4 provides scaled runtimes (training time) and scaled performances according to Table 2 for experiments considered. This table serves as a reference when deciding on the best-case model architecture in consideration of sample size and sentence lengths, in-dataset versus cross-dataset stance detection, and whether the stance detection model extracts semantic context. For example, when choosing between biLSTM-CNN and BERT for a dataset similar to MPCHI, this table suggests that although the biLSTM-CNN has lower average per target training runtime, while BERT has higher runtime, the per target performance is medium for both models. Because of this, the biLSTM-CNN can be chosen over BERT. Importantly, note that all experiments were run on a NVIDIA A40 GPU with four GPUs per task and 500GB memory. The provided categories in Table 4 are dependent on this setup. The exact runtime in seconds and all code files of the experiments in this paper are available at the following Github link: https://github.com/nlp-grp/stance_comparison

5 Discussion and Recommendations

Prior work identifies a linear relationship between the labels in stance detection and sentiment analysis — that is, `Positive = Favor` and `Negative = Against` (ALDayel and Magdy, 2021). However, an author can also express a negative sentiment, while being in favor of the target. For example, in the following tweet *"The statement of 'Guns kill people, Guns kill children' is false guns don't kill people, people kill people. Guns should be allowed everywhere GUNS ARE GOOD"*, TextBlob (Loria, 2018), a Python text processing library, predicts its sentiment as `negative`, whereas the actual stance of this tweet towards the target of Gun Rights is `Favor`. Thus, sentiment is based on the polarity of words in the text, which are more likely to persist across datasets and varying domains. On the other hand, it is evident from Table 3 that the current benchmark stance detection models generalize poorly across datasets. This is due to the expression of stance toward a specific target, and hence the dependence on semantic context. Specifically, semantic context differs with the target, in addition to the domain of the text. For example, in the SemEval dataset, targets Feminist Movement and Legalization of Abortion can be categorized to a similar domain of women's rights. However, a stance detection model trained on the target of Legalization of Abortion can only perform well when tested on the target of Feminist Movement if it has learned the semantic contextual knowledge. This is called cross-target stance detection (Conforti et al., 2021).

We can consider cross-target stance detection a subtask of cross-dataset stance detection. That is, the limitations associated with cross-target stance detection were observed in this work for cross-dataset stance detection. It is evident from Table 3 that all models trained on the SemEval dataset generalize poorly when tested on the MPCHI dataset as the model cannot adapt knowledge from one domain to another. We anticipate improved generalization of models across datasets if the targets in both datasets belong to similar domains, thus

Model	Hyperparameters	Context	Average per Target training Run Time			Per Dataset training Run Time			Per Target Performance per Dataset			Cross-Dataset Performance per Dataset		
	LR = Learning Rate		*SemEval*	*MPCHI*	*Ideological*	*SemEval*	*MPCHI*	*Ideological*	*SemEval*	*MPCHI*	*Ideological*	*SemEval*	*MPCHI*	*Ideological*
SVM	Grid('kernel': ['rbf'], 'gamma': [1e-3, 1e-4], 'C': [1, 10, 100, 1000], 'kernel': ['linear'], 'C': [1, 10, 100, 1000])	N	L	L	L	H	L	H	H	H	H	P	H	P
BiGRU	LR: 1e-3, batch size:50, Batch Size: 32, dropout: 0.3, Optimizer: Adam, activation='softmax'	N	M	L	H	M	H	H	P	P	P	H	P	H
BiGRU-CNN	LR: 1e-3, batch size:50, Batch Size: 32, dropout: 0.3, Optimizer: Adam, activation='relu'	N	M	L	M	L	M	M	M	M	M	H	H	H
biLSTM	LR: 1e-3, batch size:50, Batch Size: 32, dropout: 0.3, Optimizer: Adam, activation='softmax'	N	M	L	H	L	M	M	M	P	P	H	P	H
biLSTM-CNN	LR: 1e-3, batch size:50, Batch Size: 32, dropout: 0.3, Optimizer: Adam, activation='relu'	N	M	L	M	L	M	M	P	M	M	H	H	H
BERT	LR:2e-5, Epochs:50, Max Seq Length:[(Semeval, MPCHI): 128, Ideological: 512]	Y	H	H	L	L	M	L	H	M	M	P	P	H

Table 4: *Comparison of runtime and performance of all models for Per Target and Per Dataset stance detection.* **Per Target Run Time:** Runtime mean in seconds per model when trained per target for all datasets, categorized as L: Low, M: Medium, or H: High. **Per Target Performance:** Ranked performance of all stance detection models ranked from 1 to 6 (best to worse), with 1-2: H (High), 2-4: M (Medium), 5-6: P (Poor). **Per Dataset Run Time:** Runtime of each model when trained on the whole dataset, categorized as L: Low, M: Medium, or H: High. **Performance per Dataset:** For each model, the mean of macro F_1 scores when trained on one dataset and tested on the other two datasets, categorized as P: Poor, M: Medium, or H: High. Note that all experiments were run on a NVIDIA A40 GPU with four GPUs per task and 500GB memory.

allowing the model to leverage similar linguistic and semantic cues.

Further, we also found all deep learning stance detection methods except BERT to be trained using GLOVE embeddings. As noted previously, GLOVE embeddings do not capture context. Future work should consider the use of pre-trained models or their embeddings for training sequence models, such as BERT, Sentence Bert (Reimers and Gurevych, 2019), Universal Sentence Encoder embeddings (Cer et al., 2018), or Contextualized Word Vectors embeddings (McCann et al., 2017). This will enable the model to learn semantic contextual dependencies, likely leading to better performance.

Finally, we often observed performance degradation due to smaller dataset sizes. To cope with this, we suggest future work investigate the use of sampling techniques like random sampling, SMOTE (Synthetic Minority Over-Sampling Technique) (Chawla et al., 2002), synthetic data augmentation techniques like EDA (Easy Data Augmentation) (Wei and Zou, 2019), and synthetic data integration, such as paraphrase generation, to handle highly unbalanced data (Liu et al., 2019). Zero-shot learning has also shown improvement in these types of cases (Allaway et al., 2021).

6 Conclusion

In this paper, we replicated six popular stance detection approaches and analyzed them using three publicly available datasets. We explored how well these methods perform in stance detection per and across each dataset. Our results show that current methods generalize poorly, potentially due to the diversity in targets and the use of deep models which do not consider semantic contextual information, such as meaning and domain specificity. In our experiments, BERT is the only model which captures semantic context; all other deep learning models are trained on GLOVE embeddings which do not capture context. We also explored the SVM, another baseline stance detection model, which only captures surface-level vocabulary statistics. Our observations and recommendations for future work, such as the use of sampling techniques to increase dataset sizes and the use of pre-trained models like Sentence Bert to capture context, are also noted.

To expand this work, we will test similar methods for cross-target stance detection. We are also developing techniques to improve cross-target, cross-domain, and cross-dataset stance analyses. We will also consider larger datasets like the Will-They-Won't-They dataset proposed by Conforti et al. (2020), and other baseline models for cross-target stance detection such as those proposed by Augenstein et al. (2016), Du et al. (2017), and Xu et al. (2018).

References

Abdulrahman I. Al-Ghadir, Aqil M. Azmi, and Amir Hussain. 2021. A novel approach to stance detection in social media tweets by fusing ranked lists and sentiments. *Information Fusion*, 67:29–40.

Abeer ALDayel and Walid Magdy. 2021. Stance detection on social media: State of the art and trends. *Information Processing Management*, 58(4):102597.

Emily Allaway, Malavika Srikanth, and Kathleen McKeown. 2021. Adversarial learning for zero-shot stance detection on social media. *arXiv preprint arXiv:2105.06603*.

Isabelle Augenstein, Tim Rocktäschel, Andreas Vlachos, and Kalina Bontcheva. 2016. Stance detection with bidirectional conditional encoding. *CoRR*, abs/1606.05464.

Daniel Cer, Yinfei Yang, Sheng-yi Kong, Nan Hua, Nicole Limtiaco, Rhomni St. John, Noah Constant, Mario Guajardo-Cespedes, Steve Yuan, Chris Tar, Brian Strope, and Ray Kurzweil. 2018. Universal sentence encoder for English. In *Proceedings of the 2018 Conference on Empirical Methods in Natural Language Processing: System Demonstrations*, pages 169–174, Brussels, Belgium. Association for Computational Linguistics.

Nitesh V Chawla, Kevin W Bowyer, Lawrence O Hall, and W Philip Kegelmeyer. 2002. Smote: synthetic minority over-sampling technique. *Journal of artificial intelligence research*, 16:321–357.

Costanza Conforti, Jakob Berndt, Mohammad Taher Pilehvar, Chryssi Giannitsarou, Flavio Toxvaerd, and Nigel Collier. 2020. Will-they-won't-they: A very large dataset for stance detection on twitter.

Costanza Conforti, Jakob Berndt, Mohammad Taher Pilehvar, Chryssi Giannitsarou, Flavio Toxvaerd, and Nigel Collier. 2021. Synthetic examples improve cross-target generalization: A study on stance detection on a Twitter corpus. In *Proceedings of the Eleventh Workshop on Computational Approaches to Subjectivity, Sentiment and Social Media Analysis*, pages 181–187, Online. Association for Computational Linguistics.

Jacob Devlin, Ming-Wei Chang, Kenton Lee, and Kristina Toutanova. 2018a. Bert: Pre-training of deep bidirectional transformers for language understanding.

Jacob Devlin, Ming-Wei Chang, Kenton Lee, and Kristina Toutanova. 2018b. Bert: Pre-training of deep bidirectional transformers for language understanding. *arXiv preprint arXiv:1810.04805*.

Jiachen Du, Ruifeng Xu, Yulan He, and Lin Gui. 2017. Stance classification with target-specific neural attention networks. In *26th International Joint Conference on Artificial Intelligence, IJCAI 2017*, pages 3988–3994. International Joint Conferences on Artificial Intelligence, AUS. IJCAI International Joint Conference on Artificial Intelligence2017, Pages 3988-399426th International Joint Conference on Artificial Intelligence, IJCAI 2017; Melbourne; Australia; 19 August 2017 through 25 August 2017; Code 130864.

Douglas Eck and Juergen Schmidhuber. 2002. A first look at music composition using lstm recurrent neural networks. *Istituto Dalle Molle Di Studi Sull Intelligenza Artificiale*, 103:48.

Bilal Ghanem, Paolo Rosso, and Francisco Rangel. 2018. Stance detection in fake news a combined feature representation. In *Proceedings of the first workshop on fact extraction and VERification (FEVER)*, pages 66–71.

Shalmoli Ghosh, Prajwal Singhania, Siddharth Singh, Koustav Rudra, and Saptarshi Ghosh. 2019. Stance detection in web and social media: A comparative study. In *Experimental IR Meets Multilinguality, Multimodality, and Interaction*, pages 75–87, Cham. Springer International Publishing.

Alex Graves, Navdeep Jaitly, and Abdel-rahman Mohamed. 2013. Hybrid speech recognition with deep bidirectional lstm. In *2013 IEEE Workshop on Automatic Speech Recognition and Understanding*, pages 273–278.

Huishan Ji, Zheng Lin, Peng Fu, and Weiping Wang. 2022. Cross-target stance detection via refined meta-learning. In *ICASSP 2022 - 2022 IEEE International Conference on Acoustics, Speech and Signal Processing (ICASSP)*, pages 7822–7826.

Dilek Küçük and Fazli Can. 2020. Stance detection: A survey. *ACM Comput. Surv.*, 53(1).

Bin Liang, Yonghao Fu, Lin Gui, Min Yang, Jiachen Du, Yulan He, and Ruifeng Xu. 2021. Target-adaptive graph for cross-target stance detection. In *Proceedings of the Web Conference 2021*, WWW '21, page 3453–3464, New York, NY, USA. Association for Computing Machinery.

Yuanxin Liu, Zheng Lin, Fenglin Liu, Qinyun Dai, and Weiping Wang. 2019. Generating paraphrase with topic as prior knowledge. In *Proceedings of the 28th ACM International Conference on Information and Knowledge Management*, pages 2381–2384.

Steven Loria. 2018. textblob documentation. *Release 0.15*, 2.

Michal Lukasik, Kalina Bontcheva, Trevor Cohn, Arkaitz Zubiaga, Maria Liakata, and Rob Procter. 2019. Gaussian processes for rumour stance classification in social media. *ACM Trans. Inf. Syst.*, 37(2).

Bryan McCann, James Bradbury, Caiming Xiong, and Richard Socher. 2017. Learned in translation: Contextualized word vectors. In *Advances in Neural Information Processing Systems*, volume 30. Curran Associates, Inc.

Saif Mohammad, Svetlana Kiritchenko, Parinaz Sobhani, Xiaodan Zhu, and Colin Cherry. 2016. Semeval-2016 task 6: Detecting stance in tweets. In *Proceedings of the 10th International Workshop on Semantic Evaluation (SemEval-2016)*, pages 31–41.

Saif M. Mohammad, Parinaz Sobhani, and Svetlana Kiritchenko. 2017. Stance and sentiment in tweets. *Special Section of the ACM Transactions on Internet Technology on Argumentation in Social Media*, 17(3).

Mitra Mohtarami, Ramy Baly, James R. Glass, Preslav Nakov, Lluís Màrquez, and Alessandro Moschitti. 2018. Automatic stance detection using end-to-end memory networks. *CoRR*, abs/1804.07581.

Tempestt Neal, Kalaivani Sundararajan, Aneez Fatima, Yiming Yan, Yingfei Xiang, and Damon Woodard. 2017. Surveying stylometry techniques and applications. *ACM Comput. Surv.*, 50(6).

Jianmo Ni, Jiacheng Li, and Julian McAuley. 2019. Justifying recommendations using distantly-labeled reviews and fine-grained aspects. In *Proceedings of the 2019 Conference on Empirical Methods in Natural Language Processing and the 9th International Joint Conference on Natural Language Processing (EMNLP-IJCNLP)*, pages 188–197, Hong Kong, China. Association for Computational Linguistics.

William S Noble. 2006. What is a support vector machine? *Nature biotechnology*, 24(12):1565–1567.

Jeffrey Pennington, Richard Socher, and Christopher D. Manning. 2014. Glove: Global vectors for word representation. In *Empirical Methods in Natural Language Processing (EMNLP)*, pages 1532–1543.

Nils Reimers and Iryna Gurevych. 2019. Sentence-bert: Sentence embeddings using siamese bert-networks. *CoRR*, abs/1908.10084.

SemEval. 2016. International workshop on semantic evaluation 2016.

Anirban Sen, Manjira Sinha, Sandya Mannarswamy, and Shourya Roy. 2018. Stance classification of multi-perspective consumer health information. In *Proceedings of the ACM India Joint International Conference on Data Science and Management of Data*, CoDS-COMAD '18, page 273–281, New York, NY, USA. Association for Computing Machinery.

Parinaz Sobhani, Diana Inkpen, and Xiaodan Zhu. 2017. A dataset for multi-target stance detection. In *Proceedings of the 15th Conference of the European Chapter of the Association for Computational Linguistics: Volume 2, Short Papers*, pages 551–557.

Richard Socher, Alex Perelygin, Jean Wu, Jason Chuang, Christopher D Manning, Andrew Y Ng, and Christopher Potts. 2013. Recursive deep models for semantic compositionality over a sentiment treebank. In *Proceedings of the 2013 conference on empirical methods in natural language processing*, pages 1631–1642.

Swapna Somasundaran and Janyce Wiebe. 2010. Recognizing stances in ideological on-line debates. In *Proceedings of the NAACL HLT 2010 Workshop on Computational Approaches to Analysis and Generation of Emotion in Text*, pages 116–124, Los Angeles, CA. Association for Computational Linguistics.

Stefan Stieglitz and Linh Dang-Xuan. 2013. Emotions and information diffusion in social media—sentiment of microblogs and sharing behavior. *Journal of Management Information Systems*, 29(4):217–248.

Ming-Hsiang Su, Chung-Hsien Wu, Kun-Yi Huang, Qian-Bei Hong, and Hsin-Min Wang. 2017. A chatbot using lstm-based multi-layer embedding for elderly care. In *2017 International Conference on Orange Technologies (ICOT)*, pages 70–74.

Martin Sundermeyer, Ralf Schlüter, and Hermann Ney. 2012. Lstm neural networks for language modeling. In *Thirteenth annual conference of the international speech communication association*.

Ming Tan, Bing Xiang, and Bowen Zhou. 2015. Lstm-based deep learning models for non-factoid answer selection. *CoRR*, abs/1511.04108.

Muhammad Umer, Zainab Imtiaz, Saleem Ullah, Arif Mehmood, Gyu Sang Choi, and Byung-Won On. 2020. Fake news stance detection using deep learning architecture (cnn-lstm). *IEEE Access*, 8:156695–156706.

Cheng Wang, Haojin Yang, Christian Bartz, and Christoph Meinel. 2016. Image captioning with deep bidirectional lstms. In *Proceedings of the 24th ACM International Conference on Multimedia*, MM '16, page 988–997, New York, NY, USA. Association for Computing Machinery.

Jason W. Wei and Kai Zou. 2019. EDA: easy data augmentation techniques for boosting performance on text classification tasks. *CoRR*, abs/1901.11196.

Penghui Wei, Junjie Lin, and Wenji Mao. 2018. Multi-target stance detection via a dynamic memory-augmented network. In *The 41st International ACM SIGIR Conference on Research amp; Development in Information Retrieval*, SIGIR '18, page 1229–1232, New York, NY, USA. Association for Computing Machinery.

Penghui Wei and Wenji Mao. 2019. Modeling transferable topics for cross-target stance detection. In *Proceedings of the 42nd International ACM SIGIR Conference on Research and Development in Information Retrieval*, SIGIR'19, page 1173–1176, New York, NY, USA. Association for Computing Machinery.

Wan Wei, Xiao Zhang, Xuqin Liu, Wei Chen, and Tengjiao Wang. 2016. pkudblab at semeval-2016 task 6: A specific convolutional neural network system for effective stance detection. In *Proceedings of the 10th international workshop on semantic evaluation (SemEval-2016)*, pages 384–388.

Chang Xu, Cecile Paris, Surya Nepal, and Ross Sparks. 2018. Cross-target stance classification with self-attention networks.

Guido Zarrella and Amy Marsh. 2016. MITRE at semeval-2016 task 6: Transfer learning for stance detection. *CoRR*, abs/1606.03784.

Bowen Zhang, Min Yang, Xutao Li, Yunming Ye, Xiaofei Xu, and Kuai Dai. 2020. Enhancing cross-target stance detection with transferable semantic-emotion knowledge. In *Proceedings of the 58th Annual Meeting of the Association for Computational Linguistics*, pages 3188–3197, Online. Association for Computational Linguistics.

Yiwei Zhou, Alexandra I. Cristea, and Lei Shi. 2017. Connecting targets to tweets: Semantic attention-based model for target-specific stance detection. In *Web Information Systems Engineering – WISE 2017*, pages 18–32, Cham. Springer International Publishing.

Arkaitz Zubiaga, Elena Kochkina, Maria Liakata, Rob Procter, Michal Lukasik, Kalina Bontcheva, Trevor Cohn, and Isabelle Augenstein. 2018. Discourse-aware rumour stance classification in social media using sequential classifiers. *Information Processing Management*, 54(2):273–290.

Why is sentence similarity benchmark not predictive of application-oriented task performance?

Kaori Abe[1]**, Sho Yokoi**[1,2]**, Tomoyuki Kajiwara**[3] **and Kentaro Inui**[1,2]
[1]Tohoku University [2]RIKEN [3]Ehime University
{abe-k, yokoi, kentaro.inui}@tohoku.ac.jp, kajiwara@cs.ehime-u.ac.jp

Abstract

Computing the semantic similarity between two texts is crucial in various NLP tasks. For more than a decade, a framework, known as Semantic Textual Similarity (STS) has been used to test computational models of semantic similarity (Agirre et al., 2012). The STS evaluation framework assumes that a model that performs well for the general STS task should also perform well for specific application-oriented tasks. However, does this assumption indeed hold? This study empirically demonstrates that the answer is not always positive. We found a considerable gap between model performance in STS and each specific task. We identified three factors that contributed to the gap, namely, (i) sentence length distribution, (ii) vocabulary coverage, and (iii) granularity of gold-standard similarity scores. We believe that these findings will be considered in future research on semantic similarity.

1 Introduction

Computing the semantic similarity between two texts is crucial in various NLP tasks. One prominent cluster of application examples is the use of semantic similarity as a metric for evaluating automatically generated text (e.g., machine translation and text summarization) considering gold reference texts (Zhang et al., 2020a; Sellam et al., 2020; Rei et al., 2020). Such semantic similarity metrics are also reported effective as a loss function for training language generation models (Wieting et al., 2019; Yasui et al., 2019). Another common application of the semantic similarity can be seen in text/sentence retrieval, where estimating the relevance between a given query and retrieved texts is an essential component (Chen et al., 2017; Karpukhin et al., 2020; Gao et al., 2021a; Qu et al., 2021).

For more than a decade, a framework, known as Semantic Textual Similarity (STS) has been widely used to test computational models of semantic similarity (Agirre et al., 2012). Over the last decade, STS has emerged as the de-facto standard task for evaluating semantic similarity models, and numerous studies have been published to propose semantic similarity models over a decade (Severyn et al., 2013; Lan and Xu, 2018; Reimers and Gurevych, 2019; Li et al., 2020; Zhang et al., 2020b; Yan et al., 2021; Giorgi et al., 2021; Gao et al., 2021b; Chuang et al., 2022, etc.).

The STS evaluation framework assumes that a model that performs well for the general STS task should also perform well for specific application-oriented tasks. Based on this assumption, models proposed for and evaluated on STS have been applied to application-oriented tasks. For example, in machine translation (MT) evaluation, for the model incorporating several universal sentence encoders (USE) (Conneau et al., 2017; Logeswaran and Lee, 2018; Cer et al., 2018), which performed well on STS, had the highest performance in WMT18 (Shimanaka et al., 2018). In addition, for semantic retrieval, STS-based models such as USE have been developed and validated their effectiveness (Yang et al., 2020). These studies appear to provide empirical evidence supporting the assumption that STS performs well as a general proxy for specific application-oriented tasks.

However, in this study, we question this widely accepted assumption. Specifically, we empirically investigated whether semantic similarity models superior to the general STS task perform better on specific application-oriented tasks. In the experiments, we chose two representative application-oriented tasks, MT Metrics (MTM) and passage retrieval (PR), and investigated the correlation of the performance of numerous (> 20) sampled models between STS and each specific task. From the results, we gained several findings as follows:

- Semantic similarity models exhibited a non-negligible gap in performance on STS and each specific task (i.e., MTM or PR) (Fig. 1).

Proceedings of the 3rd Workshop on Evaluation and Comparison of NLP Systems, pages 70 - 87
November 20, 2022 ©2022 Association for Computational Linguistics

- The discrepancies appeared to be caused by the discrepancies between the STS dataset and each application-specific dataset, including (i) sentence length distribution, (ii) vocabulary coverage, and (iii) granularity of gold-standard similarity scores.

The identified gap, which we refer to as **the evaluation gap**, indicates that the assumption in question does not necessarily hold and demonstrates the potential dangers of relying solely on the current STS-based evaluation alone in studying the semantic similarity. We believe that our findings will be considered in future research on the crucial components of NLP.

2 Related work

The necessity of the semantic similarity in application-oriented tasks. Semantic similarity is required in various NLP application tasks, and STS was motivated by being a surrogate task for such application-oriented tasks (Agirre et al., 2012; Cer et al., 2017). These tasks comparing similarity can be categorized into two types, namely, (1) reference-based evaluation and (2) semantic retrieval. For example, the reference-based evaluation is commonly used in the natural language generation (NLG) fields such as MT, summarization, and simplification. Semantic retrieval includes PR, dialog retrieval, as well as machine reading comprehension. Among these application-oriented tasks, we selected (1) MT evaluation and (2) PR as representatives, respectively.

In fact, MT evaluation and semantic retrieval have several examples that incorporate STS-based models. For example, Castillo and Estrella (2012); Shimanaka et al. (2018) applied STS model for MT evaluation and demonstrated the effectiveness of those models. For semantic retrieval, Yang et al. (2020) demonstrates the effectiveness of multilingual USE as a semantic retriever. Following this success, recent semantic similarity models have also reported performance as semantic retrievers (Gao et al., 2021b; Chuang et al., 2022). However, relying on the STS evaluation for semantic similarity models could be risky when there is no sufficient correlation between the evaluation of STS and application-oriented tasks. We investigates the evaluation gap between STS and two tasks, such as MT evaluation and PR, to identify vulnerabilities in the STS evaluation in the real world.

Validity of NLP evaluation protocol. Recently, the validity of evaluation protocols, such as benchmark datasets (Bowman and Dahl, 2021) or metrics (Mathur et al., 2020; Durmus et al., 2022) has been questioned on various NLP tasks. Many studies have identified the bias or lack of certain factors in the evaluation protocol. Søgaard et al. (2021); Varis and Bojar (2021) investigated the effects of differences in the sentence length distribution between train and test sets. Additionally, a difference in vocabulary distribution (domain mismatch) is also often mentioned as an important factor affecting the evaluation (Zhang et al., 2020b; Wang et al., 2022). In terms of an STS-specific factor, Reimers et al. (2016) highlighted the difference in the granularity of similarity between STS and downstream tasks. They focus on appropriate task-intrinsic evaluation metrics for STS-based models, considering different downstream tasks; however, their thought is also based on the assumption that the STS-based models are useful for the downstream tasks. In our study, we question this assumption. Based on these previous studies, we analyze the effects of three factors, **sentence length**, **vocabulary**, and **similarity granularity**, contributing to the evaluation gap between STS and the application-oriented tasks.

Discussion of the problems of STS benchmark. While many models have been proposed using the STS evaluation, some studies have also questioned the STS or conducted an additional evaluation for specific factors that are not captured by the STS evaluation. Wang et al. (2021) argue that previous studies rely on the STS evaluation and argues that STS lacks domain adaptability. Futhermore, Liu et al. (2021) did not adopt the STS evaluation because of the lack of domain coverage and lack of consideration for context, so they created a new contextual dialog domain STS dataset. In addition, Wieting et al. (2020) extracted a more difficult subset which contains the examples with low word overlap by focusing on a specific factor such as word overlap. Wang et al. (2022) focused on the discrepancy between the evaluation of STS and single-sentence downstream tasks in SentEval, highlighting the problems of domain mismatch and ambiguous annotations. In comparison, we investigated whether STS satisfies the original motivation for application-oriented tasks *practically using semantic similarity* (Agirre et al., 2012; Cer et al., 2017).

In summary, we shed the light on the specific

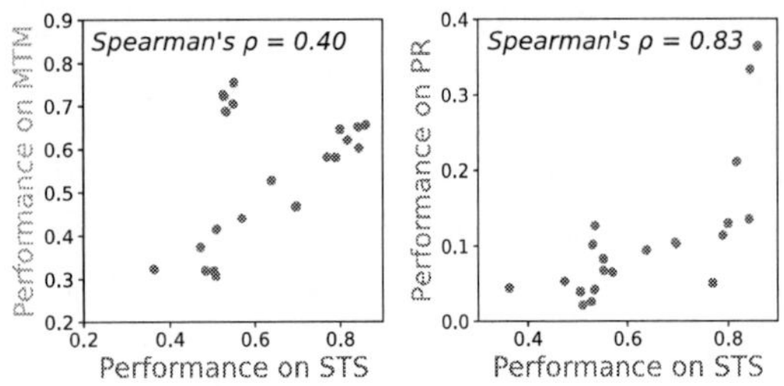

(a) STS × MT Metrics (b) STS × Passage Retrieval

Figure 1: Correlation between evaluation using STS and that using task-specific datasets, such as MT Metrics (MTM) and Passage Retrieval (PR).

factors such as sentence length, vocabulary, and similarity granularity to make the relationship to the evaluation gap explicit. We provided the first evidence that STS has a considerable evaluation gap even from two tasks, such as MT evaluation and PR that have been considered representative application tasks since the inception of STS.

3 Is there a gap between evaluation using STS and that using individual tasks?

STS dataset (Agirre et al., 2012; Cer et al., 2017) was proposed as a semantic similarity benchmark that can be directly applied to several NLP tasks and is currently the de-facto standard for evaluating semantic similarity models. In this study, to validate the STS benchmark, we conducted comprehensive experiments to examine whether there is a sufficient correlation between the evaluation results on STS and that on two specific application-oriented task datasets.

3.1 Tasks and datasets

General settings. We present the definitions of three tasks—STS and two application-oriented tasks—that must capture the semantic similarity addressed in this study. The main structure of all three tasks is comparing a sentence pair (s, s') and predicting the semantic similarity score between the two sentences. We selected two application-oriented tasks, MTM and PR, on which the STS motivation is focused. The two tasks are identical in that they require considering the semantic similarity, but they are very different in nature. MTM compares relatively similar sentence pairs and provides a gradation score as the gold standard. PR compares sentence pairs with large differences in sentence length and provides a binary label (related or not) as the gold standard. We examine the evaluation gap between these two different tasks and STS to test the adaptability of the STS evaluation to different tasks.

STS (STS-b). STS (Agirre et al., 2012) is a task that compares a sentence pair (s1, s2) and predicts a similarity score between the two sentences. The gold-standard similarity score is provided in the range of 0-5. Model prediction scores are evaluated using Pearson or Spearman correlations with the gold standard. In this study, we used Pearson correlation. We used the STS-b dataset (Cer et al., 2017) with image captions, news articles, and forum domain data over a 5-year pilot task (STS12-17).

MT Metrics (WMT17). MT Metrics (MTM) is a task that compares a (model hypothesis, reference) pair and predicts the adequacy scores of the model hypothesis relative to the reference. In this study, we use the segment-level Direct Assessment dataset (to-English) in WMT17 (Bojar et al., 2017).[1] We selected this because of the reliability of the manual scores (Zhang et al., 2020a; Sellam et al., 2020). The gold standard score is the normalized value of scores manually evaluated with 100 scales to the pair (model hypothesis, reference). The Pearson or Kendall correlation between the gold standard and the model prediction score is usually used in the evaluation. In this study, we used the Pearson correlation.

Passage Retrieval (MS-MARCO). Passage Retrieval (PR) is an important subtask of question-answering that is required to improve the performance of search systems used by many users. We use passage re-ranking data from MS-MARCO (Bajaj et al., 2018) as a dataset for PR. MS-MARCO is a highly competitive dataset that has been used as a PR benchmark in several studies (Gao et al., 2021a; Qu et al., 2021). Passage re-ranking must re-rank 1,000 candidate passages for a query in the order of their relevance to the query. Generally, the model predicts the relevance of each candidate sentence to the (query, passage) pair and extracts the sentence with the highest relevance score. Models are usually evaluated using Mean Reciprocal Rank (MRR), which determines whether passages with a gold-standard related labels appear at the top after re-ranking.

[1] We use cs–en, de–en, fi–en, lv–en, ru–en, tr–en and zh–en datasets, which are sourced from news domain texts. https://www.statmt.org/wmt17/results.html

3.2 Semantic similarity prediction model

A semantic similarity prediction model usually involves the following two steps: (i) obtaining a sentence representation and (ii) calculating the similarity between two representations.

To determine whether there is an evaluation gap between various models, we measured the correlation between the evaluation results on STS and those on the two application tasks. In this study, we used the following 23 semantic similarity prediction models: **BoW**-{raw, TFIDF}-sum, **BoV**-{Word2vec*, Glove, Fasttext}-{mean, max}, **USE**-{normal, large}, **Avg. of BERT**-{BERT-base-uncased (bbu), RoBERTa-large (rl)}, **BERTScore (BScore)**-{BERT-base-uncased, RoBERTa-large}-{precision, recall, F1-score}, **Sentence-BERT (SBERT)**-{bertbase-NLI-mean, MiniLM, mpnet}, and **SimCSE**-{supervised, unsupervised}.[2]

3.3 Experimental procedure and results

Fig. 2 compares the evaluation for each semantic similarity prediction model on STS and the two application tasks, MTM and PR. The x-axis represents the semantic similarity prediction models, which are ordered by decreasing the performance on STS from left to right. Compared with STS, the performance of each model differs largely in both MTM and PR. For the STS evaluation, SBERT (mpnet: 0.86) outperforms BScore (RoBERTa-large, F1-score: 0.55); however, in the MT evaluation task (MTM), those performances are inverse as SBERT (0.66) < BScore (0.76). By comparing STS and PR, the performances of the SBERT-bb-NLI, the original model in (Reimers and Gurevych, 2019), and BoW models are much lower with PR than with STS. Both STS and MTM, both correlation measures have a similar trend for model ranking in each task (Fig. 2), thus we used the Pearson correlation in each task's evaluation. In addition, we calculated Spearman correlation coefficients between the performance on STS and that on each task to precisely visualize these performance gaps (Fig. 1). Here, we define these correlation coefficients as the value of the evaluation gap. A lower correlation value indicated a larger evaluation gap. In Sec. 4, we examine changes in the evaluation gap when the explanatory variables (e.g., sentence length, vocabulary coverage, similarity granularity) are changed.

[2]* We remove Word2vec models due to computational order in PR.

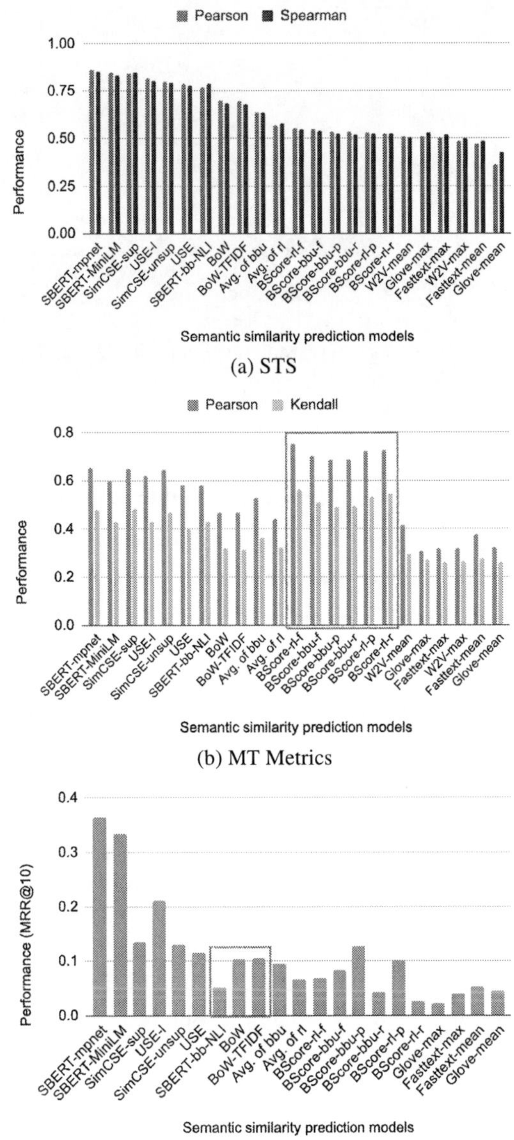

(a) STS

(b) MT Metrics

(c) Passage Retrieval

Figure 2: Performance of semantic similarity models on STS and task-specific datasets (MT Metrics and Passage Retrieval).

4 What factors cause the evaluation gap?

As mentioned in Sec. 3, there is a large gap between the specific application-oriented tasks and STS used as frameworks for evaluating the sentence similarity prediction models. In this section, we discuss three potential factors contributing to the gap between evaluation frameworks, as well as the dataset features that should considered to when using STS for evaluation.

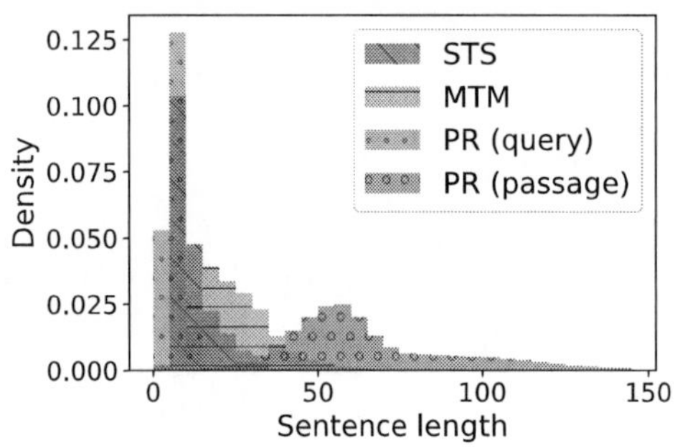

Figure 3: Histogram of sentence length in STS and two application-oriented datasets (MT Metrics: MTM and Passage Retrieval: PR).

4.1 Factor 1: difference in sentence length

In the following, we discuss the sentence length (i.e., the number of words in a sentence). Words are commonly used as the basic unit in NLP models. This is also true when making predictions of semantic similarity measures. We focused on the large variance in the number of words (i.e., sentence length) in the target text for similarity measurement. For example, in PR, the model should handle very short search snippets (queries) or very long documents (passages). Some studies reported that differences in the sentence length distributions produce different scores on different test sets (Søgaard et al., 2021; Varis and Bojar, 2021). Therefore, we hypothesize that differences in the distribution of sentence lengths by task may result in an evaluation gap.

4.1.1 Short sentence length in STS benchmark

Here, we demonstrate that the *STS dataset has shorter sentence lengths than the datasets for other specific tasks*, such as MTM and PR. Histograms of the sentence length distribution for each dataset are presented in Fig. 3. Note that the PR queries contain many short nonsentences, such as "define preventive." Compared with the sentence length distribution of the application-oriented task, STS has a biased sentence length distribution consisting of short sentences.

4.1.2 Does the sentence length gap cause the evaluation gap?

There is a difference in the sentence length distribution between STS and the application-oriented task datasets. Here, we investigate whether eliminating the difference in sentence length between the STS and the application tasks alleviates the evaluation gap.

Settings. We created subsets of the application-oriented datasets (MTM and PR) to match or differ the STS sentence length distribution, and then, compared the correlations between the STS evaluation result and each subset's result for the different models. The subset [x, y) was drawn from a range of sentence lengths [x, y) according to the STS distribution. In MTM, the subsets were split based on the average sentence length of the sentence pairs. In PR, the split was based on the length of the passage because of a large-sentence length difference between the query and passage. Histograms of the created subsets according to sentence length distribution are shown in Fig. 4. We created MTM subsets from [0, 40) to [30, 70) and PR subsets from [10, 50) to [40, 80). The shorter MTM subsets, such as [0, 40) and [5, 45), had nearly the same distribution as the STS set. Note that we could not create a subset of PR with the same distribution as STS because the original sentence length distributions were very different. We investigated whether correlations were lower in the task-specific datasets (i.e., the evaluation gap was amplified) when their sentence length distribution was more different from that of STS.

Results. Figs. 5(a) and (b) present the Spearman correlations between the performance of the models on STS and those on the MTM and PR subsets with adjusted sentence length distributions, respectively. For MTM, the greater the difference in the sentence length distribution, the lower the correlation (i.e., the larger the evaluation gap). In comparison, no trend was observed for PR. This result indicates that the difference in the sentence length distribution contributes to the evaluation gap between STS and MTM.

Analysis: In-domain vs. Out-of-domain. The STS dataset is sourced from three different domains (news, image captions, and forum), and the sentence length distribution actually differs for each domain. We conducted additional experiments for three sub-domain sets following the same procedure using subsets, and found that the similar trends that the evaluation gap increases with the larger sentence length subset (See Appendix for details).

4.2 Factor 2: difference in vocabulary coverage

Beyond sentence length, there are still other factors that may contribute to the evaluation gap between STS and the application-oriented tasks. Here, we

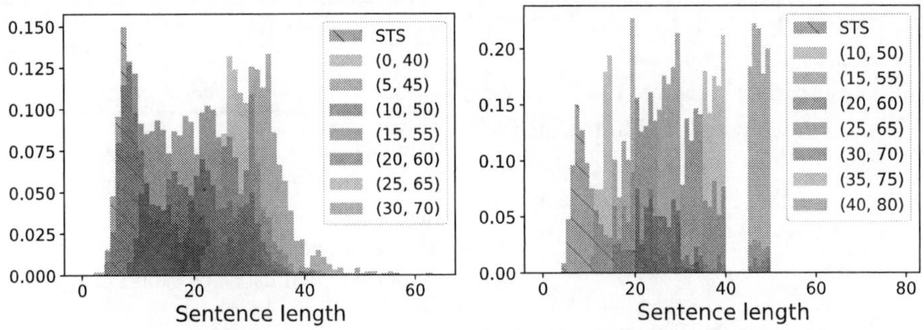

(a) MT Metrics (b) Passage Retrieval

Figure 4: Histogram of subsets extracted from two application tasks (MT Metrics and Passage Retrieval) according to sentence length.

	STS		STS
MTM-[0, 40)	0.351	PR-[10, 50)	0.613
MTM-[5, 45)	0.351	PR-[15, 55)	0.792
MTM-[10, 50)	0.390	PR-[20, 60)	0.752
MTM-[15, 55)	0.407	PR-[25, 65)	0.777
MTM-[20, 60)	0.317	PR-[30, 70)	0.779
MTM-[25, 65)	0.284	PR-[35, 75)	0.770
MTM-[30, 70)	0.313	PR-[40, 80)	0.814

(a) MT Metrics (b) Passage Retrieval

Figure 5: Spearman correlations between performance with STS and that with the subsets split according to sentence length with specific tasks (MT Metrics: MTM and Passage Retrieval: PR). The darker color represents the lower correlation (= the larger evaluation gap). [x, y) means that the subsets consist of the examples of the sentence length from x to y.

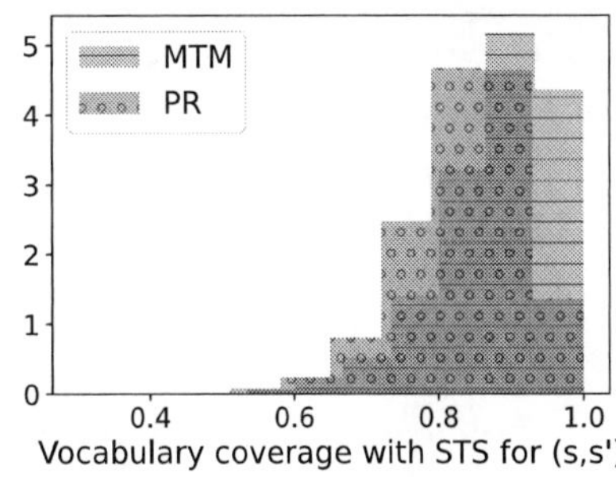

Figure 6: Histogram of the ratio of the vocabulary covered with the vocabulary of STS in the application tasks (MT Metrics: MTM and Passage Retrieval: PR) for each sentence pair.

discuss the vocabulary coverage of the application-oriented tasks using STS. One reason for focusing on this factor is that the text domains represented in the datasets are distinct. Some studies have highlighted the strong dependence of the STS-based models on domains (Zhang et al., 2020b), as well as mismatch with a dialog domain (Liu et al., 2021). Therefore, we hypothesize that differences in vocabulary coverage due to domain differences may influence the evaluation gap.

4.2.1 Low vocabulary coverage with STS for vocabulary in the applications

Here, we demonstrate that *the STS vocabulary does not adequately cover task vocabulary (MTM, PR).* For each sentence pair, we calculate the vocabulary coverage, which is the recall of vocabulary in STS (V_{sts}) to the vocabulary in the sentences in the specific task (s, s'), as follows:

$$\text{Recall}(s, s') = \frac{|(s \cup s') \cap \mathcal{V}_{\text{STS}}|}{|s \cup s'|} \quad (1)$$

Fig. 6 shows the histograms of $\text{Recall}(s, s')$ for each sentence pair in MTM and PR. In both tasks, most sentence pairs have a vocabulary coverage of less than 1, i.e., they contain vocabulary not covered by STS. Thus, STS vocabulary does not sufficiently cover the vocabulary of the other tasks.

4.2.2 Does the vocabulary distribution gap cause an evaluation gap?

We investigate whether the low vocabulary coverage with STS examined in Sec. 4.2.1 is indeed a factor contributing to the evaluation gap.

Settings. For the MTM and PR datasets, we extract the top and bottom 100 pairs as the $\text{Recall}(s, s')$-*High* and $\text{Recall}(s, s')$-*Low* subsets, respectively. The MTM Recall(s, s')-*High* subset contains all sentence pairs composed of STS vocabulary. Furthermore, the average of the PR *High* subset is 0.988 ± 0.011, which is almost all the pairs composed of STS vocabulary. In this experiment, we examine whether higher lexical coverage with the STS vocabulary for the subsets resulted in a higher correlation.

Results. Table 1 presents the Spearman correlation between the performance on STS and those on the Recall(s, s')-*High* and *Low* subsets in MTM and PR, respectively. The PR *High* subset correlated better than the *Low* subset, as hypothesized. However, no such trend was observed in MTM. A reason for the MTM result is that STS is a mix of three different domains (news, image captions, and forum). In contrast, MTM is a single news domain dataset, which might have caused a divergence in the evaluation of sentence pairs from the same or different domains.

Analysis: In-domain vs. Out-of-domain. To confirm the influence of STS inner domains, we performed an additional analysis. We created vocabulary coverage subsets for the three STS sub-domain sets (news, image captions, and forum) in the same way as for the entire STS, and calculated the correlation between the three STS sub-domain sets and MTM *High/Low* subsets. For an in-domain setting, the MTM subset with *High* vocabulary coverage using STS-news correlated better than that with *Low* vocabulary coverage ($0.438 > 0.373$), as hypothesized. For out-of-domain settings, the STS-forum set also showed that the *High* subset has a better correlation than the *Low* subset ($0.779 > 0.458$); however, in the image caption set, the correlation of the *Low* subset (0.177) is better than that of *High* subset (0.046). For the image caption domain, the correlation values are extremely low for both the subsets, indicating that the STS image caption set did not play a good role in the evaluation of application-oriented tasks such as MTM. In summary, these results indicate that the vocabulary coverage contributes to evaluating gap between STS and the two application-oriented tasks, such as MTM and PR.

4.3 Factor 3: difference in granularity of gold-standard scores

Below, we consider the granularity gap of the gold-standard similarity scores between STS and MTM. [3]

	Recall(s, s')-*Low*		Recall(s, s')-*High*
MTM	0.276	>	0.272
PR	**0.673**	<	0.851

Table 1: Spearman correlations between the performance with STS and that with the subsets split according to higher vocabulary coverage (Recall(s, s')-*High*) and lower one (Recall(s, s')-*Low*) with STS of specific tasks (MT Metrics: MTM and Passage Retrieval: PR).

We suspect that the granularity of the similarity that was considered in each task varies. The distinction between better or worse hypotheses for high-similarity sentence pairs is an arresting challenge in MTM (Ma et al., 2019). More concretely, the current semantic evaluation model for MTM is unable to finely discriminate the better outputs in highly competitive language pairs such as to-English because of high quality of recent MT output for highly competitive language pairs. Considering this application, we hypothesize that the similarity granularity of STS is insufficient to evaluate such MTM problems.

4.3.1 The discrepancy of the similarity granularity between STS and MTM

The difference in the similarity score between STS and MTM can be seen in some real examples. The actual examples in STS and MTM are illustrated in Table 2. STS provides give relatively high scores for the difference between the past and present progressive tenses, and the difference in including proper nouns such as *cholera*, as long as they generally share some elements. However, in MTM, the first example is given a relatively higher score (0.49) for the different actions between *continues to take* and *is already given*, whereas the second example (*Fresh fruit ...*) is assigned a lower score (-0.83), sharing almost similar elements but the hypothesis is somewhat difficult to understand. Can this similarity granularity gap cause the evaluation gap?

4.3.2 Does the gap in the granularity of similarity cause an evaluation gap?

Here, we investigate whether the difference in the similarity granularity mentioned in Sec. 4.3.1 results in the evaluation gap.

[3] In this section, we omit considering PR because the property of PR is different from the other tasks in terms of binary labels.

source		s1 (ref)	s2 (hyp)	gold	BScore	SimCSE
STS	(i)	A man **is riding** a mechanical bull.	A man **rode** a mechanical bull.	4	0.98	0.96
	(ii)	A total of 17 cases have been confirmed in the southern city of Basra, the Organization said.	A total of 17 confirmed cases of **cholera** were reported yesterday by the **World Health** Organisation in the southern **Iraqi** city of Basra.	3.6	0.93	0.74
MTM	(i)	This drug **continues to take** 12 months after a heart attack, which can reduce the risk of a stroke or heart attack.	The drug **is already given for** 12 months after a heart attack, reducing the risk of a stroke or another attack.	0.49	0.94	0.90
	(ii)	Fresh fruit **was replaced with** cheaper dried fruit.	Fresh fruit **is** cheap dried fruit **instead.**	**-0.83**	0.94	0.82

Table 2: Actual examples of STS and MT Metrics (MTM). The gold scores of MTM are normalized in the range (-1.81, 1.44) from with manually evaluated 100-scale scores. "BScore" and "SimCSE" mean prediction scores with BERTScore (RoBERTa-large, F1-score) and SimCSE (supervised), respectively.

Settings. For the STS and MTM datasets, we create subsets according to the similarity scores for a sentence pair. We divide the STS dataset into five subsets by considering six labels from 0 to 5. For the MTM dataset, we separated four subsets (*Sim-{Low, MidLow, MidHigh and High}*) by quartiles for human-rated golden scores. We determined the gap between the evaluations using STS and MTM subsets to confirm which range of the similarity granularity impacts the gap in the evaluation. Specifically, the correlation might be higher between the narrower range of the similarity band of STS and the wider range of that of MTM. We anticipate that the higher similarity band in STS only correlates with the MTM dataset, to consider the demand of the MTM that must distinguish higher similarity pairs.

Results. Fig. 7 shows the Spearman correlations between the similarity granularity subsets of STS and that of the MTM. As hypothesized, only the high-similarity subsets of STS, *STS-(3,4]* and *STS-(4,5]*, were highly correlated with all the MTM subsets. These results significantly show that STS is unable to evaluate discrimination performance in the fine-grained higher similarity bands.

In Fig. 8, we describe one interpretation of the above result. We suspect that STS cannot capture fine-grained granularity at higher similarity bands, as discussed (Sec 4.3.1). Not only is the evaluation of the high-similarity band of STS is higher correlated with that of MTM, but the low-similarity band of STS and MTM are nearly uncorrelated or inversely correlated (Fig. 7). We should consider introducing finer granularity in high similarity bands for STS, while also considering exclusion examples in ineffective low similarity bands as a widely

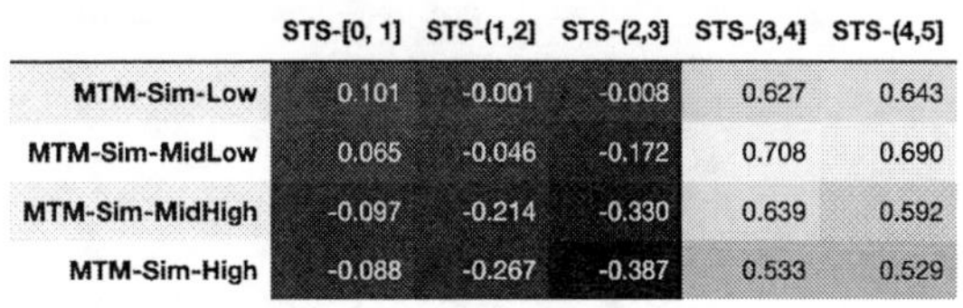

Figure 7: Spearman correlations between performance on subsets according to gold-standard similarity scores of STS and MT Metrics (MTM). The darker color represents the lower correlation (= the larger evaluation gap).

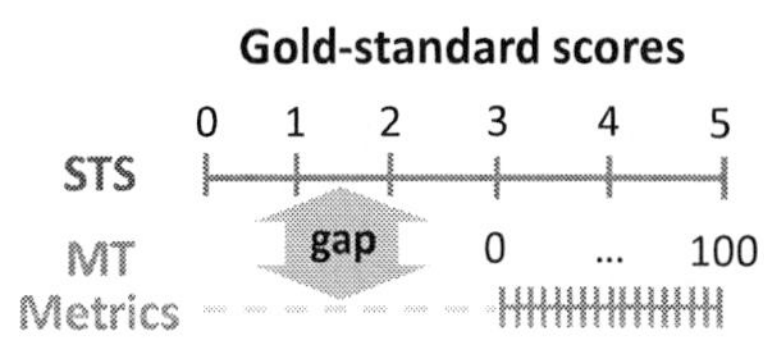

Figure 8: The relationship of the granularity of similarity scores between STS and MT Metrics.

applicable benchmark.

Analysis: Tendency for each domain. As in the previous analyses, we investigated the difference in the tendencies for each domain. The correlations between subsets and MTM similarity subsets in each STS sub-domain sets are shown in Fig. 11. For the in-domain setting (STS-news $\leftrightarrow$ MTM), only the middle similarity band showed a strong negative correlation with the MTM evaluation. For the two domains in the out-of-domain setting, the image caption set showed no correlation with MTM at lower similarity levels, whereas the forum domain set showed correlation only at very high or low similarity levels. One of the possible reasons for this strange phenomenon is the ambiguity of STS annotations due to label definition and amateur annotator discussed in (Wang et al., 2022).

	STS-news-[0, 1]	STS-news-(1,2]	STS-news-(2,3]	STS-news-(3,4]	STS-news-(4,5]
MTM-Low	0.341	0.154	-0.217	0.479	0.632
MTM-MidLow	0.379	0.566	-0.537	0.664	0.716
MTM-MidHigh	0.249	0.515	-0.632	0.595	0.650
MTM-High	0.260	0.466	-0.728	0.529	0.588

(a) news

	STS-image-[0, 1]	STS-image-(1,2]	STS-image-(2,3]	STS-image-(3,4]	STS-image-(4,5]
MTM-Low	-0.019	0.070	0.405	0.409	0.514
MTM-MidLow	-0.086	0.167	0.399	0.490	0.569
MTM-MidHigh	-0.215	0.029	0.319	0.384	0.437
MTM-High	-0.271	-0.006	0.238	0.215	0.352

(b) image captions

	STS-forum-[0, 1]	STS-forum-(1,2]	STS-forum-(2,3]	STS-forum-(3,4]	STS-forum-(4,5]
MTM-Low	0.475	0.112	-0.359	0.170	0.452
MTM-MidLow	0.587	0.165	-0.426	0.059	0.555
MTM-MidHigh	0.554	0.136	-0.239	-0.006	0.658
MTM-High	0.548	0.183	-0.079	0.016	0.688

(c) forum

Figure 9: Spearman correlations between performance on subsets divided according to gold-standard similarity scores of each STS domain (news, forum, image captions) and MT Metrics (MTM). The darker color represents the lower correlation (= the larger evaluation gap).

Particularly, there is a large gap between the definitions of 2 (*not equivalent but share some details*) and 3 (*roughly equivalent*) in terms of semantic equivalence, which can be attributed to this result.

5 Discussion and conclusions

We have investigated the gap between evaluation scores on the STS benchmark dataset and those on the evaluation datasets for MT evaluation (MTM) and Passage Retrieval (PR). We identified three factors contributing to this evaluation gap; namely, (i) sentence length distribution, (ii) vocabulary coverage ratio, and (iii) similarity granularity. These factors actually contributed to the evaluation gap, indicating that STS is not currently a directly applicable benchmark for evaluating semantic similarity at present. Future work could include checking for causal effects and controlling for covariates to rigorously identify factors, as well as investigate evaluation gaps in other tasks and domains.

Therefore, what should we do? The evaluation of semantic similarity alone must continue to be studied because of the significant demand for predicting semantic similarity (Sec. 1). One feasible approach is to evaluate and validate the model performance on multiple datasets that engage real-world tasks, rather than just STS. Wang et al. (2021) argued that the evaluation of existing semantic similarity models is biased toward STS and reported evaluation results on several datasets, including STS. Additionally, there have also been attempts to create a union of evaluation datasets from multiple task data and use it as a basis for evaluation in neighboring fields, such as PASCAL-RTE (Dagan et al., 2006) or SentEval (Conneau and Kiela, 2018). While these attempts have been achieved, there is an assumption that there are substantial costs are involved in regularly maintaining the infrastructure in each of these areas. To proceed with this approach, including STS, we should address the problem of STS shown in this study, and pursue what it should be as a benchmark for semantic similarity evaluation. Whatever approach we take, we must consider each of these factors contributing to the evaluation gap described in this study and refine them stably.

Acknowledgments This work was supported by JSPS KAKENHI Grant Number JP20J21694 and JST, ACT-X Grant Number JPMJAX200S, Japan.

References

Eneko Agirre, Daniel Cer, Mona Diab, and Aitor Gonzalez-Agirre. 2012. SemEval-2012 task 6: A pilot on semantic textual similarity. In **SEM*, pages 385–393.

Payal Bajaj, Daniel Campos, Nick Craswell, Li Deng, Jianfeng Gao, Xiaodong Liu, Rangan Majumder, Andrew McNamara, Bhaskar Mitra, Tri Nguyen, Mir Rosenberg, Xia Song, Alina Stoica, Saurabh Tiwary, and Tong Wang. 2018. Ms marco: A human generated machine reading comprehension dataset. *ArXiv*, pages 1–16.

Ondřej Bojar, Yvette Graham, and Amir Kamran. 2017. Results of the wmt17 metrics shared task. In *WMT*, pages 489–513.

Samuel R. Bowman and George Dahl. 2021. What will it take to fix benchmarking in natural language understanding? In *NAACL*, pages 4843–4855.

Julio Castillo and Paula Estrella. 2012. Semantic textual similarity for MT evaluation. In *Proceedings of the Seventh Workshop on Statistical Machine Translation*, pages 52–58.

Daniel Cer, Mona Diab, Eneko Agirre, Iñigo Lopez-Gazpio, and Lucia Specia. 2017. SemEval-2017 task 1: Semantic textual similarity multilingual and crosslingual focused evaluation. In *SemEval*, pages 1–14.

Daniel Cer, Yinfei Yang, Sheng-yi Kong, Nan Hua, Nicole Limtiaco, Rhomni St. John, Noah Constant, Mario Guajardo-Cespedes, Steve Yuan, Chris Tar, Brian Strope, and Ray Kurzweil. 2018. Universal sentence encoder for English. In *EMNLP*, pages 169–174.

Danqi Chen, Adam Fisch, Jason Weston, and Antoine Bordes. 2017. Reading Wikipedia to answer open-domain questions. In *ACL*, pages 1870–1879.

Yung-Sung Chuang, Rumen Dangovski, Hongyin Luo, Yang Zhang, Shiyu Chang, Marin Soljacic, Shang-Wen Li, Wen-tau Yih, Yoon Kim, and James Glass. 2022. DiffCSE: Difference-based contrastive learning for sentence embeddings. In *NAACL*, pages 1–12.

Alexis Conneau and Douwe Kiela. 2018. SentEval: An evaluation toolkit for universal sentence representations. In *LREC*, pages 1699–1704.

Alexis Conneau, Douwe Kiela, Holger Schwenk, Loïc Barrault, and Antoine Bordes. 2017. Supervised learning of universal sentence representations from natural language inference data. In *EMNLP*, pages 670–680.

Ido Dagan, Oren Glickman, and Bernardo Magnini. 2006. The pascal recognising textual entailment challenge. In *Machine Learning Challenges. Evaluating Predictive Uncertainty, Visual Object Classification, and Recognising Tectual Entailment*, pages 177–190, Berlin, Heidelberg. Springer Berlin Heidelberg.

Esin Durmus, Faisal Ladhak, and Tatsunori Hashimoto. 2022. Spurious correlations in reference-free evaluation of text generation. In *ACL*, pages 1443–1454.

Luyu Gao, Zhuyun Dai, and Jamie Callan. 2021a. COIL: Revisit exact lexical match in information retrieval with contextualized inverted list. In *NAACL*, pages 3030–3042.

Tianyu Gao, Xingcheng Yao, and Danqi Chen. 2021b. SimCSE: Simple contrastive learning of sentence embeddings. In *EMNLP*, pages 6894–6910.

John Giorgi, Osvald Nitski, Bo Wang, and Gary Bader. 2021. DeCLUTR: Deep contrastive learning for unsupervised textual representations. In *ACL-IJCNLP*, pages 879–895.

Junjie Hu, Sebastian Ruder, Aditya Siddhant, Graham Neubig, Orhan Firat, and Melvin Johnson. 2020. XTREME: A massively multilingual multi-task benchmark for evaluating cross-lingual generalisation. In *ICML*, pages 4411–4421.

Vladimir Karpukhin, Barlas Oguz, Sewon Min, Patrick Lewis, Ledell Wu, Sergey Edunov, Danqi Chen, and Wen-tau Yih. 2020. Dense passage retrieval for open-domain question answering. In *EMNLP*, pages 6769–6781.

J. Peter Kincaid, Robert P. Jr. Fishburne, Richard L. Rogers, , and Brad S. Chissom. 1975. Derivation of new readability formulas (automated readability index, fog count and flesch reading ease formula) for navy enlisted personnel.

Matt Kusner, Yu Sun, Nicholas Kolkin, and Kilian Weinberger. 2015. From word embeddings to document distances. In *ICML*, pages 957–966.

Wuwei Lan and Wei Xu. 2018. Neural network models for paraphrase identification, semantic textual similarity, natural language inference, and question answering. In *COLING*, pages 3890–3902.

Hang Le, Loïc Vial, Jibril Frej, Vincent Segonne, Maximin Coavoux, Benjamin Lecouteux, Alexandre Allauzen, Benoit Crabbé, Laurent Besacier, and Didier Schwab. 2020. FlauBERT: Unsupervised language model pre-training for French. In *LREC*, pages 2479–2490.

Bohan Li, Hao Zhou, Junxian He, Mingxuan Wang, Yiming Yang, and Lei Li. 2020. On the sentence embeddings from pre-trained language models. In *EMNLP*, pages 9119–9130.

Yaobo Liang, Nan Duan, Yeyun Gong, Ning Wu, Fenfei Guo, Weizhen Qi, Ming Gong, Linjun Shou, Daxin Jiang, Guihong Cao, Xiaodong Fan, Ruofei Zhang, Rahul Agrawal, Edward Cui, Sining Wei, Taroon Bharti, Ying Qiao, Jiun-Hung Chen, Winnie Wu, Shuguang Liu, Fan Yang, Daniel Campos, Rangan Majumder, and Ming Zhou. 2020. XGLUE: A new benchmark datasetfor cross-lingual pre-training, understanding and generation. In *EMNLP*, pages 6008–6018.

Che Liu, Rui Wang, Jinghua Liu, Jian Sun, Fei Huang, and Luo Si. 2021. DialogueCSE: Dialogue-based contrastive learning of sentence embeddings. In *EMNLP*, pages 2396–2406.

Lajanugen Logeswaran and Honglak Lee. 2018. An efficient framework for learning sentence representations. In *ICLR*, pages 1–16.

Qingsong Ma, Johnny Wei, Ondřej Bojar, and Yvette Graham. 2019. Results of the WMT19 metrics shared task: Segment-level and strong MT systems pose big challenges. In *WMT*, pages 62–90.

Nitika Mathur, Timothy Baldwin, and Trevor Cohn. 2020. Tangled up in BLEU: Reevaluating the evaluation of automatic machine translation evaluation metrics. In *ACL*, pages 4984–4997.

Sungjoon Park, Jihyung Moon, Sungdong Kim, Won Ik Cho, Jiyoon Han, Jangwon Park, Chisung Song, Junseong Kim, Yongsook Song, Taehwan Oh, Joohong Lee, Juhyun Oh, Sungwon Lyu, Younghoon Jeong, Inkwon Lee, Sangwoo Seo, Dongjun Lee, Hyunwoo Kim, Myeonghwa Lee, Seongbo Jang, Seungwon Do, Sunkyoung Kim, Kyungtae Lim, Jongwon Lee, Kyumin Park, Jamin Shin, Seonghyun Kim, Lucy Park, Alice Oh, Jung-Woo Ha, and Kyunghyun Cho. 2021. Klue: Korean language understanding evaluation. *ArXiv*, pages 1–76.

Yingqi Qu, Yuchen Ding, Jing Liu, Kai Liu, Ruiyang Ren, Wayne Xin Zhao, Daxiang Dong, Hua Wu, and Haifeng Wang. 2021. RocketQA: An optimized training approach to dense passage retrieval for open-domain question answering. In *NAACL*, pages 5835–5847.

Ricardo Rei, Craig Stewart, Ana C Farinha, and Alon Lavie. 2020. COMET: A neural framework for MT evaluation. In *EMNLP*, pages 2685–2702.

Nils Reimers, Philip Beyer, and Iryna Gurevych. 2016. Task-oriented intrinsic evaluation of semantic textual similarity. In *COLING*, pages 87–96.

Nils Reimers and Iryna Gurevych. 2019. Sentence-BERT: Sentence embeddings using Siamese BERT-networks. In *EMNLP-IJCNLP*, pages 3982–3992.

Thibault Sellam, Dipanjan Das, and Ankur Parikh. 2020. BLEURT: Learning robust metrics for text generation. In *ACL*, pages 7881–7892.

Aliaksei Severyn, Massimo Nicosia, and Alessandro Moschitti. 2013. Learning semantic textual similarity with structural representations. In *ACL*, pages 714–718.

Hiroki Shimanaka, Tomoyuki Kajiwara, and Mamoru Komachi. 2018. RUSE: Regressor using sentence embeddings for automatic machine translation evaluation. In *WMT*, pages 751–758.

Anders Søgaard, Sebastian Ebert, Jasmijn Bastings, and Katja Filippova. 2021. We need to talk about random splits. In *EACL*, pages 1823–1832.

Robyn Speer, Joshua Chin, Andrew Lin, Sara Jewett, and Lance Nathan. 2018. Luminosoinsight/wordfreq: v2.2.

Dusan Varis and Ondřej Bojar. 2021. Sequence length is a domain: Length-based overfitting in transformer models. In *EMNLP*, pages 8246–8257.

Alex Wang, Amanpreet Singh, Julian Michael, Felix Hill, Omer Levy, and Samuel R. Bowman. 2019. GLUE: A multi-task benchmark and analysis platform for natural language understanding. In *ICLR*, pages 1–20.

Bin Wang, C.-c. Kuo, and Haizhou Li. 2022. Just rank: Rethinking evaluation with word and sentence similarities. In *ACL*, pages 6060–6077.

Kexin Wang, Nils Reimers, and Iryna Gurevych. 2021. TSDAE: Using transformer-based sequential denoising auto-encoderfor unsupervised sentence embedding learning. In *EMNLP Findings*, pages 671–688.

John Wieting, Taylor Berg-Kirkpatrick, Kevin Gimpel, and Graham Neubig. 2019. Beyond BLEU:training neural machine translation with semantic similarity. In *ACL*, pages 4344–4355.

John Wieting, Graham Neubig, and Taylor Berg-Kirkpatrick. 2020. A bilingual generative transformer for semantic sentence embedding. In *EMNLP*, pages 1581–1594.

Yuanmeng Yan, Rumei Li, Sirui Wang, Fuzheng Zhang, Wei Wu, and Weiran Xu. 2021. ConSERT: A contrastive framework for self-supervised sentence representation transfer. In *ACL*, pages 5065–5075.

Yinfei Yang, Daniel Cer, Amin Ahmad, Mandy Guo, Jax Law, Noah Constant, Gustavo Hernandez Abrego, Steve Yuan, Chris Tar, Yun-hsuan Sung, Brian Strope, and Ray Kurzweil. 2020. Multilingual universal sentence encoder for semantic retrieval. In *ACL (System Demonstrations)*, pages 87–94.

Go Yasui, Yoshimasa Tsuruoka, and Masaaki Nagata. 2019. Using semantic similarity as reward for reinforcement learning in sentence generation. In *ACL-SRW*, pages 400–406.

Seid Muhie Yimam, Chris Biemann, Shervin Malmasi, Gustavo Paetzold, Lucia Specia, Sanja Štajner, Anaïs Tack, and Marcos Zampieri. 2018. A report on the complex word identification shared task 2018. In *Proceedings of the Thirteenth Workshop on Innovative Use of NLP for Building Educational Applications*, pages 66–78.

Tianyi Zhang, Varsha Kishore, Felix Wu, Kilian Q. Weinberger, and Yoav Artzi. 2020a. Bertscore: Evaluating text generation with bert. In *ICLR*, pages 1–43.

Yan Zhang, Ruidan He, Zuozhu Liu, Kwan Hui Lim, and Lidong Bing. 2020b. An unsupervised sentence embedding method by mutual information maximization. In *EMNLP*, pages 1601–1610.

A Appendix

A.1 Limitation: Experiments on only English STS

We would like to investigate other languages in this paper, but we are only concerned with the original English STS. Other languages than English also have benchmark datasets of the semantic similarity but are generally based on the STS framework. Since the GLUE (Wang et al., 2019), including STS, is facilitating model development for each task, a language-specific GLUE-like benchmark set (Le et al., 2020; Park et al., 2021) or cross-lingual benchmark set (Liang et al., 2020; Hu et al., 2020) are constructed. The benchmarks of the semantic similarity for each language are created in two methods: re-constriction by automatic translation or new construction by each language's expert following the original method. Crucially, the former method is likely to fundamentally face the same biases such as vocabulary distribution as those in the English benchmarks, albeit including the issue of translation quality. Regarding the latter, dataset creators may improve the original dataset creation method. For example, in the Korean GLUE (KLUE; Park et al., 2021), they added more detailed instructions on label definition when annotating the similarity by non-expert. Thus, it is necessary to re-consider the requirements for an appropriate benchmarks before straightforwardly following the original method when creating datasets.

A.2 Statistics of datasets and subsets in the experiments

Satistics of datasets. Table 3 shows statistics of three datasets (STS, MTM and PR) employed in this paper. The dataset size of STS is larger than that of MTM, whereas the total word counts are comparable between STS and MTM. The sentence length distribution (the number of of words / {s,s'}) shows that STS has very few words per sentence compared to the application-oriented tasks. As for the STS sub-domain sets, the three sets have different sentence length distributions. We additionally describe the histograms of the sentence length distributions for the three STS sub-domain sets in Fig. 10. As illustrated here, the average sentence length of the image-caption domain is particularly highly biased for shorter sentence lengths.

Statistics of subsets used in the experiment. Statistics of the subset of sentence length, vocabulary coverage, and the granularity of similarity are shown in Table 4, 6, and 7, respectively.

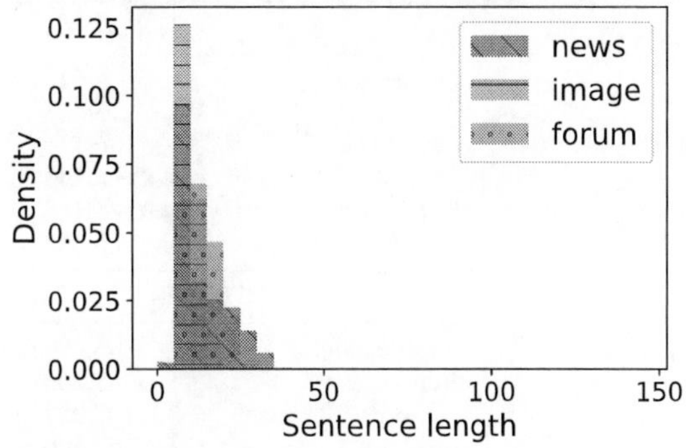

Figure 10: Histograms of sentence length in the STS sub-domain (news, image captions, forum) sets.

A.3 In-domain vs. Out-of-domain analysis in sentence length factor

Settings. We create subsets from the MTM dataset to match the sentence length distribution for each of three STS sub-domain sets. Notably, the forum and image caption domains have relatively small sentence length distributions (in Fig. 5, we thus reduced the range of the subsets from [0, 40) to [20, 60). Statistics of the subset of sentence length are shown in Table 5.

Results. Fig. 11 shows the correlation with MTM when sentence length subsets are created separately for each domain. We observed a similar tendency for all sub-domain sets that the evaluation gap increases for subsets of longer sentence lengths. This suggests that the evaluation results differ due to different sentence length distribution even within the same domain, which is consistent with a previous study's report in a different benchmark (Søgaard et al., 2021).

A.4 Extended Vocabulary analysis

STS has easier vocabulary STS contains more familiar words than that appear in the application tasks. As quantitative indicators of word familiarity, word frequency (Yimam et al., 2018) and word length (Kincaid et al., 1975) are often used mainly in the text simplification task. Intuitively, the higher the word frequency or the shorter the word length, the more familiar the word. In this case, we use "word frequency (wordfreq)" and "zipf frequency (zipffreq)" scale in `wordfreq` mod-

	STS (s1, s2)	MTM (hyp, ref)	PR (query, passage)
#sentence pairs	8,628	3,793	6,668,967
#sentences ({s, s'})	15,487	4,261	13,337,934
#words	186,134	170,565	472,778,794
#words / {s, s'}	**11.443±6.143**	23.381±11.215	35.908±35.266
#words / s	**11.450±6.188**	23.296±11.290	6.176± 2.642
#words / s'	**11.437±6.099**	23.467±11.138	65.640±26.692
	STS-news (s1, s2)	STS-forum (s1, s2)	STS-image-captions (s1, s2)
#sentence pairs	4,299	1,079	3,250
#sentences	8,268	1,913	5,306
#words	107,957	25,456	52,721
#words / {s, s'}	12.927±7.506	12.642±4.978	9.0823±2.910
#words / s	12.949±7.564	12.677±5.007	9.0585±2.906
#words / s'	12.905±7.448	12.608±4.949	9.1062±2.914

Table 3: Stats. of sentences and words and average of sentence length for STS (all and sub-domain sets) and application datasets (MT Metrics: MTM, Passage Retrieval: PR).

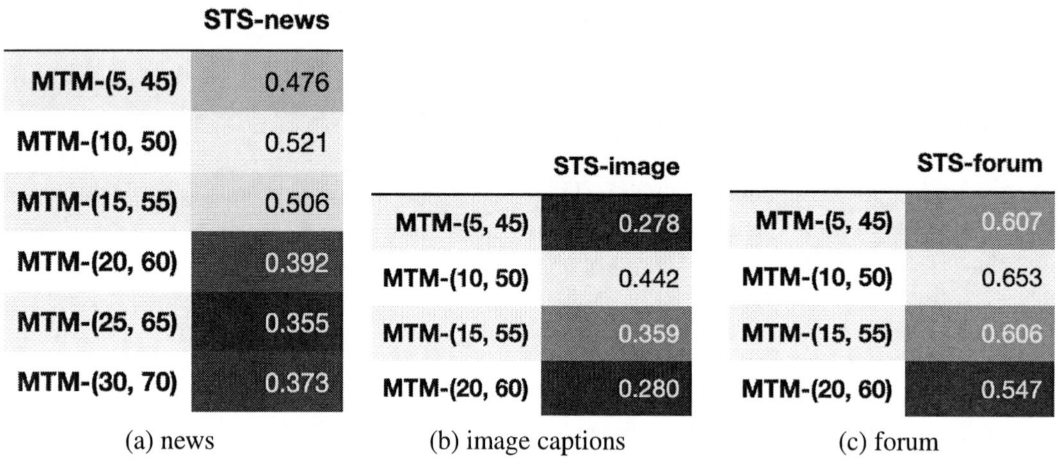

Figure 11: Spearman correlations between performance on sentence length subsets of STS-news, image captions, forum and MT Metrics (MTM) . The darker color indicates the lower correlation (= the larger evaluation gap).

	MTM		PR	
	size	avg. sent len	size	avg. sent len
[0, 40)	481	11.610±5.794	-	-
[5, 45)	481	11.790±5.979	-	-
[10, 50)	1225	16.841±5.747	67	16.045±4.420
[15, 55)	1484	21.086±5.015	119	19.849±3.759
[20, 60)	1112	24.722±4.286	199	23.704±3.285
[25, 65)	715	28.260±3.733	262	28.000±2.980
[30, 70)	465	33.184±4.462	561	34.526±3.855
[35, 75)	-	-	690	38.323±3.549
[40, 80)	-	-	932	46.987±1.390

Table 4: Stats. of sentence length subsets for MTM and PR. The "size" means the number of sentence pairs and the "avg. sent len" means the average of sentence length for each subset.

ule (Speer et al., 2018).[4] Wordfreq is the normalized frequency in the corpora, and zipffreq is the logarithmically scale of wordfreq. The word length is the number of characters in each word. We use `nltk.word_tokenize()` as word split and filtered out URLs and those with more than 50 characters.

Table 8 shows the average word frequency with the wordfreq module and word length for each dataset. In zipffreq, the average of STS is shorter than that of both the application tasks. Also in word length, we could observe that the average of STS is higher than that of MTM and PR. Thus, in both the indicators, word familiarity distribution in STS is higher than in the two application tasks.

Additionally, by comparing between "general" word frequencies (wordfreq) in the `wordfreq` module and actual word frequencies in the corpus (corpus-freq), we can identify words that appear particular high-frequently in the corpus. The words

[4] A tool to obtain word frequencies from 7 different corpora (Wikipedia, Subtitles, News, Books, Web text, Twitter, Reddit). `https://pypi.org/project/wordfreq/`

MTM						
	(STS-news-based)		(STS-forum-based)		(STS-image-captions-based)	
	size	avg. sent len.	size	avg. sent len.	size	avg. sent len.
[0, 40)	503	12.898±6.971	400	9.491±3.183	816	12.348±4.347
[5, 45)	506	13.238±7.259	398	9.521±3.162	867	13.106±4.855
[10, 50)	2150	19.356±6.201	676	13.024±2.620	1229	15.444±3.879
[15, 55)	1902	22.082±5.192	778	17.648±2.457	911	18.337±3.013
[20, 60)	1185	24.935±4.332	650	22.185±2.548	658	22.251±2.620
[25, 65)	715	28.260±3.733	-	-	-	-
[30, 70)	465	33.184±4.462	-	-	-	-

Table 5: Stats. of sentence length subsets for MTM according the sentence length distribution of STS sub-domain sets. The "size" means the number of sentence pairs and the "avg. sent len" means the average of sentence length (the average of {s, s'}) for each subset.

MTM								
	(STS-all-based)		(STS-news-based)		(STS-forum-based)		(STS-image-captions-based)	
	size	avg. Recall	size	avg. Recall	size	avg. Recall	size	avg. Recall
(all)	3,793	0.882±0.084	4,299	0.854±0.093	1,079	0.715±0.120	3,250	0.523±0.112
High	100	1.000±0.000	100	1.000±0.000	100	0.980±0.024	100	0.787±0.042
Low	100	0.631±0.060	100	0.588±0.058	100	0.418±0.063	100	0.252±0.062

PR		
	size	avg. Recall
all	6,614	0.835±0.079
High	100	0.988±0.011
Low	100	0.572±0.051

Table 6: Stats. of vocabulary subsets for MTM and PR.

STS								
	(all)		(news)		(forum)		(image captions)	
	size	avg. similarity	size	avg. similarity	size	avg. similarity	size	avg. similarity
[0, 1]	1182	0.655±0.280	594	0.522±0.393	275	0.472±0.420	931	0.360±0.353
(1, 2]	1348	1.631±0.285	640	1.631±0.283	248	1.687±0.286	460	1.601±0.283
(2, 3]	1672	2.653±0.291	876	2.678±0.291	232	2.656±0.292	564	2.615±0.286
(3, 4]	2317	3.614±0.287	1378	3.599±0.280	189	3.692±0.303	750	3.622±0.292
(4, 5]	1491	4.619±0.304	811	4.613±0.301	135	4.686±0.311	545	4.612±0.306

MTM		
	size	avg. similarity
Sim-Low: [-2, -0.47]	950	-0.820±0.266
Sim-MidLow: (-0.47, -0.03]	948	-0.240±0.126
Sim-MidHigh: (-0.03, 0.42]	943	0.193±0.127
Sim-High: (0.42, 1.5]	952	0.683±0.183

Table 7: Dataset size (#sentence pairs) and average & standard derivation of gold-standard similarity scores on STS and MTM subsets.

belongs to "corpus-freq − wordfreq > 0.001" for STS, MTM, and PR were 43, 18, and 26 words, respectively (if excluding stopwords and punctuation, 28, 3, and 6 words, respectively). Examples of higher frequent words in each dataset are shown in Table 9. As shown in this, some domain-specific words (STS: image captions, MTM: news, PR: question answering) are particularly frequent in each corpus. STS seems to be biased toward certain words (e.g., colors, present progressive forms, relatively abstract nouns such as *man* and *dog*). The results indicate that the STS has a relatively "easier" vocabulary (particularly sourced from the image-caption domain) than the application-oriented task.

Gap of proper noun in word representation distribution In actual semantic similarity predic-

	STS	MTM	PR
zipffreq (↑)	**3.59±1.24**	3.45±1.54	1.29±1.74
length (↓)	**6.97±2.76**	7.34±2.83	10.1±4.83

Table 8: Average of word frequency and word length in STS, MT Metrics: MTM, Passage Retrieval: PR. The higher (↑) the average for zipffreq (zipf scale of normalized word frequency) or the lower (↓) the average for word length, the higher the word familiarity can be considered.

tion models, words are embedded into a multi-dimensional space and treated as a soft distributed representation. Does the STS vocabulary still diverge from the vocabulary of the application-oriented tasks in the soft representations? To obtain an intuition for this, we plot word distribution in each dataset by t-SNE using the fasttext model. In the t-SNE setting, we use random initialization and set learning rate to 200 (scikit-learn), random state to 0. Fig. 12 shows the results of t-SNE plotting the top-frequency 5,000 words in each dataset. The areas surrounded with red lines are non-overlapping clusters between STS (blue) and the application tasks (MTM: orange, PR: green). Additionally, we enlarge some non-overlapping clusters in Fig. 13. These clusters mostly includes several proper nouns such as *Columbus*, *Carolina*, and *Robin* in all the datasets. In addition, to capture the quantitative distance between word distributions, we measured the Word Mover's Distance (WMD) (Kusner et al., 2015) with the above t-SNE representations. We use uniform distribution as the WMD weight and sqeuqlidian distance as the distance metric. The larger the value, the less STS covers the vocabulary of each application task. The distance between STS and MTM was 189.44 and the distance between STS and PR was 89.893. Thus, The vocabulary distribution gap between STS and the application-oriented tasks is caused by mainly the distribution of proper nouns.

A.5 NLI analysis

Various studies have found that pre-trained models of NLI dataset lead to improved performance on STS (Conneau et al., 2017; Reimers and Gurevych, 2019; Gao et al., 2021b). Gao et al. (2021b) tried several NLI and paraphrase identification datasets for model pre-training, indicating that NLI examples with the lowest lexical overlap have been the most effective. In this section, we show that the **sentence length** and **soft lexical** distribution of the NLI dataset are nearly STS-like. We suspect that the coincidence of these distributions is responsible for the improved performance of the NLI-supervised model on STS.

Sentence length analysis. Fig. 15 shows histograms of sentence length distribution for each dataset including NLI. As shown in this, NLI datasets have a relatively shorter sentence length distribution, similar to that of STS. Although MNLI contains relatively longer sentences than SNLI, there are still fewer examples of longer sentences compared to the application-oriented datasets such as MTM and PR.

Vocaburaly coverage analysis. In following, we see the vocabulary distribution on the NLI datasets. The statistics on NLI's vocabulary distribution are shown in Table 10. The Herdan's C of NLI is lower than that of STS; however, TTR of NLI close to that of MT Metrics. As the word familiarity distribution of NLI, the average of zipffreq shows that more high-frequency words appear in both SNLI and MNLI than in STS. However, the average of word length of NLI is close to that of MT Metrics. These results indicate that the words which appear in NLI are a fairly high frequent but those lengths are longer compared to STS. The visualization of the soft word distribution including NLI is shown in Fig. 14. As illustrated in this, the word distribution of NLI is similar for STS compared to the other datasets. This trend might contribute to the improvement of performances of NLI-supervised models such as SentenceBERT on STS.

A.6 Model description

Table 11 shows the descriptions of the models used in this paper.

STS	man, woman, playing, running, sitting, standing, guitar, white, black, red, dog, cat, horse, grass ⋯
MTM	said, police, olympic(, was, will, which, who, ⋯)
PR	name, definition, meaning, number, average(, what, your, ⋯)

Table 9: Examples of higher frequency words for STS, MT Metrics: MTM, Passage Retrieval: PR (stopwords in parentheses).

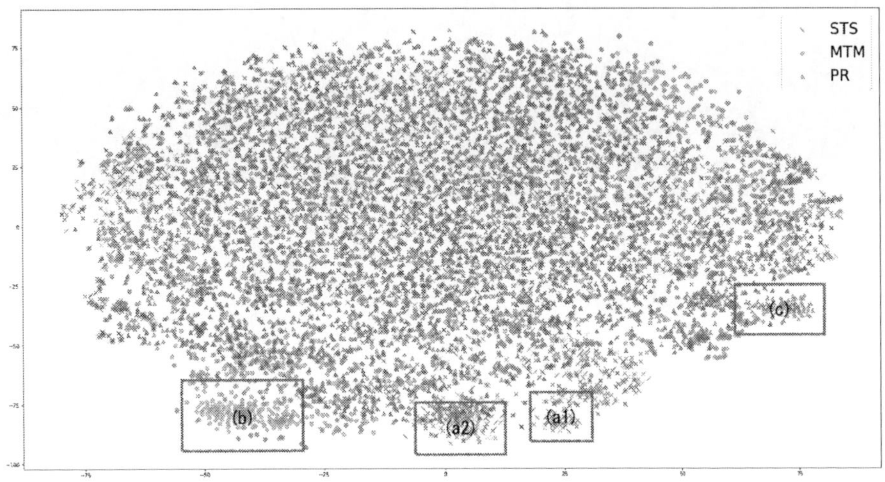

Figure 12: Word distribution of fasttext model in three datasets, STS (blue), MT Metrics (orange) and Passage Retrieval (green).

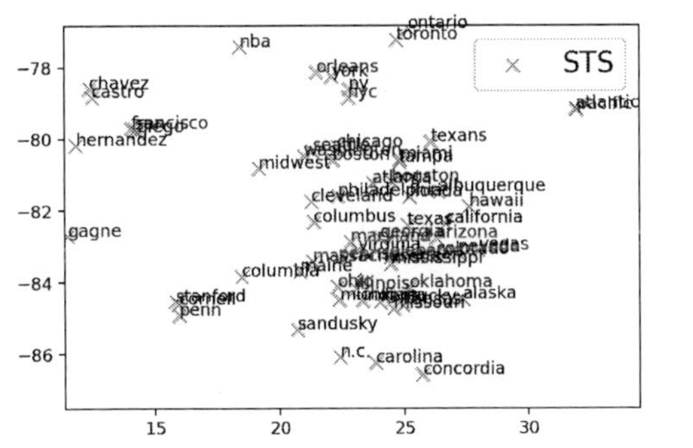

(a1) STS

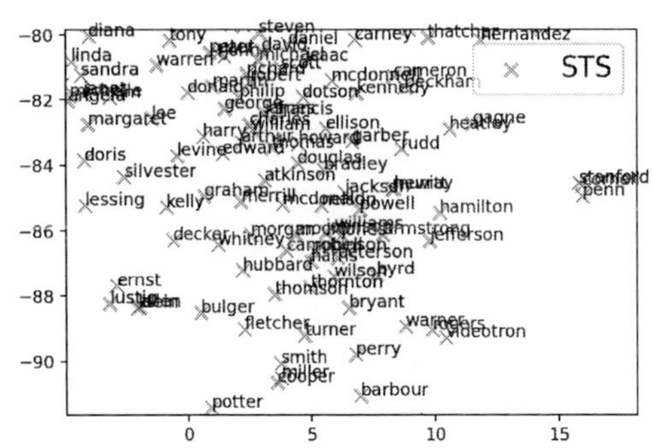

(a2) STS

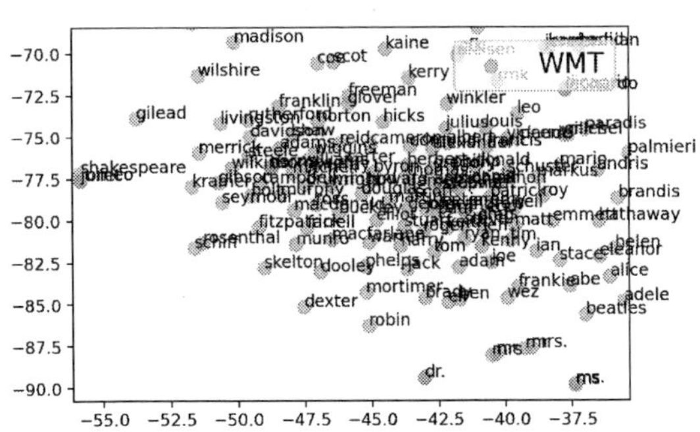

(b) Metrics

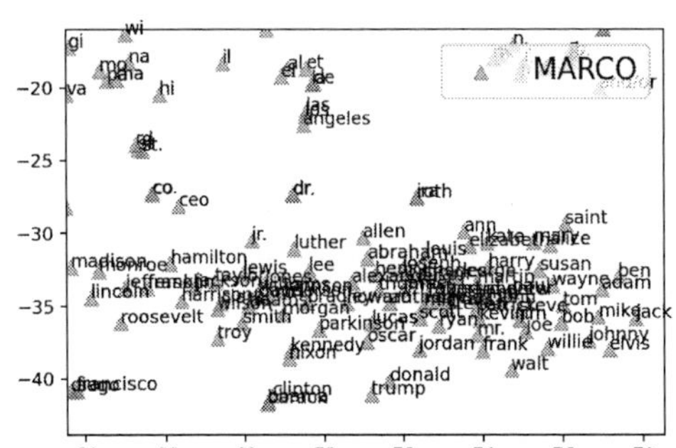

(c) Passage Retrieval

Figure 13: Expanded areas in the visualization of word distribution (Fig. 12).

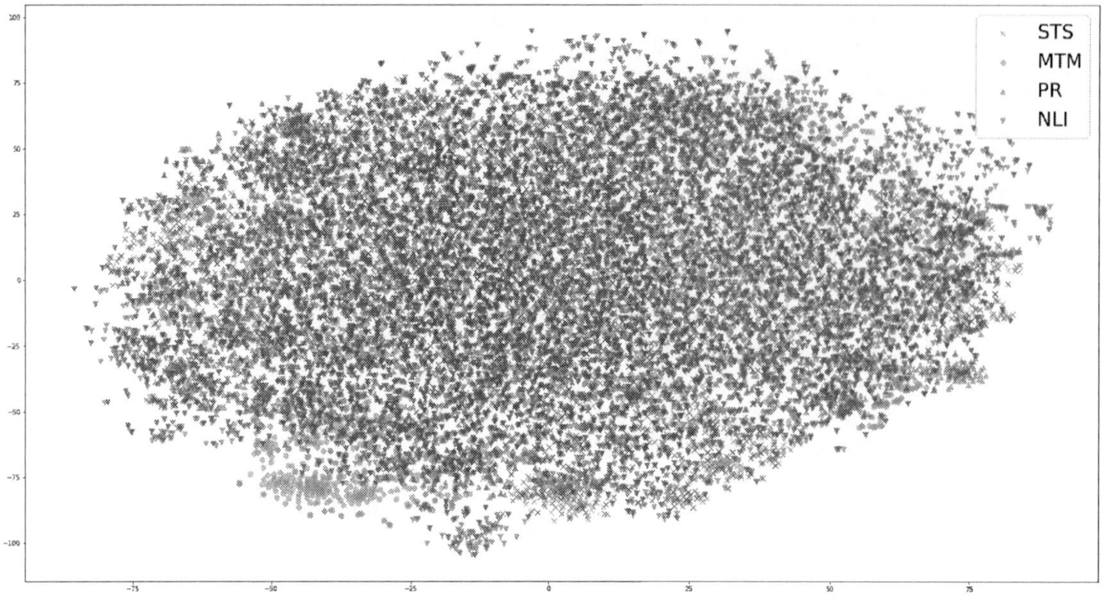

Figure 14: Word distribution of fasttext model in three datasets, STS (blue), MT Metrics (MTM: orange), Passage Retrieval (PR: green) and NLI (purple).

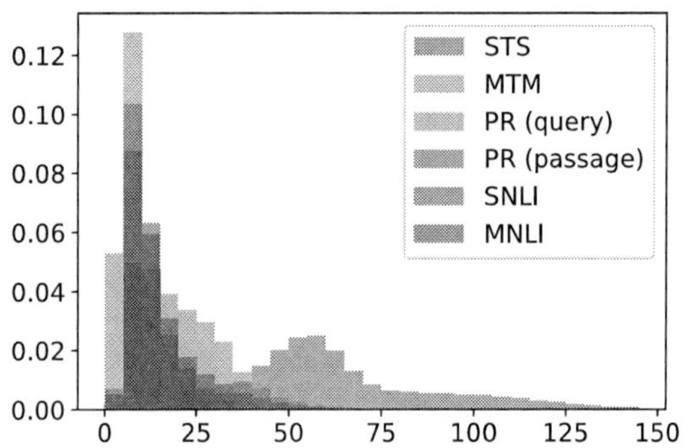

Figure 15: Histgrams of sentence length in the datasets includes NLI.

	SNLI	MNLI
#sentence pairs	570,152	402,703
#words	11,731,474	12,864,145
#types of words	37,179	85,789
TTR	0.0032	0.0067
Herdan's C	0.6465	0.6939
avg. zipffreq	2.871±1.488	2.685±1.448
avg. word len	7.544±2.613	8.206±3.313

Table 10: Statistics of vocabulary distribution on NLI datasets.

	model	dim	similarity function	pooling	others
SimCSE-sup	princeton-nlp/sup-simcse-bert-base-uncased	default	cos		
SimCSE-unsup	princeton-nlp/unsup-simcse-bert-base-uncased	default	cos		
SBERT-bb-NLI-mean	bert-base-nli-mean-tokens		cos	mean	
SBERT-MiniLM	all-MiniLM-L6-v2	384	cos	mean	
SBERT-mpnet	all-mpnet-base-v2	768	cos	mean	
BERTScore-rl-p	roberta-large	default	precision		
BERTScore-rl-r	roberta-large	default	recall		
BERTScore-rl-f	roberta-large	default	f1-score		
BERTScore-bbu-p	bert-base-uncased	default	precision		
BERTScore-bbu-r	bert-base-uncased	default	recall		
BERTScore-bbu-f	bert-base-uncased	default	f1-score		
avg. of BERT-bbl	bert-base-uncased	768	cos	mean	
avg. of BERT-rl	roberta-large	768	cos	mean	
BoV-Word2Vec (mean)	GoogleNews-vectors-negative300.magnitude	300	cos	mean	
BoV-Word2Vec (max)	GoogleNews-vectors-negative300.magnitude	300	cos	max	
BoV-Glove (mean)	glove.840B.300d.magnitude	300	cos	mean	
BoV-Glove (max)	glove.840B.300d.magnitude	300	cos	max	
BoV-fasttext (mean)	crawl-300d-2M.magnitude	300	cos	mean	
BoV-fasttext (max)	crawl-300d-2M.magnitude	300	cos	max	
BoW (sum)	CountVectorizer (sklearn, use smooth idf, stopwords)	vocab size	cos	sum	
BoW-TFIDF (sum)	TfidfVectorizer (sklearn, stopwords)	vocab size	cos	sum	norm=L2
USE	universal-sentence-encoder	512	cos		norm=L2
USE-l	universal-sentence-encoder-large	512	cos		norm=L2

Table 11: Semantic similarity model descriptions.

Chat Translation Error Detection for Assisting Cross-lingual Communications

Yunmeng Li[1] Jun Suzuki[1,3] Makoto Morishita[2] Kaori Abe[1]
Ryoko Tokuhisa[1] Ana Brassard[3,1] Kentaro Inui[1,3]
[1]Tohoku University [2]NTT [3]RIKEN
li.yunmeng.r1@dc.tohoku.ac.jp

Abstract

In this paper, we describe the development of a communication support system that detects erroneous translations to facilitate cross-lingual communications due to the limitations of current machine chat translation methods. We trained an error detector as the baseline of the system and constructed a new Japanese–English bilingual chat corpus, **BPersona-chat**, which comprises multi-turn colloquial chats augmented with crowdsourced quality ratings. The error detector can serve as an encouraging foundation for more advanced erroneous translation detection systems.

1 Introduction

With the expansion of internationalization, there is an increasing demand for cross-lingual communication. However, while machine translation technologies have demonstrated sound performance in translating documents (Barrault et al., 2019, 2020; Nakazawa et al., 2019), current methods are not always suitable for translating chat (Läubli et al., 2018; Toral et al., 2018; Farajian et al., 2020; Liang et al., 2021). When a translation system generates erroneous translations, the user may be unable to identify such errors, which can lead to confusion or misunderstanding. Thus, in this study, we developed a cross-lingual chat assistance system that reduces potential miscommunications by detecting translation errors and notifying the users of their occurrences. As a critical component of such a system, we propose the erroneous chat translation detection task and conduct an empirical study to model error detection. An illustration of the baseline task is shown in Figure 1. When the translation system generates a translation that is suspected to be incorrect or not well-connected to the context, we prompt users on the source language side that the translation may be incorrect. The warning message is expected to encourage users to modify their text into a better translatable form. Simultaneously,

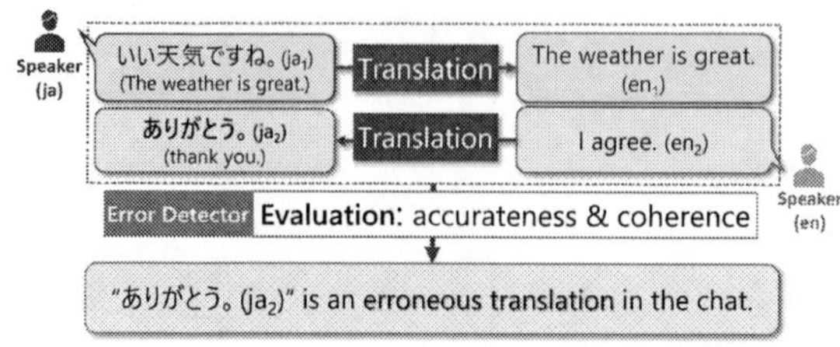

Figure 1: Illustration of the error detector predicting erroneous translations. The detector evaluates whether translation ja_2 is accurate and coherent in the chat.

users on the target language side receive the same warning message to indicate that unusual words or passages are likely translation errors.

To support this line of research, we created a new parallel chat corpus, **BPersona-chat**[1], which comprises multi-turn colloquial chats augmented with manually produced gold translations and machine-generated translations with crowdsourced quality labels (*correct* or *erroneous*). In an experiment, we trained an error detection model that classifies a given translation in a bilingual two-utterance chat as either correct or erroneous (Figure 1) and evaluated its performance on the BPersona-chat dataset. Our primary contributions are summarized as follows. (1) We propose the erroneous chat translation detection task. (2) We construct that BPersona-chat parallel chat corpus. (3) We trained the error detector, thereby providing a foundation to develop more sophisticated communication support systems.

2 Task Definition

As the baseline task, we define a *chat* as a two-utterance colloquial dialog between two humans using different languages. Here, we focus on predicting whether the second utterance, i.e., the response, was translated correctly. The preceding context, the translation of the context, the response, and the translated response are input to the error

[1]https://github.com/cl-tohoku/BPersona-chat

Proceedings of the 3rd Workshop on Evaluation and Comparison of NLP Systems, pages 88 - 95
November 20, 2022 ©2022 Association for Computational Linguistics

detector. Then, the detector predicts the translated response using the other utterances as reference data. The detector then outputs whether the translated response is erroneous.

Figure 1 shows an example target task of evaluating the Japanese translation of an English utterance. Here, the Japanese speaker's initial utterance ja_1 is translated into en_1, and the English speaker's response en_2 is translated into ja_2. In this example, the detector is assessing the utterance "ありがとう。 (*Thanks.*)," which is not an accurate translation of the utterance "I agree." The detector is given the preceding context (ja_1, en_1, and en_2) as reference data to predict whether the translation is both accurate and coherent. If the detector is predicting the translation en_2 of response ja_2, the reference data include en_1, ja_1, and ja_2 in the opposite.

3 Related Work

Translation quality estimation task Our target task is a new setting compared to quality estimation tasks (Specia et al., 2020; Fonseca et al., 2019), which primarily focus on written text, e.g., Wikipedia articles and Amazon reviews. In contrast, the target task attempts to detect errors in chat translation systems; thus, we must understand the contexts of casual conversational settings.

Parallel dialog corpus There are bilingual dialog corpora, e.g., Business Scene Dialog (Rikters et al., 2019), which includes business negotiation scenes in both Japanese and English. However, our task requires data that include cross-lingual colloquial chats with both appropriate and erroneous translations. To the best of our knowledge, no such dataset exists; thus, we must prepare a new evaluation dataset to evaluate the proposed task.

4 Evaluation Dataset

To mitigate the construction time and cost, we took advantage of existing chat corpora as a starting point. We first filtered out inappropriate chats, then asked professional translators to perform utterance-by-utterance translations in consideration of the contexts to acquire correct translation candidates. In addition, we prepared utterance-by-utterance machine translations, without considering chat contexts to acquire incorrect translation candidates. Finally, we evaluated the translations to see if they were acceptable chat translations. The details of each process are described in the following.

Speaker	Utterance
person 1	I do not like carrots. I throw them away.
person 2	really. I can sing pitch perfect. *(incoherent: carrots → sing)*
person 1	I also cook, and I ride my bike to work. *(incoherent: sing → ride)*
person 2	great! I had won an award for spelling bee. *(incoherent: ride → spelling)*

Table 1: Example of incoherent chat from Persona-chat.

4.1 Base Datasets

We constructed Japanese–English bidirectional chat translation datasets. Specifically, we focused on Persona-chat (Zhang et al., 2018) and JPersona-chat (Sugiyama et al., 2021) as our base datasets. These datasets contain multiturn chat data in English and Japanese, respectively[2]. Each chat was performed between two crowd workers assuming artificial personas. The speakers discuss a given personality trait, including but not limited to self-introduction, hobby, and others.

4.2 Filtering Incoherent Data

A preliminary manual review of the Persona-chat dataset revealed occasionally incoherent chats, e.g., unnatural topic changes or misunderstandings (Table 1). We removed such examples from the dataset by asking crowd workers to flag passages they deemed incoherent. Here, we defined "incoherence" as questions being ignored, the presence of unnatural topic changes, one speaker not addressing what the other speaker said, responses appearing to be out of order or generally difficult to follow.

We scored each chat according to the workers' answers and selected the top 200 among $1,500$ chats[3]. The selected 200 chats were marked as accurate and coherent by at least seven of the 10 workers.

4.3 Bilingual Chats with Human Translations

To construct a parallel Japanese–English chat corpus, we combined the selected top 200 top chats ($2,940$ utterances in total) from the Persona-chat dataset and 250 chats ($2,740$ utterances in total) from the JPersona-chat dataset. We then translated them into their respective target languages[4].

[2] Persona-chat and JPersona-chat are not translations of each other.

[3] See Appendix C for additional details about the crowdsourcing process.

[4] We sought consent to translate JPersona-chat with the authors.

Speaker	Original utterance in Perosona-chat (en)	Translation by professional translators (ja)
person 1	Good evening, how has your day been?	こんばんは、今日はどうだった？
person 2	It was good I met up with some friends to larp	よかったよ、ライブRPGで友達と集まった。
person 1	I wish I had time for that, working 40 hours in a bank is killing me.	そんな時間があればなあ、銀行で４０時間勤務は死にそうだよ。
person 2	... ...	... ...

Table 2: Example of the top 200 coherent chats from the Persona-chat dataset as rated by crowdsourcing workers and translated to Japanese by professional translators.

Here, we commissioned professional translators proficient in Japanese and English to ensure high-quality translations. We asked the translators to consider both the accuracy of the translation and the coherence of the dialog. The translators were given information about the personas to help adjust the speaking styles. As a result, we obtained a parallel corpus of 450 dialogs ($5,680$ utterances) and their translations, which we refer to as the Bilingual Persona-chat (BPersona-chat) corpus. Table 2 shows a sample from the BPersona-chat corpus.

4.4 Bilingual Chats with Neural Machine Translation Translations

The task of the error detector is to distinguish between accurate and poor (potentially harmful) translations. The BPersona-chat corpus provides examples of the former. Given professionally-translated bilingual chats, we also prepared low-quality alternative translations generated using a machine translation model. Here, we trained a Transformer-based neural machine translation (NMT) model A on OpenSubtitles2018 (Lison et al., 2018), achieving a BLEU score (Papineni et al., 2002) of 4.9 on the BPersona-chat corpus[5]. Note that this BLEU score is relatively low because domain mismatch is possible between OpenSubtitles2018 and the BPersona-chat corpus. However, it was a preferable setting because we required poor translations to construct our dataset. In addition, we prepared better translations with a translation model B, which achieved a BLEU score of 26.4.

4.5 Human Evaluation of Translations

To confirm that the alternative translations generated by NMT model A were erroneous to the crowds, we asked crowd workers proficient in both English and Japanese to rate each translation in the chat as either good or bad. We qualified the workers to ensure they could reach the level of native Japanese, and the level of business and academic English.

The workers rated $5,088$ of NMT model A's $5,680$ (89.58%) translations, $1,718$ of NMT model B's $5,680$ (30.25%) translations, and 597 of the $5,680$ (10.51%) human translations as bad[6]. Then, each utterance-translation pair was marked as erroneous or correct based on human evaluations.

According to our task settings, an utterance cannot be used as the referenced preceding context if none of it is correct. Thus, we deleted the 159 utterances whose human translations, model A's translations, and model B's translations were all erroneous. As a result, we obtained $2,674$ English utterances with $8,022$ corresponding labeled Japanese translations, where $3,406$ of the translations were labeled as erroneous, and the remaining $4,616$ translations were labeled as correct. In addition, we obtained $2,397$ Japanese utterances with $7,190$ corresponding labeled English translations, where $3,096$ translations were labeled as erroneous, and $4,094$ were labeled as correct. These labeled data were used to evaluate the error detector in our subsequent experiments.

5 Baseline Error Detecting Classifier

As a baseline approach, we trained and evaluated a binary BERT-based (Devlin et al., 2019; Wolf et al., 2020) classifier as the error detector[7]. Here, the input was structured as "ja_1 [SEP] en_1 [SEP] en_2 [SEP] ja_2" to predict the Japanese translation ja_2 of the corresponding source utterance en_2. The input was structured as "en_1 [SEP] ja_1 [SEP] ja_2 [SEP] en_2" to predict the translation en_2 of the corresponding source utterance ja_2 in the opposite translating direction[8].

[5] Refer to Appendix A for additional details about training NMT model A.

[6] Refer to AppendixC for additional details about the crowdsourcing process.

[7] Refer to AppendixB for additional details about training this classification model.

[8] [SEP] was used to indicate different utterances, [CLS] was used to indicate the beginning of the data and [PAD] was

	ja→en	en→ja
Majority class	56.94	57.54
Minority class	43.06	42.46
Error detector	76.27	77.06

Table 3: Accuracy of the majority class classifier, minority class classifier, and error detector.

	ja → en			en → ja		
	F	**(Pre**	**Rec)**	**F**	**(Pre**	**Rec)**
Error detector	73.30	(71.10	75.65)	75.03	(69.75	81.18)

Table 4: F-score, precision, and recall of the error detector on BPersona-chat dataset.

Similar to the original experimental settings for BERT, we applied the SoftMax function to the classification result to obtain the final prediction.

We used the OpenSubtitles2018 dataset for training with approximately one million utterances. Here, we generated negative samples with the low-quality translation model A (Section 4.4), and we fine-tuned the multilingual BERT model provided by HuggingFace[9] to construct the error detector for both the English-to-Japanese and Japanese-to-English directions.

6 Experiments

In this section, we report on our trial of the chat translation error detection task (Section 2) using the model described in Section 5. The task was evaluated with the dataset described in Section 4.

6.1 Evaluation Metrics

Majority class and minority class classifiers To confirm that the error detector is not simply making lucky guesses, we calculated the accuracy of the majority class classifier, the minority class classifier, and the error detector. Note that the majority class of the data is the correct translation, and the minority class is the erroneous translation.

F-score, precision and recall We evaluated the performance of the error detector according to the F-score (**F**). We also show the precision (**Pre**) and recall (**Rec**) values for reference. The truth (T) is set as the erroneous translation, and the positive case (P) is detecting the erroneous translation.

Confusion matrix To evaluated the performance of the error detector on different types of translations, we provide confusion matrices according to whether the translation was translated by the human translator, NMT model A, or NMT model B.

6.2 Results

The results demonstrate that the error detector is capable for classifying erroneous translations in chats. According to the accuracy values given in Table 3, we conclude that the error detector gained higher performance compared to the majority and minority classifiers. The results suggest that the current method can solve the task without relying on lucky guesses. According to the F-score, precision, and recall values shown in Table 4, the error detector could identify erroneous translations in the BPersona-chat dataset.

However, although the detector could distinguish translations with terrible translation or coherence issues, it could not successfully identify errors that were not obvious. The confusion matrix of the results is shown in Table 5, where the row headers are the actual annotations, and the column headers are the labels predicted by the detector. As can be seen, the error detector did not perform well when attempting to predict the translations generated by the high-quality NMT model B. Here, the detector labeled more than half of the erroneous translations generated by NMT model B as correct. One possible reason for this is that the detector was trained on a dataset whose erroneous examples were generated by model A, which generated low-quality translations.

To compare the error detector with the traditional BLEU calculation, we calculated the sentence-BLEU score of each utterance in the BPersona-chat dataset using the method provided by NLTK (Bird et al., 2009). The results demonstrate that the detector can help distinguish an erroneous translation even when the translation has a high BLEU score. Table 6 shows an example of a translation en_2 with a high sentence-BLEU score but incorrectly translated the Japanese word "米" into "America" rather than "rice". We found that the detector helped distinguish this case as erroneous, as was expected.

6.3 Quality of the Evaluation Dataset

The reason a considerably high score was obtained on the NMT model A's translations is not entirely straightforward. Note that we trained the classification model on OpenSubtitles2018, which has a different distribution from BPersona-chat. This

used as the padding token.

[9]https://huggingface.co/

	ja→en							
	Human			NMT model A (low-quality)			NMT model B (high-quality)	
	Correct	Erroneous		Correct	Erroneous		Correct	Erroneous
Correct	1879	207	Correct	11	155	Correct	1252	590
Erroneous	290	21	Erroneous	90	2140	Erroneous	374	181
	en→ja							
	Human			NMT model A (low-quality)			NMT model B (high-quality)	
	Correct	Erroneous		Correct	Erroneous		Correct	Erroneous
Correct	2406	176	Correct	6	265	Correct	1005	758
Erroneous	83	9	Erroneous	53	2350	Erroneous	505	406

Table 5: Confusion matrix of the error detector on BPersona-chat data (row headers are the actual annotations, and column headers are the prediction made by the detector).

en_1 (context)	What did you have for dinner?
ja_1	晩ご飯に何を食べましたか？
ja_2 (source)	晩ご飯に米を食べました。
en_2 **(translation)**	**I had America as my dinner.**
(reference)	*(I had rice as my dinner.)*
sentence-BLEU	72.7 (compared to the reference)
classifier's prediction	erroneous

Table 6: Example where the error detector successfully predicted the erroneous translation en_2 even though it had a high sentence-BLEU score.

means that the training was performed using out-of-domain data. One potential reason for the high performance may be attributed to the nature of the automatically generated translations. As with the experimental results described in Section 6.2, it was difficult for the detector to distinguish the good translations generated using the high-quality NMT model B. To improve performance, it is important to clarify the exact issue with the erroneous translation.

7 Discussions and Future Work

In this paper, we have proposed the chat translation error detection task to assist cross-lingual communication. For this purpose, we constructed a parallel Japanese–English chat corpus as the backbone for evaluation, including high-quality and low-quality translations augmented with crowdsourced quality ratings. We trained the error detector to identify erroneous translations, and the detector could help detect the erroneous translations in chat.

While this is the first trial to realize a cross-lingual chat assistance system, we hope to promote research to complete the chat translation assistance system in the future, and we aim to advance the detector's ability to indicate the translation's critical error possibility. This will allow speakers to focus on translations with high error rates. In addition, we hope to identify specific errors in the translations for users. To achieve this goal, we would like to refine the BPersona-chat dataset with multiple labels corresponding to different translation errors. The binary classification model would also be improved into multi-label, which would enable the error detector to analyze concrete problems. Thus, we would be able to identify the exact error in the current speech for revisions. We will also consider providing translation suggestions as reference information to help users modify.

When both parties cannot understand each other's language, the advanced error detecting system is expected to alert them of possible errors and guide them to modify their texts, thereby reducing translation problems in multilingual chats. Finding a balance between coherence and accuracy is always difficult in chat translation. However, we believe that advancing and refining the error detector and the corresponding dataset will help us identify and solve specific problems in chat translation systems.

Acknowledgements

This work was supported by JST (the establishment of university fellowships towards the creation of science technology innovation) Grant Number JPMJFS2102, JST CREST Grant Number JPMJCR20D2 and JST Moonshot R&D Grant Number JPMJMS2011 (fundamental research). The crowdsourcing was supported by Amazon Mechanical Turk (`https://www.mturk.com/`) and Crowdworks (`https://crowdworks.jp/`).

References

Loïc Barrault, Magdalena Biesialska, Ondřej Bojar, Marta R. Costa-jussà, Christian Federmann, Yvette Graham, Roman Grundkiewicz, Barry Haddow, Matthias Huck, Eric Joanis, Tom Kocmi, Philipp Koehn, Chi-kiu Lo, Nikola Ljubešić, Christof Monz, Makoto Morishita, Masaaki Nagata, Toshiaki Nakazawa, Santanu Pal, Matt Post, and Marcos Zampieri. 2020. Findings of the 2020 conference on machine translation (WMT20). In *Proceedings of the Fifth Conference on Machine Translation*, pages 1–55.

Loïc Barrault, Ondřej Bojar, Marta R. Costa-jussà, Christian Federmann, Mark Fishel, Yvette Graham, Barry Haddow, Matthias Huck, Philipp Koehn, Shervin Malmasi, Christof Monz, Mathias Müller, Santanu Pal, Matt Post, and Marcos Zampieri. 2019. Findings of the 2019 conference on machine translation (WMT19). In *Proceedings of the Fourth Conference on Machine Translation (Volume 2: Shared Task Papers, Day 1)*, pages 1–61.

Steven Bird, Ewan Klein, and Edward Loper. 2009. *Natural language processing with Python: analyzing text with the natural language toolkit*. " O'Reilly Media, Inc.".

Jacob Devlin, Ming-Wei Chang, Kenton Lee, and Kristina Toutanova. 2019. BERT: Pre-training of deep bidirectional transformers for language understanding. In *Proceedings of the 2019 Conference of the North American Chapter of the Association for Computational Linguistics: Human Language Technologies, Volume 1 (Long and Short Papers)*, pages 4171–4186.

M. Amin Farajian, António V. Lopes, André F. T. Martins, Sameen Maruf, and Gholamreza Haffari. 2020. Findings of the WMT 2020 shared task on chat translation. In *Proceedings of the Fifth Conference on Machine Translation*, pages 65–75.

Erick Fonseca, Lisa Yankovskaya, André F. T. Martins, Mark Fishel, and Christian Federmann. 2019. Findings of the WMT 2019 shared tasks on quality estimation. In *Proceedings of the Fourth Conference on Machine Translation (Volume 3: Shared Task Papers, Day 2)*, pages 1–10.

Diederik Kingma and Jimmy Ba. 2015. Adam: A method for stochastic optimization. In *Proceedings of the 3rd International Conference on Learning Representations (ICLR 2015)*.

Samuel Läubli, Rico Sennrich, and Martin Volk. 2018. Has machine translation achieved human parity? a case for document-level evaluation. In *Proceedings of the 2018 Conference on Empirical Methods in Natural Language Processing*, pages 4791–4796.

Yunlong Liang, Fandong Meng, Yufeng Chen, Jinan Xu, and Jie Zhou. 2021. Modeling bilingual conversational characteristics for neural chat translation.

Pierre Lison, Jörg Tiedemann, and Milen Kouylekov. 2018. OpenSubtitles2018: Statistical rescoring of sentence alignments in large, noisy parallel corpora. In *Proceedings of the Eleventh International Conference on Language Resources and Evaluation (LREC 2018)*, pages 1742–1748.

Toshiaki Nakazawa, Nobushige Doi, Shohei Higashiyama, Chenchen Ding, Raj Dabre, Hideya Mino, Isao Goto, Win Pa Pa, Anoop Kunchukuttan, Yusuke Oda, Shantipriya Parida, Ondřej Bojar, and Sadao Kurohashi. 2019. Overview of the 6th workshop on Asian translation. In *Proceedings of the 6th Workshop on Asian Translation*, pages 1–35.

Myle Ott, Sergey Edunov, Alexei Baevski, Angela Fan, Sam Gross, Nathan Ng, David Grangier, and Michael Auli. 2019. fairseq: A Fast, Extensible Toolkit for Sequence Modeling. In *Proceedings of the 2019 Conference of the North American Chapter of the Association for Computational Linguistics (Demonstrations)*, pages 48–53.

Myle Ott, Sergey Edunov, David Grangier, and Michael Auli. 2018. Scaling Neural Machine Translation. In *Proceedings of the Third Conference on Machine Translation (WMT 2018)*, pages 1–9.

Kishore Papineni, Salim Roukos, Todd Ward, and Wei-Jing Zhu. 2002. Bleu: a method for automatic evaluation of machine translation. In *Proceedings of the 40th Annual Meeting of the Association for Computational Linguistics*, pages 311–318, Philadelphia, Pennsylvania, USA. Association for Computational Linguistics.

Matīss Rikters, Ryokan Ri, Tong Li, and Toshiaki Nakazawa. 2019. Designing the business conversation corpus. In *Proceedings of the 6th Workshop on Asian Translation*, pages 54–61, Hong Kong, China. Association for Computational Linguistics.

Rico Sennrich, Barry Haddow, and Alexandra Birch. 2016. Neural machine translation of rare words with subword units. In *Proceedings of the 54th Annual Meeting of the Association for Computational Linguistics (Volume 1: Long Papers)*, pages 1715–1725, Berlin, Germany. Association for Computational Linguistics.

Lucia Specia, Frédéric Blain, Marina Fomicheva, Erick Fonseca, Vishrav Chaudhary, Francisco Guzmán, and André F. T. Martins. 2020. Findings of the WMT 2020 shared task on quality estimation. In *Proceedings of the Fifth Conference on Machine Translation*, pages 743–764.

Nitish Srivastava, Geoffrey Hinton, Alex Krizhevsky, Ilya Sutskever, and Ruslan Salakhutdinov. 2014. Dropout: A simple way to prevent neural networks from overfitting. *Journal of Machine Learning Research*, 15(56):1929–1958.

Hiroaki Sugiyama, Masahiro Mizukami, Tsunehiro Arimoto, Hiromi Narimatsu, Yuya Chiba, Hideharu

Nakajima, and Toyomi Meguro. 2021. Empirical analysis of training strategies of transformer-based japanese chit-chat systems.

Christian Szegedy, Vincent Vanhoucke, Sergey Ioffe, Jon Shlens, and Zbigniew Wojna. 2016. Rethinking the Inception Architecture for Computer Vision. In *2016 IEEE Conference on Computer Vision and Pattern Recognition (CVPR 2016)*, pages 2818–2826.

Jörg Tiedemann and Yves Scherrer. 2017. Neural machine translation with extended context. In *Proceedings of the Third Workshop on Discourse in Machine Translation*, pages 82–92.

Antonio Toral, Sheila Castilho, Ke Hu, and Andy Way. 2018. Attaining the unattainable? reassessing claims of human parity in neural machine translation. In *Proceedings of the Third Conference on Machine Translation: Research Papers*, pages 113–123.

Ashish Vaswani, Noam Shazeer, Niki Parmar, Jakob Uszkoreit, Llion Jones, Aidan N Gomez, Łukasz Kaiser, and Illia Polosukhin. 2017. Attention Is All You Need. In *Advances in Neural Information Processing Systems 31 (NIPS 2017)*, pages 5998–6008.

Thomas Wolf, Lysandre Debut, Victor Sanh, Julien Chaumond, Clement Delangue, Anthony Moi, Pierric Cistac, Tim Rault, Rémi Louf, Morgan Funtowicz, Joe Davison, Sam Shleifer, Patrick von Platen, Clara Ma, Yacine Jernite, Julien Plu, Canwen Xu, Teven Le Scao, Sylvain Gugger, Mariama Drame, Quentin Lhoest, and Alexander M. Rush. 2020. Transformers: State-of-the-art natural language processing. In *Proceedings of the 2020 Conference on Empirical Methods in Natural Language Processing: System Demonstrations*, pages 38–45.

Yonghui Wu, Mike Schuster, Zhifeng Chen, Quoc V. Le, Mohammad Norouzi, Wolfgang Macherey, Maxim Krikun, Yuan Cao, Qin Gao, Klaus Macherey, Jeff Klingner, Apurva Shah, Melvin Johnson, Xiaobing Liu, Łukasz Kaiser, Stephan Gouws, Yoshikiyo Kato, Taku Kudo, Hideto Kazawa, Keith Stevens, George Kurian, Nishant Patil, Wei Wang, Cliff Young, Jason Smith, Jason Riesa, Alex Rudnick, Oriol Vinyals, Greg Corrado, Macduff Hughes, and Jeffrey Dean. 2016. Google's neural machine translation system: Bridging the gap between human and machine translation. *CoRR*, abs/1609.08144.

Saizheng Zhang, Emily Dinan, Jack Urbanek, Arthur Szlam, Douwe Kiela, and Jason Weston. 2018. Personalizing dialogue agents: I have a dog, do you have pets too?

Architecture	2-to-2 Transformer (Vaswani et al., 2017; Tiedemann and Scherrer, 2017)
Enc-Dec layers	6
Attention heads	8
Word-embedding dimension	512
Feed-forward dimension	2,048
Share all embeddings	True
Optimizer	Adam ($\beta_1 = 0.9, \beta_2 = 0.98, \epsilon = 1 \times 10^{-8}$) (Kingma and Ba, 2015)
Learning rate schedule	Inverse square root decay
Warmup steps	4,000
Max learning rate	0.001
Initial Learning Rate	1e-07
Dropout	0.3 (Srivastava et al., 2014)
Label smoothing	$\epsilon_{ls} = 0.1$ (Szegedy et al., 2016)
Mini-batch size	8,000 tokens (Ott et al., 2018)
Number of epochs	20
Averaging	Save checkpoint for every 5000 iterations and take an average of last five checkpoints
Beam size	6 with length normalization (Wu et al., 2016)
Implementation	`fairseq` (Ott et al., 2019)

Table 7: List of hyper-parameters for training the NMT model A

Architecture	BERT (base) (Devlin et al., 2019)
Optimizer	Adam ($\beta_1 = 0.9, \beta_2 = 0.98, \epsilon = 1 \times 10^{-8}$, weight decay=0.01) (Kingma and Ba, 2015)
Learning rate schedule	Inverse square root decay
Max learning rate	0.001
Mini-batch size	16 samples
Number of epochs	1
Implementation	`transformers` (Wolf et al., 2020)

Table 8: List of hyper-parameters for training the classification model

A Settings of Machine Translation Model

This section describes the details of the training neural machine translation model. Firstly, we tokenized the corpus into subwords with BPE (Sennrich et al., 2016). We set the vocabulary size to 32,000. Then we trained the 2-to-2 Transformer-based NMT model A (Tiedemann and Scherrer, 2017), which outputs two consecutive given two input sentences to consider larger contexts. Table 7 shows the list of hyper-parameters.

B Settings of Classification Model

This section describes the details of the training classification model. Table 8 shows the list of hyper-parameters.

C Details of Crowd-sourcing Tasks

C.1 Filtering Persona-chat

We asked crowd workers on Amazon Mechanical Turk (`https://requester.mturk.com/`) to filter out incoherent data in Persona-chat. Here, we defined a chat as "incoherent" if:

- questions being ignored;
- the presence of unnatural topic changes;
- one is not addressing what the other said;
- responses seeming out of order;
- or being hard to follow in general.

Workers were instructed to disregard minor issues such as typos and focus on the general flow.

In the full round, we selected $1,500$ chats from Persona-chat. Each crowd worker was tasked to rate 5 chats at a time, and each chat was rated by 10 different workers. Eligible workers were selected with a preliminary qualification round.

C.2 Rating Translations

We asked crowd workers on Crowdworks (`https://crowdworks.jp/`) to label the human translation and the NMT translation in BPersona-chat as low-quality or high-quality. In the task, we defined a translation as bad if:

- the translation is incorrect;
- parts of the source chat are lost;
- there are serious grammatical or spelling errors that interfere with understanding;
- the person's speaking style changes from the past utterance;
- the translation is meaningless or incomprehensible;
- or the translation is terrible in general.

Workers worked on files in which one file included one complete chat; therefore, they could check the context and rate each utterance of the conversation.

To the limited number of workers, in the full round, crowd workers were tasked to rate around 50 to 300 chats in two weeks. Eligible workers were selected with a preliminary qualification round.

Evaluating the role of non-lexical markers in GPT-2's language modeling behavior

Roberta Rocca
Aarhus University
University of Texas at Austin
roberta.rocca@cas.au.dk

Alejandro de la Vega
University of Texas at Austin
delavega@utexas.edu

Abstract

Transformer-based language models are often trained on structured text where non-lexical markers of sentence and discourse structure (e.g., punctuation and casing) are present and used consistently. Transformers encode these markers and arguably benefit from the information they convey. Yet, a systematic evaluations of the contribution of non-lexical markers to model performance, and of whether models' behavior changes significantly in their absence, is currently lacking. This knowledge is both relevant from a theoretical standpoint, but also important to understand how well pretrained models may perform in common application scenarios where casing and punctuation are absent or inconsistent. Here, we analyze GPT-2's language modeling behavior in parallel corpora that differ in the presence vs. absence of consistent punctuation and casing. We compute GPT-2's precision and uncertainty in next-token prediction for multiple context sizes, and compare the resulting performance distributions across corpora. We find that absence of non-lexical markers, especially punctuation, increases model uncertainty, and it affects (but does not catastrophically disrupt) GPT-2's precision in next-token prediction. Interestingly, the absence of non-lexical markers prevents the model from benefiting from larger contexts in order to reduce the uncertainty of its predictions. Future work will extend this paradigm to a wider range of models and systematically investigate how features of training text affect both language modeling and downstream predictive performance.

1 Introduction

The advent of Transformer-based language models (Vaswani et al., 2017) and their availability through high-quality easy-to-use libraries such as huggingface's transformers (Wolf et al., 2020) has widely democratized the use of state-of-the-art models beyond the NLP community. Transformers' language modeling capabilities can be leveraged off-the-shelf — with no further training and only minimal programming required — for a large variety of applications, ranging from neuroscientific investigations of human language processing (Merkx and Frank, 2020; Schrimpf et al., 2021) to interactive and improvisational storytelling (Austin, 2019).

Transformers (Devlin et al., 2019; Radford et al., 2019; Brown et al., 2020) are often trained on large corpora including highly structured text (e.g., BooksCorpus, (Zhu et al., 2015), or the English Wikipedia), where non-lexical sentence structure and discourse markers (punctuation and casing) are present and used consistently. Tokenization preserves these markers: punctuation is encoded through dedicated tokens and (for some models) casing is preserved through case-sensitive vocabularies.

Punctuation and casing encode rich information about sentence boundaries, internal sentence structure, and discourse (Steinhauer, 2003), which transformers' language modeling capabilities arguably benefit from. Yet, systematic investigations of whether this is the case, and how sparse or inconsistent use of these markers affects models' predictive performance, is lacking[1].

This knowledge would not only be informative from a theoretical standpoint (clarifying the contribution of non-lexical structure and discourse markers to transformers' language modeling capabilities) but also to understand whether popular pretrained models' capabilities generalize to common real-world application scenarios where non-lexical markers are absent or used inconsistently (e.g., social media text, or speech-to-text transcription). Discrepancies in performance could in fact be addressed by fine-tuning models on unstructured

[1] With the exception of studies on punctuation restoration (Courtland et al., 2020; Vāravs and Salimbajevs, 2018) and dialogue act recognition (Żelasko et al., 2021).

Proceedings of the 3rd Workshop on Evaluation and Comparison of NLP Systems, pages 96 - 102
November 20, 2022

baseline	no punctuation
the date: September eighteenth. He slides over a dirty martini, **and**	the date September eighteenth He slides over a dirty martini **glass**
and 'cheapest' therapist. Before long, he understood that, knowing nothing about the subject, it was hard to figure out which **therapist**	and cheapest therapist Before long he understood that knowing nothing about the subject it was hard to figure out which **one**
cups are too big to serve wine. "You didn't get half the things on my **cup**	cups are too big to serve wine You didn't get half the things on my **list**
is now going to introduce Watson to Sherlock in hopes that, um, Sherlock and, or, **you**	is now going to introduce Watson to Sherlock in hopes that um Sherlock and or **Watson**

Table 1: Examples of model input and predictions (blue if predicted token = true token, red otherwise).

text, but in many scenarios resource- or technical limitations make this unfeasible.

In this paper, we start addressing these questions by analyzing the language modeling behavior of OpenAI's GPT-2 (Radford et al., 2019) using a corpus of narratives available both as manually curated transcriptions and as noisier force-aligned transcripts. These manipulations make it possible to evaluate the impact of punctuation and casing removal on GPT-2's language modeling precision and uncertainty with very minimal preprocessing of the input text. By comparing next-token predictive accuracy and entropy across: a) parallel version of the corpus and b) multiple context sizes, we analyze how absence of these structural markers affects the model's ability to integrate information over longer text spans in order to formulate precise next-token predictions and reduce uncertainty.

2 Methods

2.1 Dataset

We evaluated GPT-2's language modeling behavior on next-token prediction using transcripts from the Narratives dataset (Nastase et al., 2021). The Narratives dataset, originally intended as a neural benchmark for models of language processing, includes transcripts from 27 thematically diverse audio narratives, and functional imaging (fMRI) data from participants listening to those narratives [2]. Transcripts are made available in three parallel versions: a manual transcript, cased and including punctuation (henceforth referred to as "baseline"); a cased, punctuation-stripped transcript; an uncased punctuation-stripped transcript produced by a force-aligned algorithm. Overall, each parallel version includes 42,989 words, and 1,440 of these are marked as "unknown" in the force-aligned transcript (the words not recognized by the force-alignment algorithm). These parallel versions of the corpus provide incremental manipulations of the presence of punctuation and casing (and an additional manipulation introducing lexical noise), while lexical content stays the same. To disentangle the effects of casing and lexical noise, we generated one more version of the transcripts, identical to the force-aligned transcription except for unknown tokens being replaced with lower-cased original tokens.

2.2 Procedure

For each transcript type, we evaluated GPT-2 behavior in next-token prediction in a sliding window fashion, using a 1-word stride and different window sizes (5, 10, 15, 20, 25, 30, 50 words — where words are defined by whitespace boundaries). The manipulation in window size makes it possible to assess whether and how the model's ability to integrate information over longer contexts to produce more precise next-token predictions is affected by ablation of punctuation, casing, or addition of lexical noise. For each narrative and window size, the model iterates through corresponding chunks of text across all parallel corpora: at each iteration t, input to the model will include the same lexical context for all four corpora (with the exception of corrupted tokens). For a given window size s, words $w_t, w_{t+1}, ..., w_{t+s-1}$ are joined through whitespaces, tokenized, and fed to the corpus. w_{t+s} is tokenized, and the first of the resulting token is treated as true next token to compute performance metrics.

For each iteration t and each corpus, we extract a few predictive performance and uncertainty met-

[2]Both can be accessed through DataLad (Halchenko et al., 2021) at `http://datasets.datalad.org/?dir=/labs/hasson/narratives`

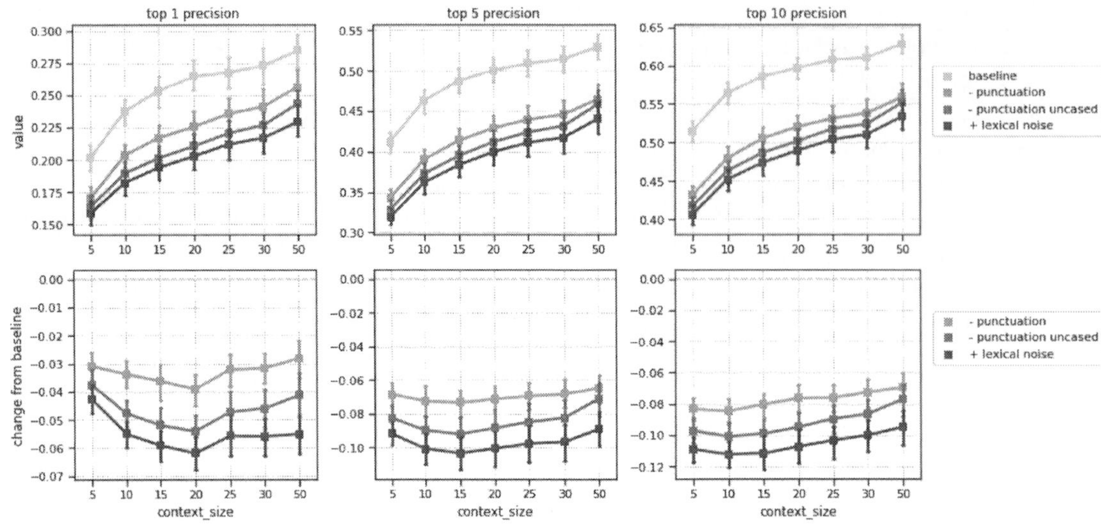

Figure 1: Proportion of cases (top: absolute values, bottom: difference from baseline) where the true word is assigned top probability (left), is among the tokens with the 5 highest probability scores (middle) or is among the tokens with the 10 highest probability scores (right), for each text type and context size. Error bars are 95% confidence intervals across narratives in the corpus.

rics. For performance, we focus on the model's precision in retrieving the true token (a more interpretable metric than cross-entropy loss). To quantify performance, we compute: a) a binary score quantifying whether the token with highest predicted probability is the true token (top 1 precision); b) a binary score quantifying whether predicted probability for the true token is one of the 5 highest predicted probability values (top 5 precision); c) a binary score quantifying whether predicted probability for the true token is among the 10 highest predicted probability values (top 10 precision). For uncertainty, we extract the entropy of the predicted probability distribution. To summarize the overall impact of punctuation, casing and lexical noise on the model's behavior, for each of these metrics we also compute correlations between values for the baseline transcript and values for each of the three manipulated versions.

3 Results

3.1 Precision

Overall, ablation of punctuation and casing and addition of lexical noise incrementally degrade precision.

Removal of punctuation contributes the most to a loss in precision (up to 4%, up to 6.5% and up to 8% for top 1, top 5 and top 10 precision respectively), while incremental casing and noise removal contribute to a smaller extent (up to 1% each for top 1 precision, and up to 2% each top 5 and top 10 precision). Overall, the model retains considerably good precision across manipulations (16-22% top 1, 35-45% top 5, and 42-53% top 10).

For all text types, precision systematically increase as context size increases, suggesting that absence of punctuation and casing does not hinder the models' ability to benefit from additional long-range information to refine its predictions. Qualitative inspection of model predictions suggests that, even when punctuation or casing are removed, the model generally produces plausible next-token predictions. Note that, for corresponding input sequences, predicted next tokens are often *different* across text types: the predicted token is the same across baseline and manipulated texts less than 10% of the time.

3.2 Uncertainty

All manipulations increase model uncertainty relative to the baseline, with punctuation having by far the largest effect. Interestingly, the effect of manipulations here interact with context size. When punctuation is available, the model benefits from the larger context to reduce its uncertainty. In absence of punctuation, however, entropy remains roughly constant across context sizes larger than 10 words (see Figure 2).

This effect is clarified by closer inspection of the predicted probability distribution (see Figure 4). In the baseline, adding context increases probability mass in the head of the distribution, which reduces entropy. In absence of punctuation, as context size increases, probabilities remain roughly the same for the highest probability token (top left panel), and they decreases for its immediate competitors (top middle panel) and for highly implausible options (bottom right panel), but the countervailing increase in probability mass in the middle of the distribution (top right to bottom center panel) causes overall model uncertainty not to decrease.

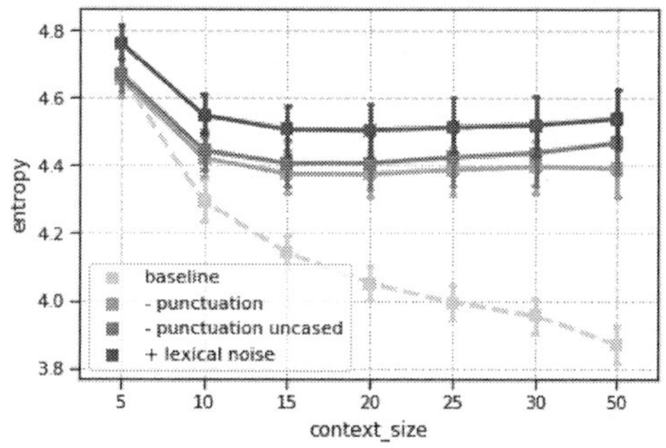

Figure 2: Entropy of the predicted probability distribution across text types and context sizes.

3.3 Overall similarity

Both next-token predictive performance metrics and entropy display medium to high correlations between baseline text and manipulated texts. Correlations range between .78 and .83 when punctuation is removed, between .72 and .77 when casing is removed, and between .69 and .73 when corrupted lexical tokens are added.

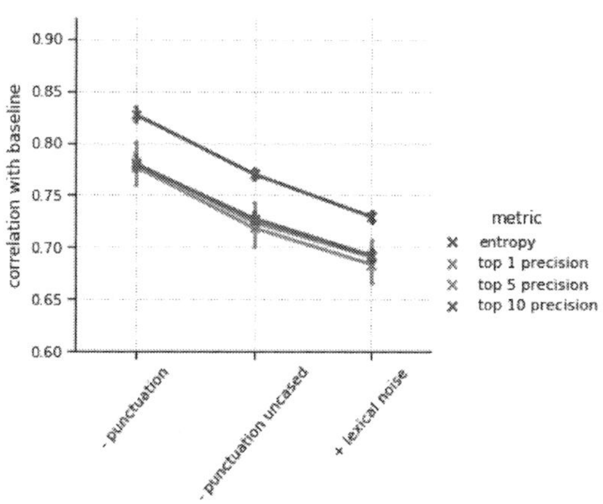

Figure 3: Correlations between baseline text and manipulated texts for both entropy and precision metrics.

4 Conclusions

We evaluated how manipulations of non-lexical markers (specifically, punctuation and casing) affects GPT-2's language modeling behavior. Absence of punctuation and casing increase uncertainty, and they decrease, but do not disrupt, model's ability to yield plausible language modeling predictions. Crucially, we observe that in absence of punctuation, GPT-2's precision increases when longer contexts are available, but — contrary to what observed for baseline text — longer contexts do *not* reduce uncertainty.

5 Limitations and future work

Our study provides a first contribution to understanding how transformers leverage structural and discourse information conveyed by non-lexical markers to perform language modeling predictions.

This study focuses uniquely on GPT-2, and the patterns observed in the present work may not generalize to other models. There are a number of factors that may modulate whether and how model behavior is significantly affected by the absence (or an inconsistent use) of non-lexical markers. Characteristics of the training corpus are one such example, with models trained on corpora including a larger proportion of unstructured text potentially being more robust than models trained mainly on highly structured text. Other relevant factors may include the mono- vs. multi-lingual nature of the model. Use of punctuation and casing is, in fact, far from consistent across languages. Multilingual models may therefore rely on non-lexical markers to a smaller extent compared to monolingual models. In a follow-up to this study, we are applying out evaluation pipeline to a wider range of pretrained models, including both models trained on forward language modeling and on masked language modeling, and including both monolingual and multilingual models.

The current study only evaluates the impact of non-lexical markers on *language modeling* performance. Yet, in most application scenarios, pretrained models are deployed in the context of downstream tasks (e.g., classification). Future iterations of this work will combine an evaluation of the effect of removing non-lexical markers on language modeling behavior with an evaluation of its impact on common downstream tasks.

Finally, this study compares GPT-2's behavior across scenarios where non-lexical markers are ei-

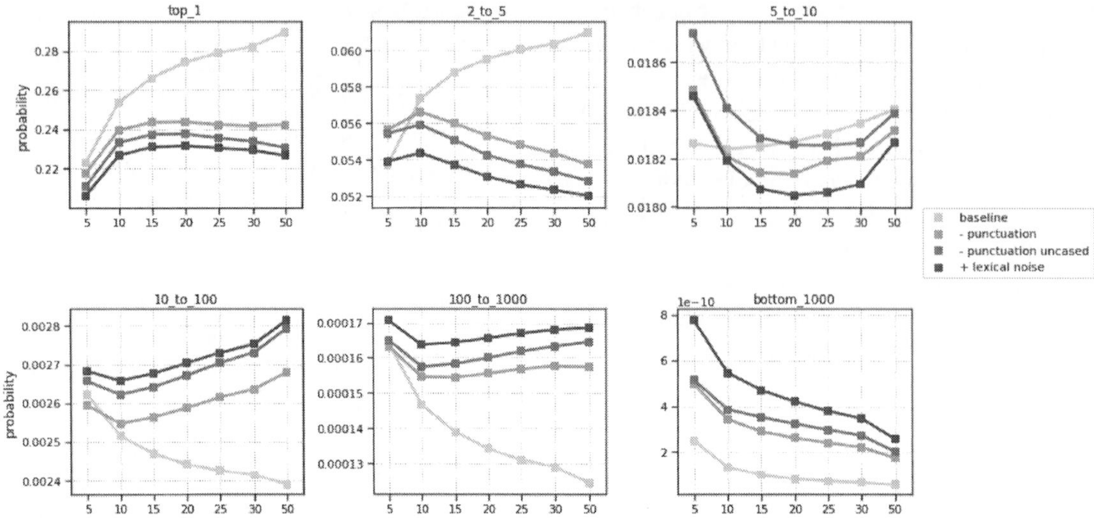

Figure 4: Average probability for the top value in the distribution (top left), 2nd to 5th top values (top middle), 5th to 10th top values (top right), 10th to 100th top values (bottom left), 100th to 1000th top values (bottom centre) and bottom 1000 values (bottom right).

ther present and used consistently or fully absent, but there are several (and perhaps more realistic) scenarios in between. Future work will also target these intermediate scenarios, using a more varied set of corpora or probabilistic text augmentation.

References

John Austin. 2019. The Book of Endless History: Authorial Use of GPT2 for Interactive Storytelling. In *Interactive Storytelling*, Lecture Notes in Computer Science, pages 429–432, Cham. Springer International Publishing.

Tom B. Brown, Benjamin Mann, Nick Ryder, Melanie Subbiah, Jared Kaplan, Prafulla Dhariwal, Arvind Neelakantan, Pranav Shyam, Girish Sastry, Amanda Askell, Sandhini Agarwal, Ariel Herbert-Voss, Gretchen Krueger, Tom Henighan, Rewon Child, Aditya Ramesh, Daniel M. Ziegler, Jeffrey Wu, Clemens Winter, Christopher Hesse, Mark Chen, Eric Sigler, Mateusz Litwin, Scott Gray, Benjamin Chess, Jack Clark, Christopher Berner, Sam McCandlish, Alec Radford, Ilya Sutskever, and Dario Amodei. 2020. Language Models are Few-Shot Learners. *arXiv:2005.14165 [cs]*. ArXiv: 2005.14165.

Maury Courtland, Adam Faulkner, and Gayle McElvain. 2020. Efficient Automatic Punctuation Restoration Using Bidirectional Transformers with Robust Inference. In *Proceedings of the 17th International Conference on Spoken Language Translation*, pages 272–279, Online. Association for Computational Linguistics.

Jacob Devlin, Ming-Wei Chang, Kenton Lee, and Kristina Toutanova. 2019. BERT: Pre-training of Deep Bidirectional Transformers for Language Understanding. *arXiv:1810.04805 [cs]*. ArXiv: 1810.04805.

Yaroslav O. Halchenko, Kyle Meyer, Benjamin Poldrack, Debanjum Singh Solanky, Adina S. Wagner, Jason Gors, Dave MacFarlane, Dorian Pustina, Vanessa Sochat, Satrajit S. Ghosh, Christian Mönch, Christopher J. Markiewicz, Laura Waite, Ilya Shlyakhter, Alejandro de la Vega, Soichi Hayashi, Christian Olaf Häusler, Jean-Baptiste Poline, Tobias Kadelka, Kusti Skytén, Dorota Jarecka, David Kennedy, Ted Strauss, Matt Cieslak, Peter Vavra, Horea-Ioan Ioanas, Robin Schneider, Mika Pflüger, James V. Haxby, Simon B. Eickhoff, and Michael Hanke. 2021. DataLad: distributed system for joint management of code, data, and their relationship. *Journal of Open Source Software*, 6(63):3262.

Danny Merkx and Stefan L. Frank. 2020. Human Sentence Processing: Recurrence or Attention? Technical report. Publication Title: arXiv e-prints ADS Bibcode: 2020arXiv200509471M Type: article.

Samuel A. Nastase, Yun-Fei Liu, Hanna Hillman, Asieh Zadbood, Liat Hasenfratz, Neggin Keshavarzian, Janice Chen, Christopher J. Honey, Yaara Yeshurun, Mor Regev, Mai Nguyen, Claire H. C. Chang, Christopher Baldassano, Olga Lositsky, Erez Simony, Michael A. Chow, Yuan Chang Leong, Paula P. Brooks, Emily Micciche, Gina Choe, Ariel Goldstein, Tamara Vanderwal, Yaroslav O. Halchenko, Kenneth A. Norman, and Uri Hasson. 2021. The "Narratives" fMRI dataset for evaluating models of naturalistic language comprehension. *Scientific Data*, 8(1).

Alec Radford, Jeffrey Wu, Rewon Child, David Luan, Dario Amodei, and Ilya Sutskever. 2019. Language Models are Unsupervised Multitask Learners.

Martin Schrimpf, Idan Asher Blank, Greta Tuckute, Carina Kauf, Eghbal A. Hosseini, Nancy Kanwisher, Joshua B. Tenenbaum, and Evelina Fedorenko. 2021. The neural architecture of language: Integrative modeling converges on predictive processing. *Proceedings of the National Academy of Sciences*, 118(45). Publisher: National Academy of Sciences Section: Biological Sciences.

Karsten Steinhauer. 2003. Electrophysiological correlates of prosody and punctuation. *Brain and Language*, 86(1):142–164.

Ashish Vaswani, Noam Shazeer, Niki Parmar, Jakob Uszkoreit, Llion Jones, Aidan N Gomez, Łukasz Kaiser, and Illia Polosukhin. 2017. Attention is All you Need. In *Advances in Neural Information Processing Systems*, volume 30. Curran Associates, Inc.

Andris Vāravs and Askars Salimbajevs. 2018. Restoring Punctuation and Capitalization Using Transformer Models. In *Statistical Language and Speech Processing*, Lecture Notes in Computer Science, pages 91–102, Cham. Springer International Publishing.

Thomas Wolf, Lysandre Debut, Victor Sanh, Julien Chaumond, Clement Delangue, Anthony Moi, Pierric Cistac, Tim Rault, Remi Louf, Morgan Funtowicz, Joe Davison, Sam Shleifer, Patrick von Platen, Clara Ma, Yacine Jernite, Julien Plu, Canwen Xu, Teven Le Scao, Sylvain Gugger, Mariama Drame, Quentin Lhoest, and Alexander Rush. 2020. Transformers: State-of-the-Art Natural Language Processing. In *Proceedings of the 2020 Conference on Empirical Methods in Natural Language Processing: System Demonstrations*, pages 38–45, Online. Association for Computational Linguistics.

Yukun Zhu, Ryan Kiros, Richard Zemel, Ruslan Salakhutdinov, Raquel Urtasun, Antonio Torralba, and Sanja Fidler. 2015. Aligning Books and Movies: Towards Story-like Visual Explanations by Watching Movies and Reading Books. *arXiv:1506.06724 [cs]*. ArXiv: 1506.06724.

Piotr Żelasko, Raghavendra Pappagari, and Najim Dehak. 2021. What Helps Transformers Recognize Conversational Structure? Importance of Context, Punctuation, and Labels in Dialog Act Recognition. *Transactions of the Association for Computational Linguistics*, 9:1163–1179.

A Appendix

original transcript. Jerry and George strolled through the airport with their suitcases. George walked quickly, grimacing as he scanned the signs to figure out which way to go. A man passing by sneezed in his direction, causing him to recoil backwards and then frantically squirt Purell onto his hands.
- punctuation. Jerry and George strolled through the airport with their suitcases George walked quickly grimacing as he scanned the signs to figure out which way to go A man passing by sneezed in his direction causing him to recoil backwards and then frantically squirt Purell onto his hands
- casing jerry and george strolled through the airport with their suitcases george walked quickly grimacing as he scanned the signs to figure out which way to go a man passing by sneezed in his direction causing him to recoil backwards and then frantically squirt purell onto his hands
- casing noised jerry and george strolled through the airport with their suitcases george walked quickly <unk> as he scanned the signs to figure out which way to go a man passing by sneezed in his direction causing him to <unk> backwards and then frantically squirt <unk> onto his hands jerry <unk> up

Table 2: Sample excerpts from different transcript types

text type	**input**	**next word**	**true token**	**predicted**
manual transcript	their suitcases. George walked quickly, grimacing as he scanned the signs to figure out which way to go. A man	passing	pass	in
- punctuation	their suitcases George walked quickly grimacing as he scanned the signs to figure out which way to go A man	passing	pass	in
- casing	their suitcases george walked quickly grimacing as he scanned the signs to figure out which way to go a man	passing	pass	in
- casing noised	their suitcases george walked quickly <unk> as he scanned the signs to figure out which way to go a man	passing	pass	was

Table 3: inputs to the model, next word, true token, and model predictions for window size 20.

Assessing Neural Referential Form Selectors on a Realistic Multilingual Dataset

Guanyi Chen[♠], **Fahime Same**[♡], and **Kees van Deemter**[♠]
[♠]Department of Information and Computing Sciences, Utrecht University
[♡]Department of Linguistics, University of Cologne
g.chen@uu.nl, f.same@uni-koeln.de, c.j.vandeemter@uu.nl

Abstract

Previous work on Neural Referring Expression Generation (REG) all uses WebNLG, an English dataset that has been shown to reflect a very limited range of referring expression (RE) use. To tackle this issue, we build a dataset based on the OntoNotes corpus that contains a broader range of RE use in both English and Chinese (a language that uses zero pronouns). We build neural Referential Form Selection (RFS) models accordingly, assess them on the dataset and conduct probing experiments. The experiments suggest that, compared to WebNLG, OntoNotes is better for assessing REG/RFS models. We compare English and Chinese RFS and confirm that in both languages BERT has the highest performance. Also, our results suggest that in line with linguistic theories, Chinese RFS depends more on discourse context than English.

1 Introduction

Referring Expression Generation (REG) In Context is a key task in the classic Natural Language Generation pipeline (Reiter and Dale, 2000; Gatt and Krahmer, 2018). Given a discourse whose referring expressions (REs) have yet to be realised and given their intended referents, it aims to develop an algorithm that generates all these REs.

Traditionally, REG In Context (hereafter REG) is a two-step process. In the first step, the Referential Form (RF) is determined, e.g. whether to use a proper name, a description, a demonstrative or a pronoun. This step is the focus of this work and will be hereafter called Referential Form Selection (RFS). In the second step, the content of the RE is determined. For example, to refer to *Joe Biden*, one needs to choose from options such as "*the president*", "*the 46th president of US*".

In recent years, many works on REG have started to use neural networks. For example, Castro Ferreira et al. (2018a); Cao and Cheung (2019); Cunha et al. (2020) have proposed to generate REs in an End2End manner, i.e., to tackle the selection of form and content simultaneously. Chen et al. (2021) used BERT (Devlin et al., 2019) to perform RFS. One commonality between these studies is that they were all tested on a benchmark dataset, namely WebNLG (Gardent et al., 2017; Castro Ferreira et al., 2018b).

However, Chen et al. (2021) and Same et al. (2022) found that WebNLG is not ideal for assessing REG/RFS algorithms because (1) it consists of rather formal texts that may not reflect everyday RE use; (2) its texts are very short and have a simple syntactic structure; and (3) most of its REs are first-mentions. These limitations led to some unexpected results when they tested their RFS models on WebNLG. For example, advanced pre-trained models (i.e., BERT) performed worse than simpler models (i.e., single-layer GRU (Cho et al., 2014)) without any pre-training. By probing[1] various RFS models, they found that though BERT encodes more linguistic information, which is crucial for RFS, it still performs worse than GRU. In this study, we are interested in *how well each RFS model performs when tested on a dataset that addresses the above limitations* – in what follows, we call this a "realistic" dataset, for short.

Additionally, all the above studies were conducted on English only. It has been pointed out that speakers of East Asian languages (e.g. Chinese and Japanese) use REs differently from speakers of Western European languages (e.g. English and Dutch; Newnham (1971)). Theoretical linguists (Huang, 1984) have suggested that East Asian languages rely more heavily on context than Western European languages (see Chen (2022) for empirical testing and computational modelling). As a result, speakers of East Asian languages frequently use Zero Pronouns (ZPs), i.e. REs that contain no words and are resolved based merely

[1]Probing is an established method to analyse whether the latent representations of a model encode certain information.

Proceedings of the 3rd Workshop on Evaluation and Comparison of NLP Systems, pages 103 - 114
November 20, 2022 ©2022 Association for Computational Linguistics

Text: Amatriciana sauce is made with Tomato. It is a traditional Italian sauce. Amatriciana is a sauce containing Tomato that comes from Italy.
Delexicialised Text: Amatriciana_sauce is made with Tomato. Amatriciana_sauce is a traditional Italy sauce. Amatriciana_sauce is a sauce containing Tomato that comes from Italy.

Table 1: An example data from the WebNLG corpus. In the delexicalised text, every entity is hlhighlighted.

on their context.[2] This poses two challenges for REG/RFS models: (1) they need to be better able to encode contextual information; (2) they need to account for an additional RF (i.e. ZP). Therefore, we are curious to see *how well each RFS model performs when tested on a language that has more RFs and relies more on context than English.*

To answer the research questions above, we construct a "realistic" multilingual dataset of English and Chinese and try different model architectures, such as models with/without pre-trained word embeddings, and models incorporating BERT. We report the results and compare model behaviours on English and Chinese subsets. The code used in this study is available at: https://github.com/a-quei/probe-neuralreg.

2 Referential Form Selection (RFS)

Using WebNLG, Castro Ferreira et al. (2018a) redefined the REG task in order to accommodate deep learning techniques. Subsequently, Chen et al. (2021) adapted the definition to fit the RFS task. The first step is to remove from each RE all information about the RF of that RE. Concretely, as shown in Table 1, Castro Ferreira et al. (2018a) first "delexicalised" each text in WebNLG by assigning a general entity tag to each entity and replacing all REs referring to that entity with that tag. In most cases, a tag is assigned to an entity by replacing whitespaces in its proper name with underscores, e.g. "*Amatriciana sauce*" to "*Amatriciana_sauce*".

For a target referent $x^{(r)}$ (e.g. the second "*Amatriciana_sauce*" in Table 1), given the referent, its pre-context in the discourse $x^{(pre)}$ (e.g. "*Amatriciana_sauce is made with Tomato.*") and its post-context $x^{(post)}$ (e.g. "*is a traditional Italy sauce. Amatriciana_sauce is a sauce containing Tomato that comes from Italy.*"), the RFS task is to decide the proper RF $\hat{f}$ (e.g., pronoun).

EN	4-Way	Demonstrative, Description, Proper Name, Pronoun
	3-Way	Description, Proper Name, Pronoun
	2-Way	Non-pronominal, Pronominal
ZH	5-Way	Demonstrative, Description, Proper Name, Pronoun, ZP
	4-Way	Description, Proper Name, Pronoun, ZP
	3-Way	Non-pronominal, Pronoun, ZP
	2-Way	Overt Referring Expression, ZP

Table 2: Types of RF classification and possible classes. Demonstratives are grouped with descriptions in 3-way EN and 4-way ZH classifications under the category *Description*. The category *Non-pronominal* contains proper names, descriptions, and demonstratives.

3 Dataset Construction

To construct a realistic multilingual REG/RFS dataset, we used the Chinese and English portions of the OntoNotes dataset[3] whose contents come from six sources, namely broadcast news, newswires, broadcast conversations, telephone conversations, web blogs, and magazines. We call the resulting Chinese subset OntoNotes-ZH and the English subset OntoNotes-EN. In the following, we describe the construction process.

First, for each RE in OntoNotes, we used the 3 previous sentences as the pre-context and the 3 subsequent sentences as the post-context. Similar to Chen et al. (2021), we are interested in different RF classification tasks. For Chinese, for example, we not only have a 2-way classification task where models have to decide whether to use a ZP or an overt RE, but also a 5-way task where models have to choose from a more fine-grained list of possible RFs. Table 2 lists all categories in both OntoNotes-EN and OntoNotes-ZH. Using the constituency syntax tree of the sentence containing the target referent and the surface form of the target, we automatically annotated each RE with its RF category. For example, an RE is considered a demonstrative if it is annotated in the syntax tree as a noun phrase and its surface form contains a demonstrative determiner.

Second, we excluded all coreferential chains consisting only of pronouns and ZPs. The pronominal

[2] For example, consider the question in Chinese: "你看见比尔了吗？" (*Have you see Bill?*). A Chinese speaker can reply "∅看见∅了。" (∅ *saw* ∅.) where the two ∅ are ZPs that refer to the speaker himself/herself and "Bill" respectively.

[3] OntoNotes is licensed under the Linguistic Data Consortium: https://catalog.ldc.upenn.edu/LDC2013T19.

	WebNLG	O-EN	O-ZH
Percentage of First Mentions	85%	43%	43%
Percentage of Proper Names	71%	21%	15%
Average Number of Tokens	18.62	106.44	139.55

Table 3: Statistics of WebNLG and OntoNotes. O-EN and O-ZH stand for OntoNotes-EN and OntoNotes-ZH.

chains consist mainly of first/second-person referents, and we do not expect much variation in referential form in these cases. In other words, we only included the chains that have *at least* one overt non-pronominal RE.

Third, we delexicalised the corpus following Castro Ferreira et al. (2018a). Additionally, since we used the Chinese BERT as one of our RFS models and it only accepts input shorter than 512 characters, we removed all samples in OntoNotes-ZH whose total length (calculated by removing all underscores introduced during delexicalisation and summing the length of pre-contexts, post-contexts, and target referents) is longer than 512 characters. Experiments with models other than BERT on the original OntoNotes-ZH show that this does not bias the conclusions of this study (see Appendix A).

Last, we split the whole dataset into a training set and a test set in accordance with the CoNLL 2012 Shared Task (Pradhan et al., 2012). Since ZPs in Chinese are only annotated in the training and development sets, following Chen and Ng (2016), Chen et al. (2018), and Yin et al. (2018), we used the development set as the test set and sampled 10% of the documents from the training set as the development data. Thus, we obtained OntoNotes-EN, where the training, development, and test sets contain 71667, 8149, and 7619 samples, respectively, and OntoNotes-ZH, where the training, development, and test sets contain 70428, 9217, and 11607 samples, respectively.

OntoNotes vs. WebNLG. Based on the nature of OntoNotes and the statistics in Table 3, we observe that: (1) the WebNLG data is all from DBPedia, while the OntoNotes data is multi-genre; (2) OntoNotes has a much smaller proportion of first mentions and proper names; and (3) the documents in OntoNotes are on average much longer than those in WebNLG.

Another difference between WebNLG and OntoNotes is in the ratio of seen and unseen entities in their test sets. Castro Ferreira et al. (2018b) divided the documents in the WebNLG's test set into *seen* (where all the data come from the same domains as the training data) and *unseen* (where all the data come from different domains than the training data). Almost all referents from the seen test set appear in the training set (9580 out of 9644), while only a few referents from the unseen test set appear in the training set (688 out of 9644). [4] In OntoNotes, 38.44% and 41.45% of the referents in the test sets of OntoNotes-EN and OntoNotes-ZH also appear in the training sets.

Having said this, OntoNotes largely mitigates the problems of WebNLG discussed in §1. If OntoNotes is a "better" and more "representative" corpus for assessing REG/RFS models, we can expect more "expected" results: models with pre-training outperform those without, and models that learn more useful linguistic information outperform those that learn less. We will detail our expectations in §5.

4 Modelling RFS

We introduce how we represent entities and how we adapt the RFS models of Chen et al. (2021).

4.1 Entity Representation

Unlike WebNLG, whose 99.34% of referents in the test set appear in the training set, the majority of referents in OntoNotes do not appear in both training and test sets. This means that RFS models should be able to handle unseen referents, but mapping each entity to a general entity tag with underscores would prevent the models from doing so (Cao and Cheung, 2019; Cunha et al., 2020) because entity tags of unseen entities are usually out-of-vocabulary (OOV) words. Additionally, when incorporating pre-trained word embeddings and language models, using entity tags prevents entity representations from benefiting from these pre-trained models (again since the entity tags of unseen entities are usually OOV words).

Similar to Cunha et al. (2020), we replaced underscores in general entity tags (e.g. "*Amatriciana_sauce*") with whitespaces (henceforth, lexical tags, e.g. "*Amatriciana sauce*"). Arguably, there is a trade-off between using entity tags and using lexical tags. In contrast to lexical tags, the use of entity tags helps models identify mentions of the same entity in discourse, which has been shown to be a crucial feature for RFS. However, using entity tags prevents models from dealing with

[4] Chen et al. (2021) used only seen entities because the size of the underlying triples of the unseen test set differs from both the training set and seen test set.

unseen entities and reduces the benefit of using pre-trained language models. In §6.3, we compare the performance of using entity tags and lexical tags.

4.2 RFS Models

To build the RFS models, we use the two neural models from Chen et al. (2021): c-RNN and ConATT. Given the task definition in §2, models take pre-context $x^{(pre)}$, target referent $x^{(r)}$, and post-context $x^{(post)}$ as inputs. As a result of using lexical tags, each target referent is no longer a single tag, but a sequence of tokens. In other words, instead of being $\{w_i\}$, $x^{(r)}$ is $\{w_i, w_{i+1}, ..., w_j\}$. The other two inputs are pre-context $x^{(pre)} = \{w_1, w_2, ..., w_{i-1}\}$ and post-context $x^{(post)} = \{w_{j+1}, w_{j+1}, ..., w_n\}$. The architectures of the models are as follows:

c-RNN. c-RNN concatenates $x^{(pre)}$, $x^{(r)}$ and $x^{(post)}$, and uses a single bidirectional GRU to encode them all. Formally, we obtain a sequence of hidden representations by $h = \text{BiGRU}([x^{(pre)}, x^{(r)}, x^{(post)}])$. We then use the summation of the hidden representations at the beginning and the end of the target referent (i.e., i and j) for calculating the final representation:

$$R = ReLU(W_f[h_i + h_j]), \quad (1)$$

where W_f is the weight in the feed-forward layer. R is then used for predicting the RF:

$$P(\hat{f}|x^{(pre)}, x^{(r)}, x^{(post)}) = \text{Softmax}(W_c R), \quad (2)$$

where W_c is the weight in the output layer. x can be initialised randomly or initialised by pre-trained word embeddings or language models. We tested both the vanilla c-RNN and c-RNN, whose input layer is initialised by pre-trained word embeddings or by BERT.

ConATT. ConATT first encodes $x^{(pre)}$, $x^{(r)}$ and $x^{(post)}$ separately using three bidirectional GRUs and three self-attention modules (Yang et al., 2016). For each input $x^{(k)}$, we first obtain $h^{(k)}$ using a BiGRU: $h^{(k)} = \text{BiGRU}(x^{(k)})$. Subsequently, given the total M steps in $h^{(k)}$, we first calculate the attention weight $\alpha_j^{(k)}$ at each step j by:

$$\alpha_j^{(k)} = \frac{\exp(e_j^{(k)})}{\sum_{m=1}^{M} \exp(e_m^{(k)})}, \quad (3)$$

where $e_j^{(k)} = v_a^{(k)T} \tanh(W_a^{(k)} h_j^{(k)})$, v_a is the attention vector and W_a is the weight in the attention layer. The context representation of $x^{(k)}$ is then the weighted sum of $h^{(k)}$: $c^{(k)} = \sum_{j=1}^{N} \alpha_j^{(k)} h^{(k)}$.

After obtaining $c^{(pre)}$, $c^{(r)}$ and $c^{(post)}$, we concatenate them with the target entity embedding $x^{(r)}$, and pass it through a feed forward network to obtain the final representation:

$$R = \text{ReLU}(W_f[c^{(pre)}, c^{(r)}, c^{(post)}]), \quad (4)$$

where $[\cdot, \cdot]$ represents a concatenation operation. The prediction is made using Equation 2. The input layer of ConATT is initialised either randomly or by pre-trained word embeddings.

5 Hypotheses

OntoNotes reflects a broader range of RE use and is, therefore, more appropriate as a source of insights into the human use of REs. Thus, it is plausible to expect that the "unexpected results" of §1 will not occur when assessing RFS models (see §4) on OntoNotes. More specifically, we expect:

$\mathcal{H}_1$ models that incorporate pre-training (i.e., pre-trained word embeddings and BERT, which has been proved to be effective in many NLP tasks) work better than those that do not;

$\mathcal{H}_2$ ConATT, which has been shown to perform well on both REG (Castro Ferreira et al., 2018a) and co-reference resolution (Yin et al., 2018), works better than c-RNN;

$\mathcal{H}_3$ models that learn more useful linguistic information (confirmed by probing experiments) perform better than those that learn less.

Comparing Chinese and English, we can see in Table 2 that Chinese has an additional category compared to English, namely ZP. Given the theory that Chinese speakers process ZPs in the same way as pronouns (Yang et al., 1999), we expect:

$\mathcal{H}_4$ RFS models that work well in English would also work well in Chinese.

Additionally, since Chinese relies more on context than English (see §1), it is plausible to expect:

$\mathcal{H}_5$ Chinese RFS models would benefit more from the use of contextual representations (i.e., BERT) than English RFS models.

Model	4-way P	4-way R	4-way F	3-way P	3-way R	3-way F	2-way P	2-way R	2-way F
XGBoost	48.96	49.69	49.12	67.78	65.78	66.44	79.11	78.01	78.42
c-RNN	65.45	60.59	62.38	68.19	69.19	68.55	76.66	75.23	75.70
+Glove	66.06	63.39	64.56	69.94	70.14	70.01	77.61	76.31	76.67
+BERT	**73.57**	**75.94**	**74.59** (+19.57%)	**80.53**	**81.81**	**81.03** (+18.21%)	**87.21**	**86.97**	**87.08** (+15.03%)
ConATT	61.29	62.21	61.58	66.34	65.87	66.01	73.19	73.21	73.19
+Glove	63.71	61.70	62.51	67.18	66.88	67.00	75.17	74.48	74.75

Table 4: Evaluation results of the English RFS systems on OntoNotes-EN with lexical tags. Best results are **boldfaced**, whereas the second best results are underlined. "P", "R" and "F" stand for macro-averaged precision, recall and F1 score. Each percentage below the F-score of BERT indicates how much c-RNN gains from using BERT compared to not using BERT.

Model	5-way P	5-way R	5-way F	4-way P	4-way R	4-way F	3-way P	3-way R	3-way F	2-way P	2-way R	2-way F
XGBoost	38.17	40.06	34.59	46.16	44.12	41.29	56.19	54.64	51.98	64.5	79.56	63.67
c-RNN	52.42	48.49	49.62	54.60	54.65	54.19	56.78	53.50	54.68	67.66	62.89	64.59
+SGNS	54.54	51.27	51.56	57.78	56.75	57.16	59.57	56.19	57.46	67.74	65.33	66.37
+BERT	**64.99**	**63.60**	**63.85** (+28.68%)	**68.22**	**69.48**	**68.17** (+25.80%)	**70.36**	**68.60**	**69.13** (+26.43%)	**78.35**	**73.51**	**75.59** (+17.03%)
ConATT	51.78	48.28	49.25	54.27	53.08	52.98	53.67	49.47	50.79	63.25	56.92	58.28
+SGNS	55.44	52.13	53.09	55.88	54.94	54.18	55.01	53.06	53.87	64.98	61.38	62.69

Table 5: Evaluation results of the Chinese RFS systems on OntoNotes-ZH.

6 Experiments

In what follows, we first provide an overview of the implementation details of the RFS models. To understand what linguistic information can be learnt by each model, we introduce a series of probing experiments. We then discuss the performance of these models and answer the hypotheses.

6.1 Baseline and Implementation Details

Following Chen et al. (2021), we used a feature-based model, XGBoost (Chen et al., 2015), as our baseline. For pre-trained word embeddings, we used Glove (Pennington et al., 2014) for English and SGNS (Li et al., 2018) for Chinese; for BERT, we used "bert-base-cased" for English and "bert-base-chinese" for Chinese.[5] Since Chinese BERT is a character-based model, we use all Chinese models character-based. The results of the word-based models can be found in Appendix B.

We tuned the hyper-parameters of each of our neural models on the development set and chose the setting with the best macro F1 score. For training, we used a single Tesla V100. For the baseline XGBoost models, we set the learning rate to 0.05, the minimum split loss to 0.01, the maximum depth of a tree to 5, and the sub-sample ratio of the training instances to 0.5. We report macro-averaged precision, recall, and F1 on the test set. We run each model 5x and report the average performance.

6.2 Probing RFS Models

To test the hypotheses in §5 (especially $\mathcal{H}_3$), we probed each RFS model using probing classifiers. Specifically, after training an RFS model, we extracted its hidden representations and used them to train a probing classifier for a particular linguistic feature. The performance of the probing classifier indicates how well the RFS model learns the feature (Belinkov et al., 2017; Giulianelli et al., 2018).

Probing Tasks. We used the probing tasks defined in Chen et al. (2021). These tasks pertain

[5](1) English Glove: https://nlp.stanford.edu/projects/glove/; (2) Chinese SGNS: https://github.com/Embedding/Chinese-Word-Vectors; (3) English BERT: huggingface.co/bert-base-cased; and (4) Chinese BERT: https://huggingface.co/bert-base-chinese.

Model	Type	DisStat	SenStat	Syn	DistAnt	IntRef	LocPro	GloPro
Random	-	49.99 (49.77)	33.06 (32.27)	50.10 (50.10)	25.17 (23.75)	33.09 (32.40)	49.94 (48.21)	50.38 (49.53)
Majority	-	55.95 (35.88)	44.05 (20.39)	50.14 (33.39)	44.05 (15.29)	44.05 (20.39)	68.08 (40.50)	63.08 (38.68)
c-RNN	4-way	64.73 (63.39)	54.41 (50.76)	74.73 (74.67)	51.66 (36.31)	50.52 (44.81)	74.57 (67.86)	63.89 (50.32)
	3-way	64.24 (63.30)	53.94 (50.45)	75.57 (75.55)	52.02 (36.78)	49.76 (42.83)	74.96 (68.26)	64.00 (49.71)
	2-way	64.45 (63.31)	53.55 (49.72)	73.90 (73.82)	51.55 (35.75)	49.67 (43.03)	73.50 (65.72)	63.39 (45.76)
c-RNN +GloVe	4-way	65.00 (64.24)	54.40 (51.39)	76.75 (76.75)	51.95 (37.09)	50.65 (44.94)	74.25 (67.26)	64.14 (51.44)
	3-way	65.17 (64.44)	55.14 (52.69)	78.06 (78.06)	52.81 (37.55)	50.73 (45.89)	75.46 (70.66)	64.67 (53.28)
	2-way	65.07 (64.26)	53.55 (49.34)	75.22 (75.06)	51.20 (35.87)	50.78 (45.04)	73.91 (67.22)	63.26 (47.49)
c-RNN +BERT	4-way	86.00 (85.67)	72.17 (69.46)	79.83 (79.73)	66.53 (50.36)	69.85 (65.99)	82.32 (80.08)	68.47 (60.06)
	3-way	83.74 (83.42)	71.56 (68.90)	81.17 (81.15)	65.35 (49.10)	68.03 (63.62)	85.05 (82.38)	67.82 (61.93)
	2-way	81.82 (81.12)	69.33 (67.07)	78.05 (77.89)	63.46 (47.97)	65.11 (62.06)	81.85 (77.45)	66.35 (53.37)
ConATT	4-way	64.37 (62.95)	52.20 (46.63)	73.37 (73.34)	49.74 (33.33)	49.55 (43.52)	74.04 (66.30)	63.57 (48.89)
	3-way	64.28 (61.87)	51.96 (45.92)	74.79 (74.76)	49.25 (31.91)	49.21 (41.64)	73.89 (67.51)	63.25 (48.61)
	2-way	62.07 (59.46)	49.45 (41.73)	64.44 (63.72)	48.05 (30.18)	47.85 (40.85)	71.24 (59.96)	63.32 (47.51)
ConATT +GloVe	4-way	65.39 (63.41)	53.51 (50.49)	79.96 (79.95)	51.51 (36.03)	50.52 (43.17)	76.05 (70.27)	63.79 (49.86)
	3-way	63.72 (61.79)	52.13 (45.39)	79.03 (79.00)	49.48 (33.03)	49.43 (41.53)	74.86 (68.46)	63.31 (48.97)
	2-way	63.77 (61.56)	50.73 (44.35)	74.20 (73.97)	48.77 (31.53)	49.24 (42.81)	72.31 (63.31)	63.15 (48.39)

Table 6: Results of the English RFS models on each probing task on the OntoNotes-EN dataset. A in A(B) is the accuracy and B is the macro F1.

to four classes of features, namely referential status (DisStat and SenStat), syntactic position (Syn), recency (DistAnt and IntRef), and discourse structure prominence (LocPro, GloPro). These features have been shown to matter for RFS in linguistic literature (Ariel, 1990; Gundel et al., 1993; Arnold, 2010; von Heusinger and Schumacher, 2019). The definition of each probing task is as follows: (1) **DisStat**: This feature has 2 values: (a) `discourse-old` (the entity appeared in the previous context), and (b) `discourse-new` (it did not); (2) **SenStat**: The sentence-level referential status feature has 3 values: (a) `sentence-new` (the RE is the first mention of the entity in the sentence), (b) `sentence-old` (the RE is not the first mention of the entity in the sentence), and (c) `first-mention` (the RE is the first mention of the entity in the discourse); (3) **Syn**: The syntax probing task is a binary classification task with values (a) `subject` and (b) `object`; (4) **DistAnt**: It contains four values: the entity and its antecedent are (a) in `same` sentence, (b) `one` sentence apart, (c) `more than one` sentence apart, and (d) the entity is a `first-mention` (to distinguish first mentions from subsequent mentions); (5) **IntRef**: This feature asks whether there is an intervening referent between the target RE and its nearest antecedent. There are 3 possible values: (a) the target entity is a `first-mention`, (b) the previous RE refers to the `same entity`, and (c) the previous RE refers to a `different entity`; (6) **LocPro**: is a hybrid of DisStat and Syn. It has 2 values: (a) `locally prominent`, and (b) `not locally prominent`. An entity is said to be locally prominent if it is both "discourse- old" and "realised as a subject"; (7) **GloPro**: This is a binary feature with two possible values: (a) globally prominent, and (b) not globally prominent. The

Model	Type	DisStat	SenStat	Syn	DistAnt	IntRef	LocPro	GloPro
Random	-	50.20 (49.93)	33.18 (32.70)	50.11 (49.79)	25.02 (23.81)	33.56 (33.01)	50.12 (46.44)	50.00 (44.27)
Majority	-	57.30 (36.43)	42.70 (19.95)	57.79 (36.62)	42.70 (14.96)	42.70 (19.95)	76.27 (43.27)	81.13 (45.09)
c-RNN	5-way	65.14 (62.80)	48.85 (45.89)	76.79 (75.94)	46.50 (28.49)	48.72 (45.78)	79.12 (65.54)	82.57 (52.03)
	4-way	64.60 (61.80)	48.76 (43.39)	76.30 (74.74)	45.75 (27.73)	47.84 (44.65)	79.11 (63.44)	81.97 (46.64)
	3-way	63.55 (61.19)	47.52 (41.52)	77.13 (76.11)	45.69 (26.43)	46.60 (41.13)	78.11 (61.70)	82.02 (45.76)
	2-way	61.32 (58.06)	46.09 (36.30)	77.95 (76.96)	45.23 (24.11)	45.71 (36.49)	77.86 (58.82)	82.11 (45.54)
c-RNN +SGNS	5-way	65.75 (63.52)	50.24 (47.24)	78.36 (77.28)	47.48 (30.71)	49.66 (46.13)	79.33 (66.11)	82.21 (50.37)
	4-way	66.07 (62.90)	50.93 (46.96)	78.41 (77.18)	47.64 (30.78)	50.57 (47.81)	80.11 (66.16)	82.24 (48.20)
	3-way	64.70 (62.87)	48.24 (42.54)	79.02 (77.81)	46.27 (27.51)	47.48 (43.59)	79.35 (64.17)	82.01 (46.11)
	2-way	62.48 (60.45)	46.30 (38.24)	78.50 (77.12)	45.38 (24.27)	44.82 (37.61)	77.72 (64.09)	81.93 (46.12)
c-RNN +BERT	5-way	76.17 (75.20)	59.58 (57.07)	79.42 (78.68)	56.14 (39.54)	59.89 (57.69)	81.86 (70.93)	82.05 (55.17)
	4-way	75.32 (73.96)	59.69 (57.66)	78.86 (78.15)	56.66 (37.12)	60.27 (56.90)	81.95 (69.68)	81.96 (46.60)
	3-way	74.46 (73.77)	58.41 (56.29)	80.48 (79.67)	55.91 (35.77)	59.39 (55.96)	82.71 (73.24)	81.91 (45.59)
	2-way	69.20 (68.10)	55.16 (52.08)	80.68 (79.84)	51.74 (29.71)	51.73 (52.36)	81.43 (71.30)	82.05 (45.07)
ConATT	5-way	65.36 (62.33)	48.50 (43.17)	75.14 (73.94)	46.44 (28.92)	48.25 (45.05)	78.90 (63.99)	82.02 (47,16)
	4-way	65.07 (61.91)	48.40 (43.15)	70.38 (67.48)	45.95 (26.41)	48.16 (44.15)	77.89 (57.31)	82.22 (47.27)
	3-way	62.93 (59.54)	45.14 (39.55)	70.38 (68.78)	43.85 (24.47)	45.28 (39.13)	77.34 (55.27)	82.06 (45.73)
	2-way	60.55 (52.10)	44.21 (32.85)	68.33 (65.67)	43.75 (21.78)	44.36 (32.66)	76.37 (49.38)	82.07 (45.35)
ConATT +SGNS	5-way	66.65 (63.48)	49.57 (45.60)	78.18 (77.27)	46.34 (29.77)	49.76 (46.84)	79.35 (64.16)	81.65 (50.72)
	4-way	66.09 (61.97)	49.43 (44.63)	75.87 (74.65)	46.04 (28.19)	49.20 (46.61)	79.50 (64.49)	82.22 (47.27)
	3-way	62.84 (58.79)	46.51 (38.78)	75.15 (74.09)	44.99 (24.66)	45.76 (38.51)	78.12 (60.19)	82.06 (45.73)
	2-way	62.65 (60.09)	46.76 (39.53)	74.17 (72.90)	44.31 (22.13)	44.84 (34.88)	77.53 (61.43)	82.07 (45.35)

Table 7: Results of the Chinese RFS models on each probing task on the OntoNotes-ZH.

most frequent entity in a text is marked as globally prominent.

Probing Classifiers. Following Chen et al. (2021), we use a logistic regression classifier as our probing classifier. When probing, we use R (see Equation 1 and 4) of the models with the best RFS performance on the development set as input representations. We evaluate probing classifiers using the accuracy and macro-averaged F1 scores. We run each probing classifier 5 times and report the averaged value. We use 2 baselines: (1) `random`: it randomly assigns a label to each input; and (2) `majority`: it assigns the most frequent label in the given probing task to the inputs.

6.3 Experimental Results

Results on each Language. Table 4 and 5 show the results of each model on OntoNotes-EN and OntoNotes-ZH. In both languages, all neural RFS models defeat the baseline in 4-way and 5-way classifications, while models that does not use BERT have on-par or worse performance in 3-way and 2-way classifications. This suggests that feature-based models with linguistically-informed features

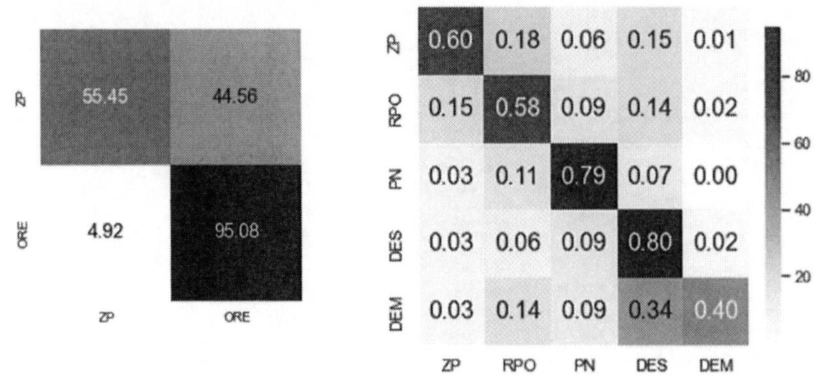

Figure 1: Confusion Matrix for Chinese 2-way c-RNN +BERT (left) and 5-way c-RNN +BERT (right) where ORE is overt RE, PRO is pronoun, PN is proper name, DES is description, and DEM is demonstrative.

	4-way			3-way			2-way		
Model	P	R	F	P	R	F	P	R	F
c-RNN	50.77	45.89	46.38	60.83	59.56	59.94	73.33	72.58	72.84
+Glove	53.47	**49.49**	**50.44**	**61.72**	**60.66**	**60.98**	**75.06**	**73.96**	**74.32**
ConATT	52.32	45.88	46.89	59.66	58.71	59.08	71.86	71.38	71.56
+Glove	**54.55**	47.56	48.14	59.75	60.05	59.85	73.84	72.32	72.66

Table 8: Evaluation results of RFS systems on OntoNotes-EN with entity tags.

can build remarkably good systems for RFS, but their performance decreases dramatically as the task becomes more fine-grained.

As for $\mathcal{H}_1$, word embeddings always improve RFS performance. The RFS tasks in both languages benefit strongly from using BERT. For instance, if we compare c-RNN +BERT to c-RNN for the full RFS tasks (i.e., 5-way classification in Chinese and 4-way classification in English), c-RNN +BERT improves the performance (F1 score) from 62.38 to 74.59 in English and from 49.62 to 63.85 in Chinese.

In both languages, contrary to our expectation $\mathcal{H}_2$, ConATT performs worse than c-RNN. Probing results presented in Tables 6 and 7 provide some explanations: in English, ConATT learns less information about referential status, syntactic position, and recency than c-RNN, and in Chinese, ConATT performs significantly worse than c-RNN in acquiring information about syntactic position.

Meanwhile, the results of the probing experiments suggest that expectation $\mathcal{H}_3$, that models that learn more useful information perform better, is true. Further evidence is provided by the observations that (1) BERT defeats all other models in almost all probing tasks and, therefore, defeats all other models by a large margin; and (2) pre-trained word embeddings (GloVe and SGNS) help each model learn significantly more information about almost every feature except GloPro, and, therefore, improve RFS performance.

English vs. Chinese. In line with our expectation $\mathcal{H}_4$, models that work well for English also work well on modelling ZP in Chinese. However, deciding whether to use a ZP or an overt RE is generally harder than pronominalisation. For example, c-RNN achieves an F-score of 75.7 for the English 2-way task, while it is only 64.6 for Chinese.

Figure 1 shows the confusion matrices for the Chinese c-RNN +BERT 2-way and 5-way classifications. By comparing them, we find that fine-grained supervision helps with the choice between ZPs and overt REs. Focusing on 5-way classification, ZPs are quite often confused with pronouns. Linguistic theory suggests that attenuated forms such as pronouns and ZPs happen when the target referent is salient enough (Ariel, 2001). It is understandable that ZPs and pronouns are confused because it is hard for a model to make such a fine-grained decision about when the target referent is salient enough for pronominalisation but not for pro-drop.

The results of both Chinese and English RFS tasks improve dramatically when using the contextual language model BERT. This is consistent with the probing results: in both languages, BERT helps a lot in acquiring all linguistic information except GloPro. To test our last hypothesis $\mathcal{H}_5$, we compute how much c-RNN gains from using BERT compared to not using BERT and report the numbers in Table 4 and 5. On average, c-RNN gains 17.60% from using BERT in English and 24.48% in Chinese. The results suggest that Chinese RFS benefits more from using BERT than English RFS. Nevertheless, we still cannot make conclusive statements about $\mathcal{H}_5$. Strictly speaking, these percentages are not directly comparable and the comparison cannot be fully controlled because for example: (1) the data is not fully parallel, and (2) the RFS tasks defined for the two languages differ from each other. For instance, unlike English RFS, Chinese RFS considers an extra category, namely ZP.

Lexical Tags vs. Entity Tags. To chart the benefits of lexical tags, we also ran models of Chen et al. (2021) on a version of OntoNotes-EN, in which entity tags are used instead of lexical tags. The results are presented in Table 8. Comparing this table to Table 4, we see that the performance of each model decreases significantly when the entity tags are used, especially in the 4-way and 3-way classifications. For example, the F-score of the 4-way c-RNN +Glove model decreases from 64.56 to 50.44. As expected, these tags prevent the models from handling unseen entities.

7 Conclusion

To address the problem that all previous assessments of neural REG/RFS models were only tested on WebNLG, we built a realistic multilingual (English and Chinese) dataset based on the OntoNotes dataset, modified the RFS models accordingly and assessed them on this dataset. Although a few outcomes were against our expectations (e.g. ConATT performed worse than c-RNN), we found that our results are explainable using probing experiments. For example, models that use BERT, which performs best in the probing experiments, also beats all other models in RFS.

We also compared the English RFS to the Chinese RFS, which uses ZPs frequently and depends more on context than English. We found that RFS models that work for English can also model Chinese ZPs. In line with the idea that Chinese relies more on context than English, the results suggest that Chinese RFS models benefited more from using contextualised language model BERT than those of English. However, as discussed, this needs to be further verified with more controlled experiments.

In future, we plan to extend our work from the following three perspectives: (1) testing other model explanation techniques, e.g., probing classifiers with control tasks (Hewitt and Liang, 2019) and attention analysis (Bibal et al., 2022); (2) assessing and probing RFS models on other languages (such as languages that are morphologically rich); and (3) trying more probing tasks based on factors that influence RFS, such as animacy, competition and positional attributes (see Same and van Deemter (2020) for more details).

References

Mira Ariel. 1990. *Accessing Noun-Phrase Antecedents*. Routledge.

Mira Ariel. 2001. Accessibility theory: An overview. In Ted Sanders, Joost Schilperoord, and Wilbert Spooren, editors, *Text Representation: Linguistic and psycholinguistic aspects*, volume 8, page 29. John Benjamins Publishing Company.

Jennifer E Arnold. 2010. How speakers refer: The role of accessibility. *Language and Linguistics Compass*, 4(4):187–203.

Yonatan Belinkov, Nadir Durrani, Fahim Dalvi, Hassan Sajjad, and James Glass. 2017. What do neural machine translation models learn about morphology? In *Proceedings of the 55th Annual Meeting of the Association for Computational Linguistics (Volume 1: Long Papers)*, pages 861–872, Vancouver, Canada. Association for Computational Linguistics.

Adrien Bibal, Rémi Cardon, David Alfter, Rodrigo Wilkens, Xiaoou Wang, Thomas François, and Patrick Watrin. 2022. Is attention explanation? an introduction to the debate. In *Proceedings of the 60th Annual Meeting of the Association for Computational Linguistics (Volume 1: Long Papers)*, pages 3889–3900, Dublin, Ireland. Association for Computational Linguistics.

Meng Cao and Jackie Chi Kit Cheung. 2019. Referring expression generation using entity profiles. In *Proceedings of the 2019 Conference on Empirical Methods in Natural Language Processing and the 9th International Joint Conference on Natural Language Processing (EMNLP-IJCNLP)*, pages 3163–3172, Hong Kong, China. Association for Computational Linguistics.

Thiago Castro Ferreira, Diego Moussallem, Ákos Kádár, Sander Wubben, and Emiel Krahmer. 2018a. NeuralREG: An end-to-end approach to referring expression generation. In *Proceedings of the 56th Annual Meeting of the Association for Computational Linguistics (Volume 1: Long Papers)*, pages 1959–1969, Melbourne, Australia. Association for Computational Linguistics.

Thiago Castro Ferreira, Diego Moussallem, Emiel Krahmer, and Sander Wubben. 2018b. Enriching the WebNLG corpus. In *Proceedings of the 11th International Conference on Natural Language Generation*, pages 171–176, Tilburg University, The Netherlands. Association for Computational Linguistics.

Chen Chen and Vincent Ng. 2016. Chinese zero pronoun resolution with deep neural networks. In *Proceedings of the 54th Annual Meeting of the Association for Computational Linguistics (Volume 1: Long Papers)*, pages 778–788, Berlin, Germany. Association for Computational Linguistics.

Guanyi Chen. 2022. *Computational Generation of Chinese Noun Phrases*. Ph.D. thesis, Utrecht University.

Guanyi Chen, Fahime Same, and Kees van Deemter. 2021. What can neural referential form selectors learn? In *Proceedings of the 14th International Conference on Natural Language Generation*, pages 154–166, Aberdeen, Scotland, UK. Association for Computational Linguistics.

Guanyi Chen, Kees van Deemter, and Chenghua Lin. 2018. Modelling pro-drop with the rational speech acts model. In *Proceedings of the 11th International Conference on Natural Language Generation*, pages 159–164, Tilburg University, The Netherlands. Association for Computational Linguistics.

Tianqi Chen, Tong He, Michael Benesty, Vadim Khotilovich, Yuan Tang, Hyunsu Cho, et al. 2015. Xgboost: extreme gradient boosting. *R package version 0.4-2*, 1(4).

Kyunghyun Cho, Bart van Merriënboer, Dzmitry Bahdanau, and Yoshua Bengio. 2014. On the properties of neural machine translation: Encoder–decoder approaches. In *Proceedings of SSST-8, Eighth Workshop on Syntax, Semantics and Structure in Statistical Translation*, pages 103–111, Doha, Qatar. Association for Computational Linguistics.

Rossana Cunha, Thiago Castro Ferreira, Adriana Pagano, and Fabio Alves. 2020. Referring to what you know and do not know: Making referring expression generation models generalize to unseen entities. In *Proceedings of the 28th International Conference on Computational Linguistics*, pages 2261–2272, Barcelona, Spain (Online). International Committee on Computational Linguistics.

Jacob Devlin, Ming-Wei Chang, Kenton Lee, and Kristina Toutanova. 2019. BERT: Pre-training of deep bidirectional transformers for language understanding. In *Proceedings of the 2019 Conference of the North American Chapter of the Association for Computational Linguistics: Human Language Technologies, Volume 1 (Long and Short Papers)*, pages 4171–4186, Minneapolis, Minnesota. Association for Computational Linguistics.

Claire Gardent, Anastasia Shimorina, Shashi Narayan, and Laura Perez-Beltrachini. 2017. Creating training corpora for NLG micro-planners. In *Proceedings of the 55th Annual Meeting of the Association for Computational Linguistics (Volume 1: Long Papers)*, pages 179–188, Vancouver, Canada. Association for Computational Linguistics.

Albert Gatt and Emiel Krahmer. 2018. Survey of the state of the art in natural language generation: Core tasks, applications and evaluation. *J. Artif. Int. Res.*, 61(1):65–170.

Mario Giulianelli, Jack Harding, Florian Mohnert, Dieuwke Hupkes, and Willem Zuidema. 2018. Under the hood: Using diagnostic classifiers to investigate and improve how language models track agreement information. In *Proceedings of the 2018 EMNLP Workshop BlackboxNLP: Analyzing and Interpreting Neural Networks for NLP*, pages 240–248, Brussels, Belgium. Association for Computational Linguistics.

Jeanette K Gundel, Nancy Hedberg, and Ron Zacharski. 1993. Cognitive status and the form of referring expressions in discourse. *Language*, pages 274–307.

John Hewitt and Percy Liang. 2019. Designing and interpreting probes with control tasks. In *Proceedings of the 2019 Conference on Empirical Methods in Natural Language Processing and the 9th International Joint Conference on Natural Language Processing (EMNLP-IJCNLP)*, pages 2733–2743, Hong Kong, China. Association for Computational Linguistics.

C-T James Huang. 1984. On the distribution and reference of empty pronouns. *Linguistic inquiry*, pages 531–574.

Shen Li, Zhe Zhao, Renfen Hu, Wensi Li, Tao Liu, and Xiaoyong Du. 2018. Analogical reasoning on Chinese morphological and semantic relations. In *Proceedings of the 56th Annual Meeting of the Association for Computational Linguistics (Volume 2: Short Papers)*, pages 138–143, Melbourne, Australia. Association for Computational Linguistics.

Richard Newnham. 1971. *About Chinese*. Penguin Books Ltd.

Jeffrey Pennington, Richard Socher, and Christopher Manning. 2014. GloVe: Global vectors for word representation. In *Proceedings of the 2014 Conference on Empirical Methods in Natural Language Processing (EMNLP)*, pages 1532–1543, Doha, Qatar. Association for Computational Linguistics.

Sameer Pradhan, Alessandro Moschitti, Nianwen Xue, Olga Uryupina, and Yuchen Zhang. 2012. CoNLL-2012 shared task: Modeling multilingual unrestricted coreference in OntoNotes. In *Joint Conference on*

EMNLP and CoNLL - Shared Task, pages 1–40, Jeju Island, Korea. Association for Computational Linguistics.

Ehud Reiter and Robert Dale. 2000. *Building Natural Language Generation Systems*. Studies in Natural Language Processing. Cambridge University Press.

Fahime Same, Guanyi Chen, and Kees Van Deemter. 2022. Non-neural models matter: a re-evaluation of neural referring expression generation systems. In *Proceedings of the 60th Annual Meeting of the Association for Computational Linguistics (Volume 1: Long Papers)*, pages 5554–5567, Dublin, Ireland. Association for Computational Linguistics.

Fahime Same and Kees van Deemter. 2020. A linguistic perspective on reference: Choosing a feature set for generating referring expressions in context. In *Proceedings of the 28th International Conference on Computational Linguistics*, pages 4575–4586, Barcelona, Spain (Online). International Committee on Computational Linguistics.

Klaus von Heusinger and Petra B Schumacher. 2019. Discourse prominence: Definition and application. *Journal of Pragmatics*, 154:117–127.

Chin Lung Yang, Peter C Gordon, Randall Hendrick, and Jei Tun Wu. 1999. Comprehension of referring expressions in chinese. *Language and Cognitive Processes*, 14(5-6):715–743.

Zichao Yang, Diyi Yang, Chris Dyer, Xiaodong He, Alex Smola, and Eduard Hovy. 2016. Hierarchical attention networks for document classification. In *Proceedings of the 2016 Conference of the North American Chapter of the Association for Computational Linguistics: Human Language Technologies*, pages 1480–1489, San Diego, California. Association for Computational Linguistics.

Qingyu Yin, Yu Zhang, Weinan Zhang, Ting Liu, and William Yang Wang. 2018. Zero pronoun resolution with attention-based neural network. In *Proceedings of the 27th International Conference on Computational Linguistics*, pages 13–23, Santa Fe, New Mexico, USA. Association for Computational Linguistics.

A Results on the Whole OntoNotes-ZH Dataset

The Chinese experiments in this paper were conducted on a subset of the original OntoNotes, each text of which contains less than 512 characters, since Chinese `BERT` can only accept texts shorter than 512 characters. For reference, we also tested models other than `BERT` on the whole OntoNotes-ZH dataset. In the whole OntoNotes-ZH dataset, there are 73607, 10008, and 12096 samples in the training, development, and test sets, respectively. Table 9 shows the results of the word-based Chinese RFS models on the whole OntoNotes-ZH dataset.

Comparing Table 9 with Table 10, we observe that the results are quite similar. The only exception is that the performance of `c-RNN` decreases from 55.16 to 53.86 in the 3-way classification, while the performance of `ConATT` does not change much.

B Results of Using Word-based Models on OntoNotes-ZH

To conduct a fair comparison between `BERT` and other models, we built all our Chinese RFS models character-based. To justify this decision, we also test word-based models on OntoNotes-ZH. Table 5 shows the results of the word-based Chinese models.

Comparing the results in Table 10 and Table 5, there are slight differences, but these differences do not change our conclusions. For example, all models still perform worse than `c-RNN +BERT` by a large margin. `ConATT` can slightly defeat `c-RNN` in the 3-way and 2-way classifications but performs significantly worse in other settings.

Model	5-way P	5-way R	5-way F	4-way P	4-way R	4-way F	3-way P	3-way R	3-way F	2-way P	2-way R	2-way F
c-RNN	52.36	47.91	48.97	54.14	52.40	53.06	55.30	52.99	53.86	64.88	62.81	63.68
+SGNS	56.67	53.82	54.30	59.38	57.40	58.23	59.58	56.66	57.78	67.75	66.28	66.91
ConATT	50.41	45.45	46.86	51.27	49.80	50.35	59.06	54.43	56.11	63.71	63.75	63.73
+SGNS	52.33	48.60	49.37	53.48	51.64	52.38	60.53	56.18	57.69	67.86	64.97	65.95

Table 9: Evaluation results of our word-based Chinese RFS systems on the whole OntoNotes-ZH dataset.

Model	5-way P	5-way R	5-way F	4-way P	4-way R	4-way F	3-way P	3-way R	3-way F	2-way P	2-way R	2-way F
c-RNN	51.13	47.14	48.63	54.70	54.02	54.18	57.63	53.79	55.16	66.19	63.22	64.40
+SGNS	53.40	53.33	53.16	57.91	59.12	58.19	60.17	57.49	58.52	70.87	65.22	67.30
ConATT	48.52	45.15	46.26	56.34	49.92	49.26	56.24	55.70	55.94	65.33	64.28	64.75
+SGNS	50.58	47.04	48.31	54.68	51.85	52.62	59.93	55.79	57.32	67.15	65.29	66.11

Table 10: Evaluation results of our word-based Chinese RFS systems on a subset of the original OntoNotes-ZH dataset, each text of which contains less than 512 characters.

Author Index

Association for Computational Linguistics
209 N. Eighth Street
Stroudsburg, Pennsylvania 18360

ISBN 978-1-7138-6315-1

CURRAN ASSOCIATES INC.
proceedings.com